T0008297

BIBLE TRIVIA DEVOTIONAL

365 DEVOTIONS TO ENLIGHTEN AND BRIGHTEN YOUR DAY

Ken Castor

BroadStreet
PUBLISHING

BroadStreet Publishing Group, LLC.
Savage, Minnesota, USA
Broadstreetpublishing.com

Bible Trivia Devotional

9781424566587
9781424566594 (eBook)

Devotional entries composed by Ken Castor.

Typesetting and design by Garborg Design Works | garborgdesign.com

Editorial services by Michelle Winger | literallyprecise.com and by Carole Holdahl.

Printed in China.

23 24 25 26 27 28 29 7 6 5 4 3 2 1

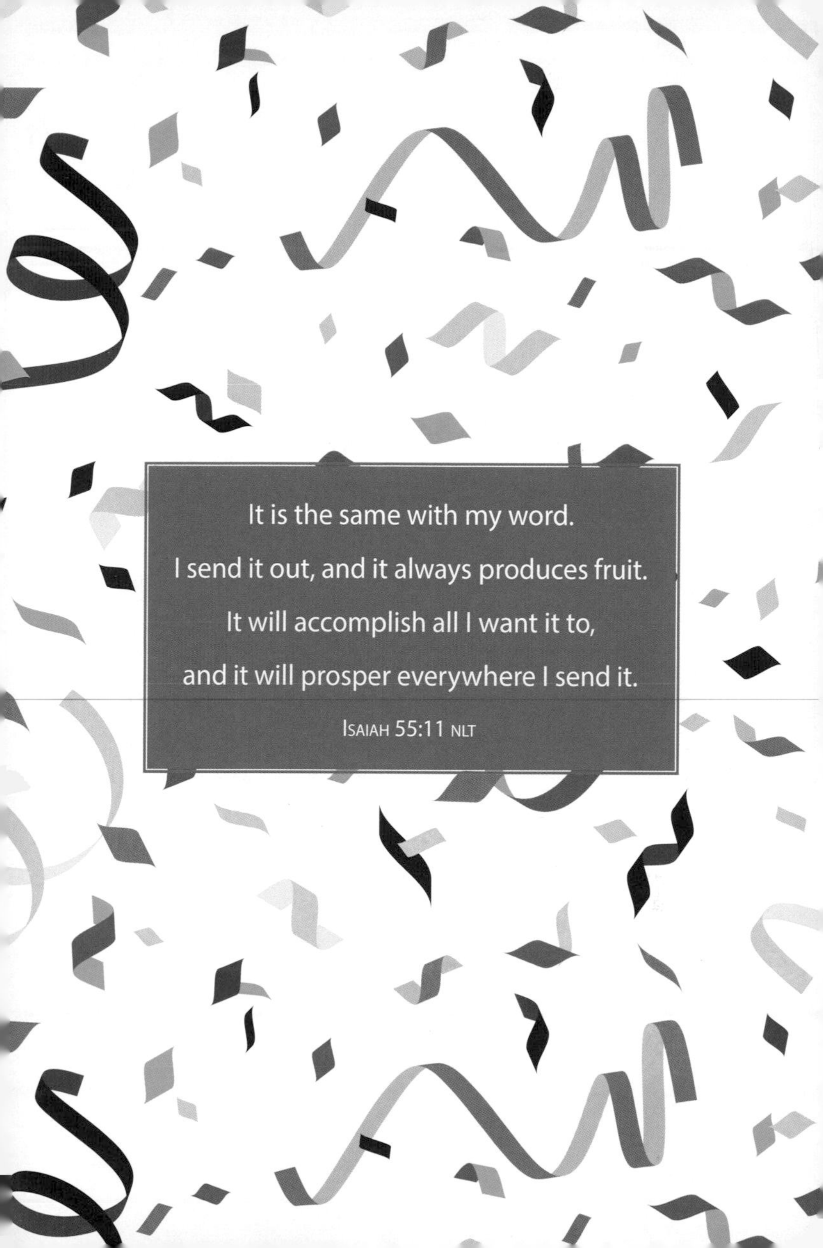
It is the same with my word.
I send it out, and it always produces fruit.
It will accomplish all I want it to,
and it will prosper everywhere I send it.
Isaiah 55:11 NLT

INTRODUCTION

You may have learned a lot about the Bible when you were growing up, or maybe you've just picked it up recently. It's good to jump back in and remember some of those facts that may have seemed a little trivial at first.

In this fun Bible Trivia Devotional, you will be challenged to think beyond the answers to their daily application. Recall Scriptures, heroes of the faith, miracles, historical places and events and discover how they are all relevant to you in this moment. Glean new insight and perspective from old, familiar passages.

The Bible is always worth studying; spending time reading it is never a waste. And the best part is that it's not trivial at all. It isn't just head knowledge or rote memory. The Word of God is alive and active! It is life-changing, brimming with hope, joy, wisdom, and peace. Dive in today!

JANUARY

JANUARY 1

A NEW CREATION

FINISH THIS VERSE

If anyone is in Christ, this person is a _______ _______;
the old things passed away;
behold, _______ _______ _______ _______.

Once we have given our lives to Jesus Christ, we are each a new creation. The old things we once considered the most important have been replaced by what God thinks is most important. The old paths we used to take have been rerouted by Jesus. The old desires of our hearts, the old focus of our eyes, the old worries of our souls, have all passed way, and the goals of God for us are alive.

The year ahead is a set of 365 days of opportunity to live in the newness of God. We are reborn because of Jesus. We are renewed through his death and resurrection. Our sins are forgiven. Our lives are redeemed. His Spirit is working in us and promises to continue working in us until the day we are fully complete.

If anyone is in Christ, this person is a new creation;
the old things passed away; behold, new things have come.

2 Corinthians 5:17 NASB

What new thing would you like Jesus to do in your life this year? Take time to dedicate this to the Lord in prayer.

Answer: new creation; new things have come

JANUARY 2

MEANING OF BABEL

TRUE OR FALSE
The name of the city of Babel is the Hebrew term that means "confusion."

The people who settled in the ancient plain of Shinar (in what today is the country of Iraq) had grown pretty confident in themselves. To highlight their own sense of greatness they conspired to build a city and a tower that reached as high as the heavens. In doing so, they planned to expand their reputation across the earth as the central gathering place for all people. Their egotistical vision was arrogant against God's authority and ignorant of God's glory.

The Lord challenged them. It's as if he said, "You think you are great, do you? Well, let's see what happens if I disrupt your communication." He confused their language which meant that the people could no longer understand one another. These arrogant, ignorant people were quickly thrown into such disorder that they scattered and went their own ways. Their building projects were halted. Their arrogance was humiliated. Their ignorance was revealed.

> Its name was called Babel, because there the Lord confused the language of all the earth. And from there the Lord dispersed them over the face of all the earth.
>
> Genesis 11:9 ESV

What areas of pride in your life do you need to submit to God?

Answer: true

JANUARY 3

A NEW NAME

Abraham's original name was
A. Bobo
B. Ham
C. Samuel
D. Abram

Abram was a very old man when God changed his name. Interestingly, his original name, Abram, meant "exalted father," but Abram had no children. He and his wife were barren. He was a son to his dad, Terah, and he was an uncle to his nephew, Lot, but Abram's name was a misnomer. It was a mocking reminder that he was not the father of anyone.

God wanted to do something miraculous. He wanted to reveal his remarkable plan of salvation for the world by turning Abram's ironic name into a truly exalted one. God turned the name of Abram into Abraham, which meant the "father of many." He promised Abraham that he would become very fruitful, that nations would descend from him, that kings would come from him, and that his offspring would bless all people on earth. Soon after his name change, Abraham's son Isaac was born. From Isaac came Jacob. From Jacob came Judah and all eleven of the other tribes of Israel. And from Judah's lineage came David. And from David's lineage, came Jesus, the promised Savior of the world.

"No longer will you be called Abram, but your name will be Abraham, for I have made you a father of a multitude of nations."

Genesis 17:5 NIV

What does Abraham's name change tell you about God's long-range plan for the world?

Answer: D) Abram

BREAD FROM HEAVEN

What does the word *manna* mean?

The Hebrew word *manna* means, "What is it?" When God rained manna down in the desert, the Israelites had trouble comprehending this mysterious wafer-like bread. But the Lord had promised to take care of Israel during their years wandering in the desert. He provided enough quail and manna for everyone to eat every day. He simply wanted Israel to trust him to provide.

Later, Jesus would instruct his followers to pray for their daily bread (Matthew 6:11). He would also reveal that he is the true bread from heaven (John 6:32) and the living bread that came down from heaven (v. 51). Again, the Lord wants people to trust him and turn to him for both the daily needs of life and for life everlasting.

When the dew had gone up, there was on the face of the wilderness a fine, flake-like thing, fine as frost on the ground. When the people of Israel saw it, they said to one another, "What is it?" For they did not know what it was. And Moses said to them, "It is the bread that the LORD has given you to eat…Now the house of Israel called its name manna. It was like coriander seed, white, and the taste of it was like wafers made with honey.

EXODUS 16:14-15, 31 ESV

My Father in heaven, give me this day my daily bread. Let me trust you for everything I truly need.

Answer: What is it?

PAYMENT FOR BETRAYAL

What payment did Judas receive for betraying Jesus?

When it seemed like the crowds were starting to turn against Jesus, Judas decided to capitalize on the moment. He met Israel's leaders in order to make a plan to turn Jesus over to them and, in turn, to benefit financially from the transaction. And his plan worked. Later that week while sharing the Passover meal with Jesus and his disciples in the upper room of a house in Jerusalem, Judas left to alert the leaders. Judas led a mob with swords and clubs to arrest Jesus and delivered him into the hands of the high council.

When Jesus was sentenced to be executed on a cross, Judas realized he had sinned and deeply regretted what he had done. He was so distraught that he "brought back the thirty pieces of silver" and threw down the money into the temple. He then went and hanged himself (Matthew 27:3-5).

One of the twelve, whose name was Judas Iscariot, went to the chief priests and said, "What will you give me if I deliver him over to you?" And they paid him thirty pieces of silver.

Matthew 26:14-15 ESV

Why did his betrayal of Jesus disturb Judas so deeply? Ponder this and take a moment to pray for strength to remain faithful to Jesus today.

Answer: thirty pieces of silver

JANUARY 6

OTHER STONES

David killed Goliath using his sling and one smooth stone.
How many more stones did he have left in his shepherd's bag?

The account of David's victory over the giant, Goliath, is one of the most famous stories ever told. It is a story that is meant to show that God is more powerful than any man, any army, or any weapon. It is a story that teaches us to stand up for God, even when the odds seem frightfully stacked against us.

First Samuel 17 records the moment: "As Goliath moved closer to attack, David quickly ran out to meet him. Reaching into his shepherd's bag and taking out a stone, he hurled it with his sling and hit the Philistine in the forehead. The stone sank in, and Goliath stumbled and fell face down on the ground. David triumphed over the Philistine that day with only a sling and a stone, for he had no sword" (vv. 48-50). David believed in God. He never even needed the other four stones in his bag. With God, he only needed the one.

He picked up five smooth stones from a stream and put them into his shepherd's bag. Then, armed only with his shepherd's staff and sling, he started across the valley to fight the Philistine.

1 Samuel 17:40 NLT

What battle are you facing today? If you saw the situation from God's point of view, how might that change the way you approached the struggle?

Answer: four

PAUL SHIPWRECKED

On what island was Paul shipwrecked?

Paul had been arrested and imprisoned for preaching about Jesus. As a Roman citizen, he appealed to Caesar and was eventually sent under armed guard by ship to Rome to await a trial. During a long, difficult journey, a violent storm overcame their ship. Trying to stay afloat, they threw most of their cargo overboard and even began stripping off the heavy equipment from the ship itself. For two weeks, the storm drove the 276 people onboard the ship across the Adriatic Sea. Eventually the fierce waves and winds pushed them against a reef and started to break the ship apart.

The soldiers wanted to kill all the prisoners including Paul in order to keep them from escaping, but the centurion assigned to Paul wanted to keep Paul alive. He commanded everyone to abandon the ship and make their way to shore. They stayed on the island of Malta until they were able to secure safe passage to Rome where Paul was under house arrest for at least two more years. This, however, allowed Paul to teach about Jesus Christ to many people unhindered by threats or violence.

When they had been brought safely through,
then we found out that the island was called Malta.

Acts 28:1 NASB

Why do you think God spared Paul's life but kept him a prisoner to the Roman soldiers?

Answer: Malta

AN ALARMING MOMENT

Whose ear did Peter cut off?

To say that Peter had a roller coaster of emotions on the night that Jesus was arrested would be an understatement. He had been told by Jesus that he would betray his Lord three times before the rooster crowed. He had fallen asleep despite Jesus' passionate plea to stay awake and pray with him. He had seen the mob approach Jesus with swords and clubs. He had seen Judas betray Jesus with a kiss. Overcome with rage and stress, Peter gripped the handle of his knife and swung wildly at the nearest person in the mob. In the scuffle, Peter missed most of the person's head, but he was successful in cutting off his right ear. We know his name. Malchus. This was the name of the high priest's servant, and it's forever etched into the Bible.

But this alarming encounter between Peter and Malchus gives us another glimpse into the passion of the Lord. Jesus told Peter to put away his sword. Then he touched Malchus' ear and healed him (Luke 22:50-51). Jesus allowed himself to be arrested and was led away to the trial that ended in his death. Simon Peter followed Jesus for a while, but when the questioning about his affiliations began, his commitment wavered.

Simon Peter drew a sword and slashed off the right ear of Malchus, the high priest's slave.

John 18:10 NLT

Where do you find yourself jumping ahead of God's plan?

Answer: Malchus, the high priest's slave

JANUARY 9

THIS ISN'T GOOD

What was the first thing God said was not good?

In the first chapter of the Bible in the book of Genesis, we learn that at the end of each day of creation, God looked at all he had made and saw that it was good. But in the second chapter of the Genesis, God looked at Adam and declared that something was not quite right. God wanted to put the world on notice that it is not good for humans to be alone. Adam needed a companion.

It is not good for humans to be independent, isolated, surviving on their own, or deprived of community. God wanted it to be known that humans were made to walk with God and with one another. God created Eve who was a true companion for Adam. And when God looked upon all of his creation with Adam and Eve together as his image-bearers, he saw that it was "very good" (Genesis 1:31).

Then the LORD God said, "It is not good for the man to be alone.
I will make a helper who is just right for him."

GENESIS 2:18 NLT

From what you know about the nature of God, why would God consider Adam's aloneness as not being good?

Answer: for man to be alone

JANUARY 10

SONS OF SIMON

What were the names of the sons of Simon of Cyrene?

The only person in the world to have carried the cross of Jesus is Simon of Cyrene. We know very little about him except what we can glean from a few verses in the Bible. We know that he was seized by Roman soldiers and made to carry the cross as Jesus was led to his execution on the hill of Golgotha. We know that he was from Cyrene, a Greek city located in northern Africa in what is now Libya. At that time, Cyrene had a large Jewish community.

In the book of Mark, we also learn that he had two sons named Alexander and Rufus. This leads us to believe that Mark's original readers could very well have known these two men. Some scholars have wondered if Simon's son, Rufus, is the same as the one mentioned with such familiarity later in Romans 16:13 by Paul.

They compelled a passer-by coming from the country, Simon of Cyrene (the father of Alexander and Rufus), to carry His cross.

Mark 15:21 NASB

What could Simon of Cyrene have experienced while carrying the cross of Jesus? What impact must this have had on his two sons? What impact does picking up the cross have on future generations?

Answer: Alexander and Rufus

JANUARY 11

JACOB'S PILLOW

When Jacob had his famous dream of a staircase,
what did he use as a pillow for his head?

At night on his journey to Paddan Aram to find a wife, Jacob laid down to sleep. He placed his head on a stone. That night he dreamed of a ladder that extended from earth to heaven with angels ascending and descending on it. God then spoke to Jacob in the dream, declaring that he would bless Jacob the way he had blessed Jacob's grandfather, Abraham, and his father, Isaac. He promised that the land where he now slept would belong one day to Jacob and his offspring, and they would become so numerous that they would spread around the world. The line of descendants through Jacob would come to bless all the families of the earth.

When Jacob woke up, he took the stone he had been sleeping against, put a pillar around it, poured oil over it, and named it *Bethel*, meaning "house of God."

He came to a certain place and stayed there that night, because the sun had set. Taking one of the stones of the place, he put it under his head and lay down in that place to sleep.

Genesis 28:11 esv

Bonus Trivia: Amongst many other significant events, Bethel would later become the place where Jacob received his new name, Israel.

Answer: a stone

JANUARY 12

GIVING UP WHAT'S INSIDE

Where did Jonah try to go instead of going to Nineveh?

God wanted Jonah to deliver a message to the wicked people of Nineveh. Jonah, however, didn't want to go because he knew that if the people repented, God would forgive them. Jonah hated the people of Nineveh, and he did not want God to give them a second chance. Instead of obeying, Jonah tried to flee as far away as possible.

The ironic twist to Jonah's story is that everyone in the story had to give up something that they were holding onto inside of themselves; everyone, that is, except for Jonah. The sailors gave up their other belief systems and turned to God. The huge fish gave up the contents of his belly when it vomited Jonah onto dry land. The people of Nineveh gave up their evil ways and promised to serve God. But Jonah doubled down on his struggle with God and instead of giving in, he grew in his bitterness.

Jonah ran away from the Lord and headed for Tarshish.
He went down to Joppa, where he found a ship bound for that port.
After paying the fare, he went aboard and sailed for Tarshish to flee from the Lord.

Jonah 1:3 NIV

How do you react when you are confronted with God's holy character?

Answer: Tarshish (Spain)

LOVE FOR THE WORLD

FINISH THIS VERSE

For God so loved the world that he gave his _______ _______ _______ _______, that whoever believes in him shall not perish but have _______ _______.

There are a few verses in the Bible that seem to sum up the most wonderful truths of Scripture. John 3:16 is one of those. In this verse we learn, first of all, that God loves the world profoundly, deeply, faithfully. Next, we learn that God loved the world so much that he was willing to give up his own Son. Third, we learn that anyone can choose to believe in God. And finally, we learn that whoever believes in him will have eternal life.

Jesus came to the earth in order to die on the cross. The reason this happened was because God loved people so much that he was willing to take the consequence of sin (death) upon himself rather than have people perish for eternity apart from him. But because Jesus overcame death through his resurrection, he also offers us eternal life if we believe in him.

For God so loved the world that he gave his one and only Son, that whoever believes in him shall not perish but have eternal life.

John 3:16 NIV

Do you believe in Jesus? Have you accepted that God loves you so much that he sent his one and only Son to die on your behalf so that you would have eternal life?

Answer: one and only Son; eternal life

JANUARY 14

HOW TO TREAT A PROPHET

What happened to the group of young men who ridiculed the prophet Elisha by calling him "baldy?"

Elisha was God's prophet. Until this moment in 2 Kings, however, he had always accompanied Elijah, his mentor. But Elijah had passed his mantle to Elisha and then had gone up to heaven in a chariot of fire. Shortly after Elijah left, Elisha was walking into the town of Bethel. He was now God's anointed voice for Israel. But as he entered the town, a large group of young men began to taunt him. They mocked him and ridiculed the way he looked. In doing so, they were also ridiculing the Lord who had chosen Elisha to represent him to the people.

When they didn't stop, Elisha called upon the Lord to defend his name. That's when two bears came out of the woods and mauled forty-two young men. These people had unrepentantly insulted God by insulting his prophet. The alarming punishment warned the people to respect God and his appointed prophet.

From there Elisha went up to Bethel. As he was walking along the road, some boys came out of the town and jeered at him. "Get out of here, baldy!" they said. "Get out of here, baldy!" He turned around, looked at them and called down a curse on them in the name of the Lord. Then two bears came out of the woods and mauled forty-two of the boys.

2 Kings 2:23-24 niv

When Jesus was ridiculed, he could have called down a curse on those who mocked him. Why do you think he didn't do that?

Answer: forty-two of them were mauled by two bears

MUCH WITH LITTLE

Jesus fed the crowd of five-thousand with ______ loaves of bread and ______ fish.

Jesus had become so popular in the region around the Sea of Galilee that great crowds consisting of thousands of people began to gather everywhere he went. It became a problem when it was getting late and there was not enough food for everyone. The disciples were worried that other, significant problems could erupt in the crowd, so they begged Jesus to send everyone home. But Jesus wasn't worried. He replied, "They don't need to go away. You give them something to eat" (v. 16). The disciples were flabbergasted. They only had five loaves and two fish! There were at least five-thousand men in attendance, not to mention the women and children in this vast sea of people!

Jesus sat everyone down, looked up to heaven, gave thanks, and broke the bread. The disciples started distributing the food and then kept serving and serving and serving. Finally, after everyone had had their fill, the disciples collected twelve baskets full of leftover pieces of bread and fish.

"We have here only five loaves of bread and two fish," they answered. "Bring them here to me," he said.

MATTHEW 14:17-18 NIV

From this event, what did Jesus want everyone to know about him?

Answer: five; two

FREAK WEATHER

TRUE OR FALSE
God once stopped both the sun and the moon in the middle of the sky.

The verse immediately following this incredible event proclaims, "Never has there been a day like it before or since!" (v. 14). Joshua was in a very difficult situation. Rather than serve God, five enemy kings had allied together to attack his people in Gibeon. Joshua prayed that the Lord would fight for Israel.

He certainly fought! God threw the enemies into confusion through freak weather patterns! God hurled large hailstones down on the armies as they fled, killing more of them from the hail than had been killed by sword. He also caused the sun to stand still which lengthened the day enough to route the five armies and allow the enemy kings to be captured.

On the day the Lord gave the Amorites over to Israel, Joshua said to the Lord in the presence of Israel:
"Sun, stand still over Gibeon,
and you, moon over the Valley of Aijalon,"
So the sun stood still, and the moon stopped,
till the nation avenged itself on its enemies,
as it is written in the Book of Jashar.
The sun stopped in the middle of the sky and delayed going down about a full day.

Joshua 10:12-13 NIV

What do you think God wanted to prove by using unnatural as well as natural weather events to fight against Israel's enemies?

Answer: true

JANUARY 17

A SIGNIFICANT NUMBER

How many sons did Jacob have?

Throughout the Bible, the number twelve is significant. There are twelve sons of Jacob, twelve tribes of Israel, which are descended from Jacob's sons, twelve disciples of Jesus, and dozens of more references. There is no magic formula with these appearances, but God did choose the number twelve to be a recurring indication of his plan of salvation for the world.

When the number twelve is used in the Bible, it echoes God's covenant to bless the world through the offspring of Jacob, specifically Judah's descendants. Despite their struggles and sins, it is through Jacob's sons that the Messiah would later be born. Despite their wanderings and sins, it is through the tribes of Israel that the Savior would be revealed. And despite their fears and faults, it is through the twelve followers of Jesus that the world would come to know Jesus Christ.

The sons of Leah: Reuben the firstborn of Jacob,
Simeon, Levi, Judah, Issachar and Zebulun.
The sons of Rachel: Joseph and Benjamin.
The sons of Rachel's servant Bilhah: Dan and Naphtali.
The sons of Leah's servant Zilpah: Gad and Asher.
These were the sons of Jacob,
who were born to him in Paddan Aram.

Genesis 35:23-26 NIV

Look through the Bible and find as many references to the number twelve as possible. Which of these stand out to you and why?

Answer: twelve

JANUARY 18

SITE OF REVELATION

John received the vision of Revelation while exiled to ______________________.

A. Babylon
B. Rome
C. Patmos
D. Philadelphia

John was exiled to an island in the Aegean Sea, between modern day Greece and Turkey. The intention of this imprisonment was to prohibit him from continually spreading the message about Jesus to the people throughout the Roman Empire.

Ironically, his landlocked confinement may have served to increase the impact of the gospel. It gave John significant opportunity to worship and pray which led to a vision that would become known throughout history and all over the world. The Revelation of John is filled with apocalyptic wonders but also of intimate personal invitation. His vision is both deeply disturbing and eternally encouraging. What impacts people about John's vision most of all, however, is the revelation that Jesus Christ is the central figure for every human being and for all history. Jesus is the Lamb of God who was slain for the sins of humanity, the conquering King returning in glory, the author of redemption and re-creation for the world.

I was exiled to the island of Patmos for preaching the word of God and for my testimony about Jesus.

Revelation 1:9 NLT

What do you find to be the strangest or most comforting part of the book of Revelation?

Answer: C) Patmos

JANUARY 19

FOURTH BOOK

What is the fourth book of the New Testament?

The New Testament begins with four small books called the Gospels. The books of Matthew, Mark, Luke, and John are all accounts of the life of Jesus, with the four together covering his birth to his resurrection. All four Gospels focus on the final three years of Jesus' ministry, his miracles, his death on the cross, and his resurrection. The first three books, Matthew, Mark, and Luke have several coordinated stories, words, and themes.

John's Gospel, while still sharing many of the same stories, gives a unique, eyewitness testimony of what Jesus did and who Jesus is. The book of John is bold in its proclamations that Jesus is God and that it is only through him that a person can be saved from sin. And the book of John is remarkably personal, having transformed the writer to the point where he referred to himself as the disciple whom Jesus loved.

This is the disciple who testifies to these things and who wrote them down. We know that his testimony is true.

John 21:24 NIV

What is your favorite verse from the book of John?

Answer: John

CALMING THE STORM

What question did the disciples ask themselves after Jesus calmed the storm?

A. When do we eat?
B. Who is this man?
C. Where's Judas?
D. When can we go home?

The disciples feared for their lives during the storm. They were in a boat on the Sea of Galilee when the fierce storm hit them, and waves began breaking into the boat. But Jesus had been sleeping. He wasn't worried. They woke him up and begged him to save them from drowning. He responded with a question, "Why are you so afraid?"

When he rebuked the winds and waves, there was an immediate calm. In that moment it is hard to say whether the disciples were more afraid of Jesus or the storm. They were amazed. They were bewildered by the discovery that Jesus had the power to control the elements of nature. They couldn't help but ask, "Who is this man?"

Jesus responded, "Why are you afraid? You have so little faith!"
Then he got up and rebuked the wind and waves,
and suddenly there was a great calm.
The disciples were amazed. "Who is this man?" they asked.
"Even the winds and waves obey him!"

MATTHEW 8:26-27 NLT

In the storms of life, who do you turn to?

Answer: B) Who is this man?

WIDOW'S SON

Before the son of the widow from Zarephath came back to life, how many times did Elijah stretch himself over the boy's dead body?

Zarephath was a small town between the cities of Tyre and Sidon. It was on the western coast of what is now Lebanon. At God's instructions, the prophet Elijah traveled there to take refuge in the home of a wary, yet generous, widow. Because of Elijah's presence and the widow's obedience, God had blessed her household.

While Elijah was there, her son contracted a severe illness and died. The distraught widow lashed out at Elijah, wondering if he had brought a curse upon her home. But Elijah cried out to the Lord, stretched himself over the boy three times, and asked God to bring the child back to life. When he did, the woman exclaimed, "Now I know that you are a man of God, and that the word of the Lord in your mouth is truth".

He stretched himself upon the child three times and cried to the Lord, "O Lord my God, let this child's life come into him again." And the Lord listened to the voice of Elijah. And the life of the child came into him again, and he revived.

1 Kings 17:21-22 ESV

Why do you think God allowed the widow's son to get sick and die while Elijah was staying in their home?

Answer: three

THE LONGEST NAME

What is the longest name in the Bible?

In a time when the kingdom of Judah was under attack and Jerusalem was being besieged, God instructed the prophet Isaiah to give his second son a symbolic name, Maher-shalal-hash-baz. The boy's name is made up of four words that mean, "swift to spoil, quick to plunder." While his name sounds ominous, it was a prophetic sign of what God was going to do to Judah's enemies.

The kingdoms of Syria and Israel allied against the kingdom of Judah and inflicted significant destruction. The situation looked dire for Judah and for God's promise to bring a Messiah through Judah. But God instructed Isaiah to give the name Maher-shalal-hash-baz to his son, informing him that before the boy was old enough to cry "my father" or "my mother," Syria and Samaria would be destroyed by the King of Assyria. And that's what happened. In 732 BC, Assyria swept in and conquered Syria and Samaria. To the people of Judah, it was a fearful and powerful reminder that God is the orchestrator of history and will make sure his plans succeed.

Then the LORD said to me, "Take a large tablet and write on it in common characters, 'Belonging to Maher-shalal-hash-baz.'"

ISAIAH 8:1 ESV

What promises of God do you know to be true even in the midst of challenging situations?

Answer: Mahershalalhashbaz

A LOT OF FOXES

How many foxes did Samson use to defeat the Philistines?

Samson's life was a dysfunctional mess. Again and again, Samson compromised his faithfulness to God. Samson decided to marry a Philistine woman. Unfortunately, the Philistines were enemies of Israel. During the weeklong wedding ceremony, he became so frustrated with the tricks of his new bride and her friends that he left and went home to live with his parents. His bride was then given to Samson's best man at the wedding (Judges 3:1-20).

Some time later, Samson went back to his bride only to discover that his best man was married to her instead. Samson said he couldn't be blamed for everything he would do to the Philistines. Then he caught three hundred foxes, tied their tails together, and lit them on fire. The foxes ran through the Philistine grain fields and burned the crops to the ground. This sparked a series of violent clashes between the Philistines and Samson. In this way, Samson became both a judge of Israel and a warrior against its enemies.

He went out and caught 300 foxes.
He tied their tails together in pairs,
and he fastened a torch to each pair of tails.

JUDGES 15:4 NLT

Why do you think God used a compromised person like Samson to still accomplish his purpose to save Israel?

Answer: three hundred

BROTHERLY JEALOUSY

Why did Joseph's brothers become jealous of him?

You could say that Jacob created a bit of a dysfunctional family dynamic, but he couldn't have predicted the tragic mess that would result from it. Jacob had multiple children through multiple women over span of multiple years. In his old age, his most beloved wife, Rachel, gave birth to Joseph. Jacob immediately favored the boy more than all of his other sons. At one point, Jacob gave Joseph an elaborate, beautiful coat as a show of his affection for his young son.

The other brothers grew jealous and angry at their younger brother's privileged status. They devised a plan to beat Joseph nearly to death and sell him into slavery. They brought his bloodied coat back to Jacob and claimed that Jacob's favored son had been mauled by a vicious animal and was dead.

> When his brothers saw that their father loved him more than all his brothers, they hated him and could not bring themselves to speak peaceably to him.
>
> Genesis 37:4 CSB

How does God use this tragic, dysfunctional situation to bring redemption to the family and ultimately to the whole world?

Answer: because their father, Jacob, loved Joseph the most

JANUARY 25

JUDGE IBZAN

How many sons and daughters did Israel's judge, Ibzan, have?

Ibzan is considered a minor judge of Israel because his story is only three verses, his influence was only seven years, and he was not associated with any major historical campaigns.

Izban's greatest achievement was that he had tremendous influence in Bethlehem through his significantly large family. It's unclear whether it's the Bethlehem in Zebulun or the one in Judea. He was likely a prosperous man who formed strategic alliances among leaders in Israel by way of the marriages of his many children. In this way, Ibzan banded the people of Israel together and became a powerful orchestrator of regional politics, business, and peace.

> After Jephthah died, Ibzan from Bethlehem judged Israel. He had thirty sons and thirty daughters. He sent his daughters to marry men outside his clan, and he brought in thirty young women from outside his clan to marry his sons. Ibzan judged Israel for seven years.

Judges 12:8-9 NLT

God fulfills his promises to rescue his people. Sometimes he uses people in unexpected situations to accomplish his plans. How might God want to use you uniquely for his purposes today?

Answer: thirty sons and thirty daughters

JANUARY 26

DAVID'S STRONG MEN

How many men did Abishai, one of David's strong men, kill with a spear in a single battle?

David was a mighty warrior who, as a boy, killed Goliath. He had a difficult time staying alive because he had a lot of enemies. First Chronicles 11 gives us fascinating insight into the men who fought valiantly for him. Jashobeam killed hundreds of enemy soldiers in a single battle. Eleazar stood with David in a barley field and held off the Philistines when all the other soldiers fled. Abishai was the leader of a contingent of thirty mighty men. He was known for killing three hundred enemies in a single battle.

Every one of David's thirty mighty men is listed in 1 Chronicles 11. These men became famous around Israel for their battle skills. It was their deep love for David and their willingness to die for him that enabled David to unite all of Israel under his reign as king.

Abishai, the brother of Joab, was the leader of the Thirty. He once used his spear to kill 300 enemy warriors in a single battle. It was by such feats that he became as famous as the Three. Abishai was the most famous of the Thirty and was their commander, though he was not one of the Three.

1 Chronicles 11:20-21 NLT

Why is it important to be surrounded by people who loyally support you?

Answer: three hundred

JANUARY 27

RISKING IT ALL

Who came with Joseph of Arimethea to ask Pilate for permission to bury Jesus' body after the crucifixion?

Nicodemus was a member of the Pharisees, a religious class of leaders and teachers committed to helping Israel follow God's commandments. However, to help people follow God's standards, the Pharisees would often add layer upon layer of strict bylaws and customs to ordinary daily routines. The Pharisees were regular challengers to Jesus' authority and many of them eventually plotted to murder him. But Nicodemus was drawn to Jesus. In the third chapter of the book of John, Nicodemus came to Jesus at night, probably so that he wouldn't be seen, to learn more about who Jesus was. Jesus turned that conversation with Nicodemus into a deep discussion about being born again through the Holy Spirit. Jesus told the Pharisee that whoever believes in him, the Son of God, would have eternal life. This conversation must have deeply impacted Nicodemus.

A couple of years later on the afternoon that Jesus died, Nicodemus and Joseph of Arimethea went to care for Jesus' body. He was willing to put his own life and career on the line by giving Jesus' body a proper burial before the Sabbath began.

With him came Nicodemus, the man who had come to Jesus at night. He brought about seventy-five pounds of perfumed ointment made from myrrh and aloes. Following Jewish burial custom, they wrapped Jesus' body with the spices in long sheets of linen cloth.

John 19:39-40 NLT

What do you risk by believing in Jesus?

Answer: Nicodemus

JANUARY 28

AT ONCE

What was Matthew's job before becoming a disciple of Jesus?

The job of tax collector had a rather notorious designation. The men who took this job were helping the oppressive government of the Roman Empire to subdue the Jewish people. Many people considered tax collectors to be ultimate betrayers of Israel, and therefore of God. People in this profession were so disrespected that a tax collector was paired in the common vernacular with the word *sinner*. Jesus was often accused of hanging out with tax collectors and sinners as if it was such a despicable profession that it didn't even warrant inclusion with bad individuals.

It was a remarkable moment when Jesus stopped at the booth of a young man named Matthew and asked him to become his disciple. A deep, internal motivation erupted within Matthew, and he responded immediately to Jesus' invitation by getting up and following him.

As Jesus left the town, he saw a tax collector named Levi sitting at his tax collector's booth. "Follow me and be my disciple," Jesus said to him. So Levi got up, left everything, and followed him.

Luke 5:27-28 NLT

Jesus is asking you to follow him today. What would an immediate response to his invitation look like for you?

Answer: he was a tax collector

BLINDED BY JESUS

Where was Paul blinded?

The movement of the first Christians spread quickly. But a zealous young Pharisee, Saul of Tarsus, was hunting followers of "the Way" because he was intent on suppressing the movement. He had overseen the mob execution of Stephen, one of the early church's first leaders. He initiated a wave of persecution within the church in Jerusalem that scattered believers into hiding around the city and beyond. Acts 8:3 informs us that Saul was going everywhere to destroy the church. He would go from house to house, dragging out men and women and throwing them into prison.

On his way from Jerusalem to Damascus, Saul's life was changed forever. As he approached city, a light from heaven shone around him. He fell to the ground and heard a voice saying, "Saul, Saul! Why are you persecuting me?" Saul asked who was speaking, and the voice replied, "I am Jesus, the one you are persecuting!" Saul was temporarily blinded until Jesus sent a Christian named Ananias, who healed him. Saul stayed in Damascus for a while, then began preaching the truth about Jesus in the synagogues and the streets, attesting that Jesus Christ is the Son of God.

Saul picked himself up off the ground,
but when he opened his eyes he was blind.
So his companions led him by the hand to Damascus.

Acts 9:8 NLT

If you were to truly meet Jesus, face-to-face, what do you believe that encounter would be like?

Answer: on the road to Damascus

JANUARY 30

POOR IN SPIRIT

According to Jesus, why are the poor in spirit blessed?

When people start to recognize their need for God, they begin to receive everything they were created to have. People were created to have a relationship with God. We need the daily bread that only God provides. "The Lord is my shepherd," Psalm 23:1 proclaims; "I lack nothing". Jesus fulfills those who cease pursuing of other interests and start to recognize that their deepest longings can only be met in Jesus Christ.

Being poor in spirit doesn't mean that someone has been trampled and broken, but rather that someone has cast aside their pride to humbly seek God. Pride is the false sense of being deserving, while poverty of the heart is knowing that we can never have enough of God. We need to therefore pursue him, and we will be rewarded with the relationship and the royal status that only God can provide.

"Blessed are the poor in spirit,
for theirs is the kingdom of heaven."

MATTHEW 5:3 NIV

What might you have in your life that is supplanting your pursuit of God?

Answer: theirs is the kingdom of heaven

NETWORK OF BELIEVERS

Who was the deacon in the church in Cenchrea?

Paul wrote his magnum opus to the believers in Rome. He wanted them to have a solid theological foundation living as believers in the most powerful city in the Roman Empire. His letter, the book of Romans, is filled with some of the most important statements about God ever written. Yet more important than all the profound faith statements in Romans is the fact that it was a real letter, sent at a real time, by a real person, to real people.

The final chapter of Romans is a long list of names. There are roughly three dozen people mentioned specifically, and scores of other people beyond that—sisters and brothers and churches and apostles, etc. Phoebe was a deacon in Cenchrea and the first name mentioned. It is likely that she carried this letter from Paul to the Christians in Rome. Paul wrote this letter before he had ever been to Rome, yet he knew and loved these people because of his commitment to the network of the church. Even at this early stage, the church was an incredible family of believers that crossed the boundaries of age, geography, ethnicity, language, and socio-economic status.

I commend to you our sister Phoebe, who is a deacon in the church in Cenchrea. Welcome her in the Lord as one who is worthy of honor among God's people. Help her in whatever she needs, for she has been helpful to many, and especially to me.

Romans 16:1-2 NLT

What does your network of believers look like?

Answer: Phoebe

FEBRUARY

PRICE OF A BIRTHRIGHT

For what price did Esau sell his rights as firstborn to his younger twin brother, Jacob?

We learn in Genesis 25 that Isaac's twin sons had unique traits. Esau was born with a red color to his skin, and Jacob was born clasping his brother's heel. Esau, whose name means "hairy," became a skillful hunter and was comfortable outdoors. Jacob, whose name means "heel" or "deceiver," grew into a quiet man who enjoyed living indoors. Esau appears to have been brash, while Jacob seems to have been a patient plotter. Their household dynamics added to the brotherly tensions since Isaac loved Esau whereas their mother, Rebekah, loved Jacob.

One day while Jacob was cooking a stew, Esau came in from working in the fields, exhausted and hungry. Esau begged Jacob for some of the stew. Jacob said he could have some if he sold him his rights as the firstborn son. In a moment of desperation, Esau agreed.

Jacob gave Esau bread and lentil stew, and he ate and drank and rose and went his way. Thus Esau despised his birthright.

GENESIS 25:34 ESV

What teachable moments for your life can you find in this remarkable story?

Answer: some bread and lentil stew

FEBRUARY 2

THE LITTLE SEA

The Sea of Galilee is ____ miles long and ____ miles wide.

The Sea of Galilee is really a large freshwater lake. Despite its relatively small size for a sea, this body of water carries a disproportional importance for the world. Also known as the Sea of Tiberias (John 6:1) or Lake Gennesaret (Luke 5:1), this freshwater lake is the sight of significant world-changing events.

The prophet Isaiah predicted that God would reveal the world's Savior from the Galilee region (Isaiah 9:1). This is where Jesus called his first disciples. This sea is also where Jesus walked on water and calmed a storm. Along its shores Jesus healed people, preached, and fed over five thousand people with five loaves of bread and two fish. Read through the gospel of Mark for descriptions of all these events.

One day as Jesus was walking along the shore of the Sea of Galilee, he saw Simon and his brother Andrew throwing a net into the water, for they fished for a living. Jesus called out to them, "Come, follow me, and I will show you how to fish for people!"

Mark 1:16-17 NLT

What is your favorite event from the Sea of Galilee? Why is that event so significant to you?

Answer: thirteen; over eight

FEBRUARY 3

THE FIRST PROFESSIONS

Abel was a shepherd and Cain was a ______.

The fourth chapter of Genesis provides a sad and dramatic backdrop for human history. Cain and Abel were the first sons of Adam and Eve. Cain cultivated the ground and produced crops. Cain's name means "to produce" or "to acquire." His brother, Abel, was a shepherd. Abel's name, perhaps ironically, means "breath" or "vapor."

In a moment of jealous rage, Cain killed his brother out in a field. When God confronted him, Cain responded arrogantly and indignantly. As punishment for taking Abel's life—and breath—the Lord proclaimed that the ground would become difficult to cultivate, and it would cause Cain to become a drifter in search of better land. Miserable, Cain left the presence of God and eventually settled in a land east of Eden.

She gave birth to his brother Abel.
Now Abel was a keeper of flocks,
but Cain was a cultivator of the ground.

Genesis 4:2 NASB

What foundational truths about humanity are learned through the account of Cain and Abel?

Answer: farmer

IMPROMPTU BAPTISM

After leaving Samaria, who did Philip baptize?

An angel of the Lord told Philip to go south down the desert road that runs from Jerusalem to Gaza. As he started out, he met a eunuch who served the Queen of Ethiopia as the nation's treasurer. As a man who feared God, the eunuch had been in Jerusalem to worship God.

As he came up to the Ethiopian's carriage, Philip could hear him reading aloud from Isaiah 53, which prophecies about the Messiah being led away like a lamb to the slaughter. When Philip explained how Jesus was the Lamb of God who takes away the sin of the world, the Ethiopian was ready to give his life to Jesus. When they came across a body of water, the Ethiopian asked to be baptized. Generations upon generations of believers in Ethiopia have traced their spiritual heritage back to this moment, two thousand years ago.

As they traveled along the road, they came to some water, and the eunuch said, "Look, here is water. What can stand in the way of my being baptized?" And he gave orders to stop the chariot. Then both Philip and the eunich went down into the water and Philip baptized him.

Acts 8:36-38 NIV

Who can you share God's good news with today?

Answer: the Ethiopian eunuch

HOLDING COATS

Who held the coats of the people who were stoning Stephen?

Before he became the apostle who changed the world, Paul was a zealous Pharisee who persecuted the followers of Jesus. He was known by his Jewish name, Saul. At an early point in his crusade against the church, Saul eagerly supported the execution of Stephen, who was one of the early leaders of the church.

Stephen angered a bunch of people by preaching the good news about Jesus. When he confronted the crowd, they turned on him. Stephen looked up to heaven and claimed to see Jesus. The crowd reacted hysterically, putting their hands over their ears and shouting at him. They grabbed him and threw him out of the city and began to throw rocks at him. Saul agreed with the vindictive spirit of the crowd against Stephen, eager to encourage violence against the church. He offered to hold the coats of the mob so they could easily throw stones. This began a wave of persecution against the early believers which caused them to flee Jerusalem and scatter to other cities.

They put their hands over their ears and began shouting. They rushed at him and dragged him out of the city and began to stone him. His accusers took off their coats and laid them at the feet of a young man named Saul.

Acts 7:57-58 NLT

If God could transform Saul into a committed Christian, what can he do with you today?

Answer: Saul, who became the Apostle Paul

WASHING HANDS

Who washed his hands clean of the crucifixion of Jesus?

Pilate knew Jesus was innocent. He was troubled that the religious leaders were demanding his death. He was bothered that the mobs outside his palace were screaming for his crucifixion. He was surprised that the people wanted a murderer, Barabbas, released while wanting Jesus, who was innocent, to be executed. He was alarmed when his wife begged him to leave the innocent man alone because she had a nightmare about him.

When it came time to sentence Jesus to death, Pilate tried to absolve himself of any guilt. He ordered a bowl of water be brought, and he made a show of washing his hands as a sign of his own innocence in the matter. Then he ordered Barabbas to be released and Jesus to be flogged with a lead-tipped whip and then to be crucified.

Pilate saw that he wasn't getting anywhere and that a riot was developing. So he sent for a bowl of water and washed his hands before the crowd, saying, "I am innocent of this man's blood. The responsibilty is yours!"

Matthew 27:24 NLT

Read Romans 3:23-25. What do you think about innocence, guilt, and forgiveness?

Answer: Pontius Pilate

WHEN GOD MADE ADAM

TRUE OR FALSE
God breathed into Adam's nostrils.

The name Adam, in Hebrew *Adamah,* means "earth" or "dirt." Adam was an "earth-man." When God created Adam, he sculpted some dusty, dirty earth into the form of a person. But it wasn't until God breathed into the man's nostrils that life began. It is God's breath that gave life to Adam. The Hebrew word used here is *ruach*, which means "breath," "wind," or "spirit." It could be understood that God breathed his Spirit into Adam.

With this in mind, it makes sense that the skeletons in the valley of Ezekiel's vision came to life when the Spirit of God breathed into them (Ezekiel 36). Likewise, it is not a surprise when Jesus tells Nicodemus that eternal life is given to someone who is born again by the Holy Spirit (John 3:3-8). God wants all humanity to know this truth: the breath of God is the essential component of true life.

The Lord God formed the man from the dust of the ground.
He breathed the breath of life into the man's nostrils,
and the man became a living person.

Genesis 2:7 NLT

How is your reliance upon the Holy Spirit today?

Answer: true

FEBRUARY 8

FIRST MIRACLE

What was Jesus' first recorded miracle?

It may be surprising that the first record of Jesus performing a miracle was at a wedding when Jesus turned water into wine. In the town of Cana in Galilee, Jesus and his disciples were invited to attend the ceremony. Jesus' mother was one of the organizers of the wedding, though it is unclear whether or not it was an official position for her. During the festivities, Mary told Jesus they had run out of wine. Jesus' response was surprising. "My time has not yet come" (John 2:4). Readers of the story get the impression that Mary was encouraging Jesus to reveal his glory while also helping out the guests of the wedding. Maybe Jesus was testing her. Mary simply turned to some workers and instructed them to do whatever Jesus told them to (v. 5).

Jesus had the servants take six jars that each held thirty gallons and fill them with water. After they had done so, he told them to draw some out and give it to the master of ceremonies. Miraculously, the water had turned to the best wine of the wedding.

This miraculous sign at Cana in Galilee was the first time Jesus revealed his glory. And his disciples believed in him.

John 2:11 NLT

Why do you think Jesus chose this moment for his first miraculous sign?

Answer: turning water into wine

STEP OF TRUST

What river did Joshua and the nation of Israel cross as they entered the Promised Land?

Forty years after they had crossed the Red Sea, God's people were finally ready to enter the Promised Land. Joshua told the Israelites that the priests would carry the ark of the covenant into the river and lead the people across. "As soon as their feet touch the water," he told them, "the flow of water will be cut off upstream, and the river will stand up like a wall" (Joshua 3:13).

As soon as the feet of the priests carrying the ark touched the water, it began backing up a great distance upstream until the riverbed was dry. When all the people had crossed the Jordan River near the town of Jericho, they set up twelve stones from the dry riverbed, one for each tribe. This was a memorial of the work of the Lord to get them to their homeland. Joshua became a great leader in the eyes of God's people that day.

The priests who were carrying the Ark of the LORD's Covenant stood on dry ground in the middle of the riverbed as the people passed by. They waited there until the whole nation of Israel had crossed the Jordan on dry ground.

JOSHUA 3:17 NLT

What might you need to trust the Lord today?

Answer: the Jordan River

FEBRUARY 10

TRAVELING COMPANIONS

Who traveled with Paul on his first missionary journey?

The church in Antioch was a dynamic community for the Christian movement. It was the first place to call the followers of Jesus Christ, Christians (Acts 11:26). The church was determined to bless more people with the good news about Jesus, so they sent out missionaries. Two of its young leaders, Barnabas and Saul, went to Jerusalem to help the believers there prepare for a severe famine. The Antioch church generously gave as much as they could (v. 29) to the elders of the church in Jerusalem. While in Jerusalem, Barnabas and Saul connected with a young John Mark, a friend of Peter's, and invited him to accompany them back to Antioch.

As the church was worshipping and fasting one day, the Holy Spirit told them to appoint Barnabas and Saul for a mission. They commissioned the men, who invited John Mark to join them as their assistant.

Barnabas and Saul were sent out by the Holy Spirit. They went down to the seaport of Seleucia and then sailed for the island of Cyprus. There, in the town of Salamis, they went ot the Jewish synagogues and preached the word of God. John Mark went with them as their assistant.

Acts 13:4-5 NLT

From the example of the church of Antioch, what would you say are the marks of a vibrant church community?

Answer: Barnabas and John Mark

FEBRUARY 11

LAST WORDS

What are the last words of the Bible?

The very last words of the Bible extend a prayer of blessing to those who follow Jesus. They are going to need his grace as they live out their faith in their present-day circumstances. The book of Revelation makes it clear that is it not going to be easy to be a faithful follower of Jesus. There will be plenty of hostility against Christians and many opportunities for Christians to flee the faith.

The book of Revelation is written as a prophetic reminder to God's people to be holy and faithful through whatever circumstances unfold. Yet there is a constant reminder that Jesus, the Lamb of God who was slain for the forgiveness of sin, is alive and on the throne. John reminds his readers that Jesus will return to make everything right on the earth. Knowing this long-term truth and longing for Jesus because of it gives Christians the resiliency to continue to be faithful in all circumstances.

He who is the faithful witness to all these things says,
"Yes, I am coming soon!" Amen! Come, Lord Jesus!
May the grace of the Lord Jesus be with God's holy people.

Revelation 22:20-21 NLT

What eternal perspective do you need in your current situations?

Answer: May the grace of the Lord Jesus be with God's holy people.

ALPHA AND OMEGA

When Jesus is called the "Alpha and Omega," what does that mean?

God created everything. He is the one who began all things. God is also the eternal one who will end all sin and hostility and who will renew all things at the end of time. God proclaimed about himself through the prophet Isaiah, "I am the First and the Last; there is no other God" (Isaiah 44:6).

The Gospel of John launches with this incredible statement: "In the beginning the Word already existed. The Word was with God, and the Word was God. He existed in the beginning with God. God created everything through him, and nothing was created except through him" (1:1-3). The book of Colossians says that Jesus existed before anything was created, and he is supreme over all creation (1:15). The book of Hebrews boldly says that Jesus is the champion who initiates and perfects our faith (12:2). The book of Revelation points out again and again that Jesus himself proclaims the title of the Alpha and Omega (1:8, 21:6, 22:13), and he is worshipped as the Creator of all things. To know Jesus is to know God.

"I am the Alpha and the Omega—the beginning and the end," says the Lord God. "I am the one who is, who always was, and who is still to come—the Almighty One."

Revelation 1:8 NLT

Take some time to be in awe of the Lord Jesus Christ, the Alpha and Omega.

Answer: the beginning and the end

LOVE WHO

"'Love the Lord your God with all your __________ and with all your __________ and with all your __________ and with all your __________'; and, 'Love your __________ as __________.'"

Today's verse is one that every believer should memorize. It sums up the gist of the whole Bible. The backstory of this verse is that a religious expert had asked Jesus what someone needed to do to inherit eternal life. Jesus turned the question back on the man and asked what the Word of God had to say. The man responded to Jesus with the correct answer. Jesus agreed and instructed the man to do this, and he would live.

The man wasn't satisfied. He wanted to know exactly who his neighbor was so he could justify only loving some people and not others. This prompted Jesus to tell one of the most famous parables in history: the story of the good Samaritan.

"'Love the Lord your God with all your heart and with all your soul and with all your strength and with all your mind'; and, 'Love your neighbor as yourself.'"

Luke 10:27 NIV

How can you love with all your heart, soul, strength, and mind?

Answer: heart; soul; strength; mind; neighbor; yourself

CHURCHES OF REVELATION

How many churches did John send the book of Revelation to?

The book of Revelation holds timeless prophetic truths for today and for the future. It also offers a profound insight into the realities of seven first-century churches in Asia Minor, now known as Turkey. These churches were each significant communities in the growing movement of Christianity in the Roman Empire. They represented hundreds of other churches in cities and towns and provinces throughout the known world. Christianity was spreading quickly, and it was planting deeply within the ancient world despite constant pressures and persecutions against the believers.

John first saw a different vision where sin was overcome by Jesus, and God's throne was established in a new heaven and a new earth. He then began to describe the vision of the future that God gave him and wrote this in his personal notes to those specific seven churches listed in our verse today. The notes, however, were not from him but directly from Jesus. To each church Jesus offered a message, usually of encouragement, but often of conviction. He urged his followers to continue to live for him in their present circumstances even while knowing that he had the future in his hands.

"Write in a book everything you see, and send it to the seven churches in the cities of Ephesus, Smyrna, Pergamum, Thyatira, Sardis, Philadelphia, and Laodicea."

Revelation 1:11 NLT

Take some time to read Jesus' letters to each of the seven churches. What present day encouragement or convictions can you take from these letters?

Answer: seven

THE SUFFERING KING

On the cross when Jesus cried out, "My God, My God, why have you forsaken me?" what psalm was he quoting?

The psalm of the suffering King is Psalm 22. It was considered a prophetic psalm that spoke about the future Messiah. This psalm was written by David during a time when he was being threatened and rejected. In it, he launched into a lament, "My God, my God, why have you abandoned me?" When Jesus cried out the famous words on the cross, those who knew the psalms would have recognized that he was reciting the psalm of the suffering King.

Psalm 22 went on to describe David's difficult circumstances. He said an evil gang was closing in on him and they had pierced his hands and feet. That, of course, is how Jesus was killed on the cross. David said his enemies divided his garments and threw dice for his clothing. The Roman soldiers later divided Jesus' clothes among themselves and took his robe and threw dice for it. David said everyone was mocking him and he asked the Lord to rescue him When Jesus was crucified, the crowds ridiculed him and said, "Let him save himself if he's really God's Messiah, the Chosen One!" (Luke 23:35)

At three o'clock Jesus called out with a loud voice, "Eloi, Eloi, lema sabachtani?" which means "My God, my God, why have you abandoned me?"

MARK 15:34 NLT

How does Psalm 22 prepare the way for the Messiah's death on the cross.

Answer: Psalm 22

FEBRUARY 16

ABRAHAM'S NEPHEW

Who was Abraham's nephew?

When Abraham moved his family to Canaan, God promised to make him into a great nation and to bless him and make him famous. The Lord used Abraham's close relationship with his nephew, Lot, to establish which land Abraham's descendants would inherit.

After accumulating large flocks and many tents and herdsmen, Abraham and Lot had become quite wealthy. But the new land in Canaan could not support both their estates with all the goats, sheep, and livestock. Abraham didn't want conflict with Lot's people, so he invited his nephew to choose any section of land he desired. Lot chose the fertile land east of the Jordan River, and Abraham consequently chose the land to the west of the Jordan toward the Mediterranean as far as he could see in every direction. God promised Abraham that this land would become the permanent possession for his descendants (Genesis 13:15).

He took his wife Sarai, his nephew Lot, all the possessions they had accumulated and the people they had acquired in Harran, and they set out for the land of Canaan, and they arrived there.

GENESIS 12:5 NIV

If someone were to ask you how Abraham's story is connected to Jesus, how would you answer?

Answer: Lot

STORYTELLING

The story of the good Samaritan is an example of what kind of storytelling technique?

The writer of Psalm 78 indicates that he is going to tell about the lessons learned from their ancestors by using a parable. This narrative story-telling technique had been employed frequently by God's people both in Scripture and in oral tradition. It was a good method to share about all God had done for them throughout history. The prophet Nathan famously shared a story to King David about a rich man stealing a poor man's lamb. Isaiah used illustrations of vineyards and flocks to help Israel understand their relationship with God.

Jesus used parables to engage people in truths about God's Kingdom. He wanted them to listen, to think, to wrestle, and to remember his teachings. He spoke about being salt and light to the earth. He taught about wise and foolish builders. He told stories about sowing seeds and fertile soil. He discussed businessmen and inheritances and marriage ceremonies. He shared about prodigal sons and lost sheep and hidden treasure. Jesus wanted people to be surprised and challenged by his parables so that his truth would be heard and then understood deeply within a person's soul.

O my people, listen to my instructions.
Open your ears to what I am saying,
for I will speak to you in a parable.
I will teach you hidden lessons from our past.

Psalm 78:1-2 NLT

Which parable of Jesus is the most memorable for you? What is it that Jesus wants you to learn about him through that parable?

Answer: parable

FEBRUARY 18

IN THE BEGINNING

What significant term does John use to refer to Jesus at the beginning of his Gospel?

"In the beginning God created the heavens and the earth." These are the famous first words in the Bible. When John started his gospel account of the life of Jesus, he wanted his readers to think about creation. John wanted people to consider who was present at the beginning of the world and then to really consider how the world was made. Recall that the Spirit of God was hovering over the waters before God commanded there to be light (Genesis 1:2-3).

John refers to Jesus as the Word—the Word that already existed in the beginning. The Word was there with God. The Word was God. The Word created everything. The Word gives life and light to everyone. The Word is more powerful than chaos and darkness. That Word, John says, is Jesus.

In the beginning was the Word, and the Word was with God,
and the Word was God. He was with God in the beginning.
Through him all things were made;
without him nothing was made that has been made.

John 1:1-3 NIV

What life and light do you need Jesus to speak into you today?

Answer: the Word

FEBRUARY 19

FIFTH BOOK

What is the fifth book in the New Testament?

Many scholars consider the book of Acts to be the sequel to Luke's Gospel. "In my former book," Luke tells his friend Theophilus, "I wrote about all that Jesus began to do and to teach until the day he was taken up to heaven" (Acts1:1-2). Luke was a doctor and a missionary companion to the apostle Paul. While traveling with Paul, he researched and compiled the awe-inspiring account of Jesus' life, death, and resurrection into the book of Luke. He then tackled an engaging record of the Spirit-empowered, stratospheric beginnings of the early Church in the book of Acts.

It is important to Luke that his readers understand that all of the world-impacting events of the growth of the Christian movement was grounded in the work of the Holy Spirit. Jesus told his followers he would send the Spirit who would empower them to be his witnesses around the world. The book of Acts is the account of that movement from Jerusalem to the ends of the earth.

"You will receive power when the Holy Spirit comes on you; and you will be my witnesses in Jerusalem, and in all Judea and Samaria, and to the ends of the earth."

Acts 1:8 NIV

What convictions might you have if you were to compare your current experience of "church" with the dynamic stories of the book of Acts?

Answer: Acts

STRANGE RESPONSE

When Elisha raised the Shunammite woman's son back to life, what did the boy do before he opened his eyes?

Shunem was a small town near Mount Carmel in Israel. The prophet Elisha would often pass through there, so a wealthy couple offered to build him a room where he could stay and be refreshed. As a way of showing his gratitude, Elisha prayed for the woman to be able to bear a son. A year later, her son was born.

Years later the son complained to his dad about his head hurting. He was carried to his mother, laid upon her lap, and died. The boy's body was laid on the same bed that Elisha used when he was visiting. The mother of the dead boy urgently rode to get Elisha from Mount Carmel and when she found him, she cried out in anguish. Elisha followed her back to the house, shut the door to the boy's room, and like Elijah had done for the son of the widow from Zarephath, stretched himself across the boy and prayed. The boy warmed, then sneezed seven times, and opened his eyes. When the woman saw her son, healthy and alive, she fell at Elisha's feet, bowed to the ground, then picked up her son.

He got up again and walked once back and forth in the house, and went up and stretched himself upon him. The child sneezed seven times, and the child opened his eyes.

2 Kings 4:35 ESV

What experiences does Jesus have later on that are similar to this event? What does God want us to learn from these moments when people are raised from the dead?

Answer: sneezed seven times

FEBRUARY 21

TASKS TO GREATNESS

Which of the following items did David's father, Jesse, ask him to bring to his brothers on the front lines of the battle?

A. A basket of roasted grain
B. Ten loaves of bread
C. Ten cuts of cheese
D. Five smooth stones

David was only a boy when his dad sent him to the front lines of the battle carrying supplies for his brothers. From his home in Bethlehem to the warfront in the Valley of Elah (over fourteen miles), he brought them a basket of roasted grain and ten loaves of bread. He also brought cuts of cheese for the army captain so that David could then ask about how things were going.

What happened next is legendary. David noticed the Philistine champion, Goliath, taunting the Israelite army. He heard Goliath defying God. As a shepherd, David protected his flocks from bears and lions. And as a young man, David faithfully walked with God. David passionately convinced King Saul to let him fight Goliath. Instead of Saul's military armor, however, David chose to confront Goliath with only his shepherding tools—his staff, his sling, and five smooth stones from his bag.

One day Jesse said to David his son, "Take for your brothers an ephah of this parched grain, and these ten loaves, and carry them quickly to the camp to your brothers. Also take these ten cheeses to the commander."

1 Samuel 17:17-18 NLT

What would the world be like if David had not been faithful in the menial tasks he'd been given?

Answer: A) and B); C) was for their commander

FEBRUARY 22

UNKNOWN GOD

In what city did Paul discover an altar to an unknown god?

Paul was distressed by the number of idols in Athens. He reasoned with the Jews and the God-fearing Greeks in the synagogue and also with the Greek philosophers in the marketplace. He found the philosophers eager to debate with him about his teachings, and he received an invitation to teach the leaders of the Areopagus, which was the center of political and religious governance in Athens. These curious thinkers wanted to hear the new teaching and strange ideas that Paul presented.

Paul affirmed the religious interests of the people of Athens, noting that he had seen first-hand how many objects of worship they had around them. He noted that he had even found an altar with an inscription dedicated to an unknown god. Paul continued, by revealing to them that the unknown god was actually Almighty God. This God made everything and held it all together just as their own philosophers had figured. Paul shared about Jesus and called for the people of Athens to repent of sin and align themselves with him. Several people including a member of the Areopagus named Dionysius, became followers of Paul and believed his message about Jesus.

"People of Athens! I see that in every way you are very religious. For as I walked around and looked carefully at your objects of worship, I even found an altar with this inscription: to an unknown god.

ACTS 17:22-23 NIV

How would you share the good news with someone who was religious but had never heard of Jesus?

Answer: Athens

FEBRUARY 23

A FLY'S STENCH

According to Ecclesiasties, what kind of flies make perfume stink?

A. dead flies
B. horse flies
C. fruit flies
D. dragonflies

It doesn't matter how many good things we do or how many smart things we say, one slip of foolishness can be the only thing people remember about us. It is easy to ruin a good reputation. It doesn't take much to wreck a long track record of integrity. People are generally good lie detectors. Most are ready to call out hypocrisy among those who claim to follow God. Living in purity is the only way to keep the pleasing aroma of Christ from becoming a stench that people turn their noses from.

The Bible speaks frequently of getting rid of anything in our lives that can compromise our walk with God. The Holy Spirit works to make us holy and to sanctify us. He convicts us of sin and restores the reflection of God within our lives.

Dead flies make the perfumer's ointment give off a stench;
so a little folly outweighs wisdom and honor.

Ecclesiasties 10:1 ESV

What folly do you need to get rid of today so you can reflect the wisdom and honor of Christ?

Answer: A) dead flies

LONG OBEDIENCE

TRUE OR FALSE
Pharaoh made Joseph the second most powerful person in Egypt.

Joseph was exalted by his father, Jacob, and lavished with an elaborate coat. He also had prophetic dreams of being elevated above his brothers. Joseph's brothers were so jealous of him that they severely beat him and sold him into slavery. Throughout this process, Joseph remained faithful to God and was eventually elevated by his Egyptian owner, Potiphar, to run his estate. After an alarming incident in Potiphar's house, Joseph was falsely accused and thrown into prison. There, Joseph still remained faithful and interpreted the dreams of some fellow prisoners.

When Pharaoh heard that Joseph's interpretations had come true, he sent for him to interpret his own dreams. Pharaoh was so impressed with Joseph's wisdom and consistent leadership skills that he elevated him to the second most important person in all of Egypt. Pharaoh put Joseph in charge of delegating all the food for Egypt during a time of abundance and then during a time of famine. When his brothers came to Egypt seeking rations to survive the food shortages, they didn't realize that it would be Joseph who would decide their fate.

"You will be over my house, and all my people will obey your commands. Only I, as king, will be greater than you."

GENESIS 41:40 CSB

What impresses you most about the long obedience of Joseph throughout the unpredictable experiences of his life?

Answer: true

JUDGE ABDON

How many donkeys did Abdon's sons and grandsons ride?

There are some interesting, random facts scattered throughout the Bible. Here we learn some details about a man named Abdon. He was raised up by God to become a judge for Israel, a role he had for eight years. He was buried in a place called Pirathon in Ephraim, a region that was constantly being contested by the Amalekites, the Canaanites and the nation of Israel, especially the by tribe of Ephraim. But most interesting is that Abdon had forty sons, thirty grandsons, and that they all rode on donkeys. One wonders why this detail is included in the Bible.

The Ephraimites were decimated in some wars in the lifetime of Abdon, and they were struggling to bring prosperity and safety to the land. The fact that Abdon was able to have such a large multi-generation family and a large drove of donkeys indicates that he had become prosperous and had a significant influence in the region. It is noteworthy that he would become the focal point of leadership for Israel after accumulating remarkable affluence in his life.

After Elon died, Abdon son of Hillel, from Pirathon, judged Israel. He had forty sons and thirty grandsons, who rode on seventy donkeys. He judged Israel for eight years. When he died, he was buried at Pirathon in Ephraim, in the hill country of the Amalekites.

Judges 12:13-15 NLT

How might God want to use your faithfulness today to prepare you for his calling later in your life?

Answer: seventy

FEBRUARY 26

DAVID'S BEST FRIEND

Who was David's best friend?

On multiple occasions King Saul tried to kill David. He had grown jealous of David's popularity and was threatened by David's claim to the throne. But Saul's son Jonathan felt differently. He loved David deeply and was willing to forfeit his own rights to the throne so that David could become king. Jonathan protected David from his father's schemes and pledged his loyalty to David. Saul became so enraged by Jonathan's commitment to David that he once threw a spear at Jonathan in an attempt to kill him.

David also found companionship with Jonathan. Not many people would be able to understand the strain David was under. He found likemindedness with Jonathan, who was a man of honor and kept his promises even during difficulties. They made a vow to one another that if Jonathan was killed in his attempts to protect David, that David would care for Jonathan's children as his own. In the end, King Saul became unrelentingly determined to kill David. Jonathan made arrangements for his friend to escape. When it came to time to say goodbye, David and Jonathan embraced and wept.

Jonathan made David reaffirm his vow of friendship again,
for Jonathan loved David as he loved himself.

1 Samuel 20:17 NLT

How does Jonathan's friendship with David represent the second greatest commandment to love your neighbor as yourself?

Answer: Jonathan, the son of King Saul

THOSE WHO MOURN

Why does Jesus say that those who mourn are blessed?

Those who mourn have lost someone or something that they cared for deeply. The pain, the grief, the stress, the worry, all leave a void in the soul. It would seem that those who mourn are not blessed at all.

In the Beatitudes, Jesus offers one stark revolutionary statement after another. Each "Blessed are…" statement stands in contrast to the common pursuit of riches, health, and security. In those few sentences Jesus tackles the raw reality of the human condition and offers the radical promises of God's kingdom. Those who mourn because of love and loss will be comforted. God sees them. God knows their hurt. God loves them. God is present with them in their time of need. A person who does not mourn cannot be comforted, for their heart is closed and calloused. It is only the soft hearted who has cared deeply that may receive the deep care of God.

"Blessed are those who mourn,
for they will be comforted."
MATTHEW 5:4 NIV

How can you extend compassion to someone you know who is grieving?

Answer: they will be comforted

FEBRUARY 28

THE GARDENER

On the morning of the resurrection,
who did Mary mistake as the gardener?

Mary was overwhelmed by the events of the morning. She had gone to the tomb to anoint Jesus' body with perfumes but was startled to find the stone rolled away from the entrance and no body inside. Now she was looking for Jesus. As she wept, she looked inside the tomb again. This time, instead of an empty tomb, she saw two angels seated where Jesus' body had been. They asked her, "Why are you crying?" She responded that someone had taken her Lord away and she didn't know where his body was. A man who she thought was the gardener appeared and asked her, "Why are you crying? Who are looking for?" He then called her by name, "Mary." She cried out in Aramaic, "*Rabboni*" which means "teacher."

At creation, God came to a garden looking for Adam and Eve who were hiding due to their sin. Here at the resurrection of Jesus, Mary came to a garden looking for Jesus who had died for all sin and was now alive.

She turned around and saw Jesus standing there, but she did not realize that it was Jesus. He asked her, "Woman, why are you crying? Who is it you are looking for?" Thinking he was the gardener, she said, "Sir, if you have carried him away, tell me where you have put him, and I will get him."

John 20:14-15 NIV

How do the great gardens of the Bible tell the story of God's good news through Jesus Christ?

Answer: Jesus

MARCH

HUMAN LIFESPAN

Who was the oldest person in history?

The Bible teaches that human lifespans used to be considerably longer than they are now. After the flood, God choose to reduce the span of human life to 120 years because he did not want to abide in man forever. There were some epic lifespans among the first humans. Genesis 5 says that Adam lived to be 930 years old, Seth to 912, Enosh to 905, Kenan to 910, and Jared to 962. But the title of the longest living human of all time belongs to Methuselah, who lived to be 969.

Later we learn that Noah lived 350 years after the Flood and his son Shem lived 502 years after the Flood. Eventually the generations began to live shorter and shorter lives. By the end of the book of Genesis, Joseph lived to be 110 years old, a lifespan that by then was considered a remarkable, respected old age.

All the days of Methuselah were 969 years,
and he died.

Genesis 5:27 NASB

Why do you think God created humans with such long lifespans and then later decided to reduce them?

Answer: Methuselah at 969 years old

TEN LEPERS

How many of the ten lepers that Jesus healed came back to thank him?

On his way to Jerusalem, Jesus crossed the border between Galilee and Samaria. As he entered a village, ten men stood at a distance and cried out for Jesus to have mercy on them. The ten men had leprosy. Jesus told them to go show themselves to the priests. As they obeyed Jesus and started towards the priests, Luke said that they were cleansed of their disease. One of the ten, a Samaritan man, came back to Jesus. He shouted, "Praise God!" He fell at Jesus' feet and thanked him.

Jesus asked why only one of the ten men returned to him. "Didn't I heal ten men?" he asked. "Has no one returned to give glory to God except this foreigner?" Jesus then turned his attention to the man and told him that his faith had healed him.

One of them, when he saw that he was healed, came back to Jesus, shouting, "Praise God!" He fell to the ground at Jesus' feet, thanking him for what he had done. This man was a Samaritan.
Jesus asked, "Didn't I heal ten men? Where are the other nine?"

LUKE 17:15-17 NLT

What surprises you most in this story about the healing of the ten lepers?

Answer: one

THE CENSUS

From the first census that Moses took, which tribe was the largest?

The size of the Israelite exodus from Egypt is astonishing. In the second year after coming out of Egypt, the Lord ordered them to take a census so that they could organize their army and government. The results were measured according to the number of men capable of serving in the army. The tribe of Reuben had 46,500 fighting men; Simeon had 59,300; Gad had 45,650; Judah had 74,600; Issachar had 54,400; Zebulun had 57,400; Ephraim had 40,500; Manasseh had 32,200; Benjamin had 35,400; Dan had 62,700; Asher had 41,500; and Naphtali had 53,400.

Altogether there were 603,550 men able to serve in Israel's army. Joseph's tribe was split between his two sons, Ephraim and Manasseh. The tribe of Levi was not counted in this census because of their priestly responsibilities.

From the descendants of Judah: All the men twenty years old or more who were able to serve in the army were listed by name, according to the records of their clans and families. The number from the tribe of Judah was 74,600.

Numbers 1:26-27 NIV

What are the implications of such a large population and fighting force wandering in the wilderness for another thirty-nine years before entering the Promised Land?

Answer: the tribe of Judah

MARCH 4

SAME FAITH

What were the names of the three men thrown into the fiery furnace?

The three men thrown into the fiery furnace are best known to us today by their Babylonian names: Shadrach, Meshach, and Abednego. Along with Daniel, they were among the early captives taken into exile from Judah and brought to Babylon to serve King Nebuchadnezzar. The first chapter of the book of Daniel says that the men were all given new names to cover up their Jewish names. Daniel's name was changed to Belteshazzar. Hananiah was changed to Shadrach. Mishael was changed to Meshach. And Azariah was changed to Abednego.

When the King built a statue of himself and ordered people to bow down to it, the men refused. Angry, Nebuchadnezzar threw them into the furnace for not revoking their faith in God. But the Lord spared them in the furnace and astonished the King.

Nebuchadnezzar was furious with Shadrach, Meshach and Abednego, and his attitude toward them changed. He ordered the furnace heated seven times hotter than usual and commanded some of the strongest soldiers in his army to tie up Shadrach, Meshach and Abednego and throw them into the blazing furnace.

DANIEL 3:19-20 NIV

In the face of severe opposition, would you be willing to lose your identity in order to follow the Lord?

Answer: Shadrach, Meshach, and Abednego

BURNING COAL

Which prophet had a vision of his lips being touched with burning coal?

Isaiah was overwhelmed by the presence of God whom he saw sitting on his throne, his robe filling the temple. There were seraphim who covered their faces with two of their wings. The seraphim called to one another, "Holy, holy, holy, is the Lord of hosts; the whole earth is filled with his glory!" (Isaiah 6:3) The foundations of the temple shook and was filled with smoke. Isaiah felt unworthy. He became aware of his own unclean lips, and of the fact that he dwelled in a land filled with people of unclean lips.

One of the seraphim flew toward him with a burning coal from the altar. The seraphim touched Isaiah's lips with the coal and declared that God had forgiven Isaiah's guilt.

> One of the seraphim flew to me, having in his hand a burning coal that he had taken with tongs from the altar. And he touched my mouth and said: "Behold, this has touched your lips; your guilt is taken away, and your sin atoned for."
>
> Isaiah 6:6-7 ESV

If you were to summarize what Isaiah discovered about himself and about the Lord in this experience, what would you say?

Answer: Isaiah

MARCH 6

DISCOVERING GOD'S WORD

What did King Josiah do when he heard the words from the book of the law for the first time?

King Josiah did what was right in the eyes of the Lord. He was only eight years old when he became king, but he tried to follow the ways of his ancestor, David. When he was twenty-six years old, Josiah hired carpenters, builders, and stone masons to repair the temple. It had fallen into disrepair during prior generations. During construction, Hilkiah, the high priest told Josiah's secretary, Shaphan, that he had found the book of the Law in the temple. Almost as an afterthought while going through the accounts of the work, Shaphan informed King Josiah that the high priest had found a book. Josiah asked him to read it and immediately realized that the readings were from the Torah, the original five books of Moses. They contained the foundations of the nation of Israel and the revelation of their relationship with God.

Josiah was overcome with grief and fear as he realized how far from God's commands the nation had drifted. This launched a dramatic time of revival. Josiah steered the nation back into alignment with the ways of God.

Shaphan the secretary informed the king, "Hilkiah the priest has given me a book." And Shaphan read from it in the presence of the king. When the king heard the words of the Book of the Law, he tore his robes.

2 Kings 22:10-11 NIV

Read part of the first five books of the Bible. How do you think you would respond if you were hearing this for the first time in the day of King Josiah?

Answer: he tore his robes

MARCH 7

FIRST COMMANDMENT

What is the first of the Ten Commandments?

The first priority for every person is God, whether they realize it or not. Many choose to prioritize their own pursuits or even the desires of others, instead of prioritizing God. But what or who could be more important in our daily and eternal lives than God? He is our Creator, our Sustainer, and the author and perfecter of each of us. He made us to be in relationship with him. He pursues us and draws us toward him. He rescues us from our sin and calls us by our names. He knows us intimately and he never forsakes us.

Yet, we are tempted to forsake him. We turn our eyes toward other things. We gaze on other objects of worship. We focus our attention on other values, worries, and lusts. We spend our energy pursuing temporal things, rather than investing in the everlasting provisions of God.

"You shall have no other gods before me."

Exodus 20:3 NIV

How sad is it that God needs to remind us of this first commandment?

Answer: you shall have no other gods

MARCH 8

THE DRY BONES

Who had the vision of the valley of dry bones that come to life?

God gave a special prophet a vision. He saw of an entire valley filled with an army of dried-up skeletons which took on flesh and skin, and then came back to life. Only God could take lifeless bodies and cause his breath to enter into them. He wanted this prohpehet to understand that this is what he would do for Israel. "I will put my Spirit within you, and you shall live, and I will place you in your own land" (Ezekiel 37:14). He promised him that the people of Israel would know he was God when their graves were opened and his Spirit was put within them.

Generations later, Jesus declared that the kingdom of God was near. He brought people back to life and sent his Spirit to dwell within his people.

"I will lay sinews upon you, and will cause flesh to come upon you, and cover you with skin, and put breath in you, and you shall live, and you shall know that I am the Lord."

Ezekiel 37:6 ESV

What effect does this passage have on you?

Answer: Ezekiel

MARCH 9

LONGEST REIGN

What was the name of the king who had the longest reign in Israel?

The northern kingdom of Israel was marked by generations of corrupt kings. Jeroboam II was able to keep his reign in the northern kingdom longer than any other ruler. Second Kings notes that he did evil in the eyes of the Lord and contributed greatly to the suffering of the people of Israel. He reigned from Samaria and reestablished a significant hold on the land from the northern end of what is today Syria down to the northern end of the Dead Sea.

Like the other northern kings before and after him, Jeroboam II encouraged the worship of God through idols and also encouraged the worship of other gods. He treated the people badly and relied on slavery to accomplish his aims as king. Soon after his harsh reign, the kingdom began to disintegrate and was eventually conquered by the Assyrians.

In the fifteenth year of Amaziah son of Joash king of Judah, Jeroboam son of Jehoash king of Israel became king in Samaria, and he reigned forty-one years.

2 Kings 14:23 NIV

Why do you think God put up with the compromised faith of his people for so long?

Answer: Jeroboam II

MARCH 10

THE TEN PLAGUES

How many of the ten plagues that God sent against Egypt can you name?

It is estimated that there were about a million Jews enslaved in the Egyptian empire during this time. Much of the construction and infrastructure of the economy was built on their backs. It was not likely that Pharaoh would have responded favorably to Moses' demand to let God's people go. But Pharaoh wasn't really dealing with Moses; he was dealing with God. God was going to free his people from their misery and oppression.

God sent one plague after another, restoring the faith of his people. He wore down Pharaoh's resolve and struck fear into the Egyptians. By the end of the ninth plague, the tide of popular opinion had turned in favor of the Jews and of Moses (v. 3). But Pharaoh hardened his heart and refused to compromise. It was the tenth plague that broke the obstinacy of Pharaoh. And so it was with a mixture of mourning and fear and relief when the people of Israel were urged to leave the country.

> The Lord had said to Moses, "I will bring one more plague on Pharaoh and on Egypt. After that, he will let you go from here, and when he does, he will drive you out completely."
>
> Exodus 11:1 NIV

Which of the plagues would have had you running back to God and pleading with him?

Answer: blood, frogs, gnats, flies, livestock, boils, hail, locusts, darkness, death

MARCH 11

DAVID'S FATHER

Who was David's father?

Jesse had eight sons. When the prophet, Samuel, arrived in Bethlehem, Jesse invited seven sons to join in the meeting. The youngest, David, he left in charge of the sheep in the fields. Jesse often gave David tasks like this during important moments. When King Saul needed a harp player to sooth his tormented spirit, Jesse allowed David to serve the king. When Jesse wanted to send supplies sent his sons fighting against the Philistines, he sent David.

But Jesse understood that David, though young, was bright and capable. David had proven himself to be a warrior, strong enough to kill a lion and a bear that attacked his flock. David had proven himself to be a skilled manager, wise enough to put other workers in charge when he was ordered to bring supplies to his brothers. David had proven himself to be a talented musician, able to impress the king. And Jesse came to understand that David was anointed by God to become the king of God's people.

The Lord said to Samuel, "How long will you mourn for Saul, since I have rejected him as king over Israel? Fill your horn with oil and be on your way; I am sending you to Jesse of Bethlehem. I have chosen one of his sons to be king."

1 Samuel 16:1 NIV

How did David's upbringing prepare him for the future?

Answer: Jesse

MARCH 12

MEETING GOD

How does God appear to Moses the first time?

Moses was going about his daily routines, tending the flock for his father-in-law. He herded the flock to Horeb, which was known as the mountain of God. There Moses was startled by a bush that was on fire but was not burning up. Moses cautiously approached the bush. That's when God called to him from within the bush, "Moses! Moses!" He told Moses to remove his sandals, for he was standing holy ground. Then he introduced himself to Moses. It was unexpected, since Moses was a former prince of Egypt, a murderer who fled to Midian and married the daughter of a pagan priest.

Moses hid his face in fear. God described to Moses how he had seen the misery of the Jewish people enslaved in Egypt and it was time to rescue them. And he had chosen Moses to confront Pharaoh and lead the people to freedom.

There the angel of the Lord appeared to him in flames of fire from within a bush. Moses saw that though the bush was on fire it did not burn up.

Exodus 3:2 NIV

Put yourself in Moses' situation for a moment. What emotions and thoughts would you be experiencing?

Answer: in a burning bush

WHAT A RIOT

In which city did Paul's teaching about Jesus start a riot?

Paul was traveling in what is now known as eastern Turkey. In one city his message about Jesus stirred the city large city with a quarter of a million people. It was the seat of the Temple of Artemis, known in Hellenic times as one of the seven wonders of the world. Artemis was worshipped as a goddess of fertility, which led to an influential economic system of sexual practices and trades.

Paul and his companions went throughout the city sharing about Jesus. Paul argued frequently in the synagogue and lectured in the hall of Tyrannus. He did this for over two years, so that all the Jews and Greeks who lived in the province of Asia heard the word of the Lord (v. 10). But the effective preaching and the miraculous power that accompanied it, was impacting the infrastructure of the religious system. A large mob stirred up by a silversmith named Demetrius seized two of Paul's traveling partners and threatened them in the city's theater shouting, "Great is Artemis of the Ephesians!" Ironically, the uproar further cemented the faith of the Ephesian Christians and spread the news about Jesus throughout the province.

When they heard this, they were furious and began shouting: "Great is Artemis of the Ephesians!" Soon the whole city was in an uproar. The people seized Gaius and Aristarchus, Paul's traveling companions from Macedonia, and all of them rushed into the theater together.

Acts 19:28-29 NIV

How can you be bold in your faith today?

Answer: Ephesus

MARCH 14

GARDEN OF PRAYER

In which garden did Jesus pray on the night he was arrested?

Jesus shared his Last Supper with the disciples. During this final meal, Judas left to betray him, and Peter insisted that he would never deny his Lord. Afterward, Jesus went with his disciples to a garden to pray. This garden of olive trees was a short walk across the Kidron Valley, east of the Temple Mount and the city of Jerusalem. Jesus wanted to spend the last moments before his death in prayer to his Father. He asked his disciples to keep watch with him as his soul was overwhelmed with sorrow to the point of death.

Jesus fell with his face to the ground and prayed a remarkably humble prayer. "Father, may this cup be taken from me. Yet not my will but yours be done" (Matthew 26:39). When he looked back to his disciples, he was disheartened that they had fallen asleep. Luke's Gospel tells us that he was so distressed and fervent in his prayer that his sweat fell to the ground like great drops of blood.

Jesus went with his disciples to a place called Gethsemane, and he said to them, "Sit here while I go over there and pray."

MATTHEW 26:36 NIV

What does it mean to you that Jesus felt this way, yet he still faced the suffering ahead?

Answer: Gethsemane

UNDESERVED

FINISH THIS VERSE

The wages of sin is _______, but the gift of God is _______ _______ in Christ Jesus our Lord.

If builders construct a home, or teachers instruct students at school, or pilots fly passengers from one town to another, they earn wages. But what happens if a person's effort is sinful? What payment does someone receive if they lie, or steal, or hurt someone? What wages does someone earn if their actions go against God's standards? The Bible is very clear about this. Only God is holy, without sin, and therefore wholly alive. God is the way, the truth, and the life. Humans were created to be holy with God, but because we have sinned and gone our own way, we have earned only separation from the living God.

Still, because God so loved the world, he didn't give humans what they deserve but offered an alternative. God presented humanity with a gift in the form of eternal life through Jesus Christ so that whoever believes in him will not perish.

The wages of sin is death, but the gift of God is eternal life in Christ Jesus our Lord.

Romans 6:23 NIV

Do you feel as though some of the sin in your life is too big for God to forgive? Do you know that isn't true?

Answer: death; eternal life

MARCH 16

MOST CHAPTERS

What book of the Bible has the most chapters?

The book of Psalms has the most chapters of any book in the Bible at one hundred and fifty; the next closest is the book of Isaiah with only sixty-six. In English, Psalms have more words than any other book except for Jeremiah and Genesis depending on the translation. Its poetic structure with stanzas and songs requires it to take more up more printed space than any other book. Psalms also took the longest to collect, having been written by multiple authors over a period of several hundreds of years.

The goal of the book and one of the reasons for there being so many psalms, is that people can meditate on God's Word. The psalms are meant to be sung repeatedly, memorized frequently, and remembered constantly. Jesus quotes more from Psalms than from any other book, and almost half the Old Testament quotes in the New Testament are from Psalms. Psalms give prayerful and praise-full expressions to God's Word. God's people are encouraged to delight in it, think upon it, and let it take root in their lives.

Whose delight is in the law of the Lord,
and who meditates on his law day and night.

Psalm 1:2 NIV

Plant yourself in God's Word today. Where will you begin?

Answer: Psalms

MARCH 17

JUDGING OTHERS

Before you judge someone else, what does Jesus say you should remove from your own eye?

Jesus warns people to not judge others. If someone judges another person, then they themselves stand to be judged. The standard people use to judge others will be the standard by which they are also judged. Why worry about a speck in your friend's eye when you have a log in your own? The relatively minor issue of someone removing a small irritant from their eye pales in comparison to the ridiculous image of a person with a log sticking out of their eye. This brilliantly creative and humorous parable reveals how people are so easily blinded to their own spiritual condition while attacking the condition of others.

The irony, of course, is that God's holiness is the ultimate standard, and everyone falls short of that. It is of no use judging the condition of others, for every single person already stands judged before God's glory (Romans 3:23).

"Hypocrite! First get rid of the log in your own eye; then you will see well enough to deal with the speck in your friend's eye."

MATTHEW 7:5 NLT

What blindness to your own spiritual condition should you deal with today?

Answer: a log

PHILEMON'S CHALLENGE

Who did Paul write to so he would receive Philemon back as his brother?

The letter that Paul sends to Philemon is one of the most candid and personal notes in ancient literature. It reveals how the spread of Christianity was beginning to upend the systems of the Roman Empire. The letter concerns two men: Philemon, who had become Paul's friend when he gave his life to Christ, and Onesimus, who was a former slave of Philemon. Onesimus was likely carrying this letter along with the letter to the Colossians.

At some point Onesimus fled Philemon's estate and then came across the apostle Paul. Paul indicated that Onesimus became like a son to him during Paul's stay in prison. Even though Paul would like Onesimus to remain with him, Onesimus was going to return home. Paul appealed to Philemon that because of Jesus, Onesimus was no longer a slave but a brother. It was time to reconcile. If Onesimus owes anything, Paul informs Philemon, he himself would pay it outright. Paul adds a digging reminder in the letter that Philemon himself owes Paul his very soul.

It seems you lost Onesimus for a little while so that you could have him back forever. He is no longer like a slave to you. He is more than a slave, for he is a beloved brother, especially to me. Now he will mean much more to you, both as a man and as a brother in the Lord.

PHILEMON 15-16 NLT

How has the gospel of Jesus changed the system of your life?

Answer: Onesimus

MARCH 19

LAST OF THE OLD

What is the last book of the Old Testament?

The last book of the Old Testament prepared people for the coming of the Messiah. It says that there will be another prophet like Elijah, a messenger of God, who will prepare the way before God. We recognize this person now as John the Baptist who urged people to turn from judgment to repentance through Jesus. Like John the Baptist, Malachi warns of the consequences for those who claim to be God's people but fail to be obedient to him.

In this way, Malachi is a difficult book to absorb. It speaks of God's unchanging standard compared to the hypocritical behavior of people. It speaks of God pouring out his blessings on those who respond to him, but curses for those who cheat against him. It speaks about the Sun of Righteousness who will rise with healing in his wings, yet also the coming Day of Judgment. This is the last prophetic message given to Israel before a long-lasting, silent era of hundreds of years until the angel appears to Mary.

This is the message that the LORD gave to Israel
through the prophet Malachi.

MALACHI 1:1 NLT

How can you prepare your own life today to receive Jesus?

Answer: Malachi

BACK TO LIFE

A man came back to life when his corpse was thrown into the tomb of which prophet?

Elisha was a powerful prophet. His life was marked by miracles and messages. He confronted kings and servants, wealthy and poor. He orchestrated major political upheavals and minor, behind the scenes, blessings. Elisha, known as the "man of God," represented holy power in a time when God's people struggled to survive.

Shortly after Elisha died a remarkable thing happened. Some marauders were harassing a community near a cemetery where a man was being buried. This same cemetery was the location of Elisha's tomb. Afraid for their lives, the Israelites threw the man's body into Elisha's tomb and fled. But when the dead man's body touched Elisha's bones, he came back to life and jumped to his feet! It seems that God wanted Israel to be in awe of the power he granted to Elisha, and to remind them that he had power to give life to anyone.

Once when some Israelites were burying a man, they spied a band of these raiders. So they hastily threw the corpse into the tomb of Elisha and fled. But as soon as the body touched Elisha's bones, the dead man revived and jumped to his feet!

2 Kings 13:21 NLT

How do you think the revived man lived his life after this experience? How would you be changed if you were given a chance to have life again after dying?

Answer: Elisha

SOLOMON'S WIVES

How many wives did Solomon have?

A. seven

B. seventeen

C. seventy

D. seven hundred

The beginning of the eleventh chapter of 1 Kings is alarming. King Solomon, who was once wiser than anyone on earth, was growing increasingly foolish in his decisions and behaviors. We are told that King Solomon married Pharaoh's daughter and women from Moab, Ammon, Edom, Sidon and the Hittites. These foreign wives brought their own gods to Jerusalem and turned Solomon's heart away from God, yet Solomon insisted on loving them anyway. It is a sad commentary on Solomon as he got older.

In all, Solomon had seven hundred wives and three hundred concubines. While some of these marriages were likely politically expedient, Solomon was compromised by the marriages. In his old age he turned his heart to other gods. Solomon even began worshipping gods of enemy nations. Because he turned his back, God would not allow Solomon's son to keep the kingdom intact.

He had 700 wives of royal birth and 300 concubines.
And in fact, they did turn his heart away from the LORD.

1 KINGS 11:3 NLT

How does someone who is wise and committed to God fall into sin over the course of their lifetime?

Answer: D) seven hundred

ABSALOM'S HAIR

What happened to Absalom's hair as he tried to escape the battle with David's men?

King David's charismatic son, Absalom, became frustrated with his father's leadership. Second Samuel says that Absalom was exceedingly handsome with no blemish to his physique. Absalom had thick hair that he let grow long every year (14:25-26). He was arrogant and bullish. As time went on, Absalom had an increasingly dysfunctional relationship with his aging father.

Absalom started a brutal rebellion against his father. In an attempt to keep him from destroying Jerusalem, David fled the city with a contingent of guards who remained loyal to him. Eventually, this led to a bloody battle in the forest of Ephraim. The brutal insurrection cost the lives of twenty thousand men. As Absalom's men began to lose the battle, the prince attempted to escape. Unfortunately, his hair became trapped in a tree where he remained hanging. When David's general, Joab, found Absalom, he plunged three daggers into Absalom's heart. Ten more of Joab's armor bearers then surrounded Absalom and killed him.

During the battle, Absalom happened to come upon some of David's men. He tried to escape on his mule, but as he rode beneath the thick branches of a great tree, his hair got caught in the tree. His mule kept going and left him dangling in the air.

2 Samuel 18:9 NLT

How do you reconcile the violent drama of the history of Israel with their need for a Savior in Jesus?

Answer: it became entangled in a tree leaving him hanging

MARCH 23

AARON'S STAFF

When Pharaoh demanded a miracle,
what did Aaron's staff turn into?

God knew Pharaoh would demand a miracle. For Pharaoh to believe that Moses and Aaron had been sent by the God of the Israelites, they would have to demonstrate his power. He instructed them to be prepared to have Aaron throw down his staff so it would turn into a serpent. Moses and Aaron did as God instructed. In an attempt to dimmish the significance of their miracle, Pharaoh's sorcerers also turned their rods into serpents. Then Aaron's serpent devoured the others.

Pharaoh ignored this warning that the gods of Egypt were no match for the God of Israel, and he hardened his heart. God continued to use Aaron's staff to initiate several of the plagues (e.g. water turned to blood, the infestation of frogs) in order to reveal to Pharaoh who truly was in power. Later, Aaron's staff became a sign of the authority God gave him among the tribes. He caused the staff to sprout blossoms and almonds and it was placed in the Ark of the Covenant as a sign of God's promise to lead the Israelites (Numbers 16-17).

Moses and Aaron came to Pharaoh, and so they did, just as the LORD had commanded; and Aaron threw his staff down before Pharaoh and his servants, and it turned into a serpent.

EXODUS 7:10 NASB

Can you think of other instances where a shepherd's staff is used as a symbol in Scripture?

Answer: a serpent

INTERPRETING DREAMS

Pharaoh told Joseph about his dream with seven healthy cows and seven sick cows along the bank of the Nile. What did Joseph say the dream meant?

When Pharaoh asked Joseph if he could provide the meaning of his dreams, he said he couldn't, but God could. The first dream Pharaoh described involved seven healthy cows followed by seven sickly cows which all walked up from the Nile. The second dream involved seven healthy, plump heads of grain that sprouted followed by seven scorched heads of grain dried by the winds.

When Joseph interpreted the dreams as representing seven years of abundance followed by seven years of famine, Pharaoh was certainly impressed. When Joseph followed that up by suggesting that Pharaoh appoint overseers to store up food during the abundant years so that they would have plenty through the years of famine, Pharaoh found Joseph's discernment remarkable and he elevated him to the second most powerful position in the land.

Seven years of great abundance are coming throughout the land of Egypt. After them, seven years of famine will take place, and all the abundance in the land of Egypt will be forgotten. The famine will devastate the land.

Genesis 41:29-30 CSB

In Egypt where Pharaoh was treated like a god, what level of conviction did Joseph have in his belief in the God of Israel?

Answer: seven years of abundance followed by seven years of famine

NAME OF A JUDGE

Which of the following modern day names was also the name of a judge in Israel?

A. Barack
B. Elon
C. Orpah

In Judges 4, Barak (not Barack) was the name of a general who served alongside Israel's judge, Deborah. In the first chapter of Ruth, Orpah (not Oprah) is mentioned as the name of Ruth's sister-in-law. While answers A and C are not correct, they do hold similarities to some modern-day celebrities.

Elon, however, was one of Israel's judges. In Judges 12, he was mentioned briefly in a shortlist of minor judges who served as rescuers and leaders of Israel during a turbulent period in history. There is little to learn about Elon except that he was from the tribe of Zebulun, that he led Israel for ten years, and he was buried in a town in Zebulun. The territory of Zebulun, between the Mediterranean Sea and the Sea of Galilee, was a strategic geographical region. The reference to Elon as a judge means that his influence and leadership would have been very important in uniting the northern tribes of Israel.

After Ibzan died, Elon from the tribe of Zebulun judged Israel for ten years. When he died, he was buried at Aijalon in Zebulun.

JUDGES 12:11-12 NLT

What do you know about the period of time in the book of Judges? How did Israel's judges foreshadow the need for Jesus?

Answer: B) Elon

SAUL AND THE MEDIUM

What dead prophet did King Saul want the medium of Endor to call up?

King Saul banned any kind of medium that would consult dead spirits. But when he saw the vast Philistine army that gathered for battle against him, he grew afraid. He sought God's help, but he didn't hear anything. Panicking, King Saul sought a medium so that he could talk to the recently dead prophet, Samuel. When he approached the medium, he troubled her, because she didn't want to get punished for breaking the law. But Saul assured her that he would not prosecute her in any way.

The medium relented and described that she could see someone like a god coming up from the earth. She said it was an old man wearing a robe and that he looked annoyed. Saul fell to his knees and begged this specter to help him defeat the Philistines. But the specter informed Saul that God had left him for his disobedience and that the Philistines would kill him and his sons the next day. Saul became so distraught that he fell to the ground like he was paralyzed.

Finally, the woman said, "Well, whose spirit do you want me to call up?" "Call up Samuel," Saul replied.

1 Samuel 28:11 NLT

What does this odd story teach you about Saul's compromised faith in the Lord? How does someone's faith start to deconstruct?

Answer: Samuel

MARCH 27

QUEEN OF SHEBA

Why did the Queen of Sheba visit Israel?

Solomon's fame spread throughout the world. Rulers far and wide sent Solomon tributes of gold, weapons, and provisions to honor him and to be in good standing with him. The Queen of Sheba was one of the visiting royalty who were overwhelmed by Solomon's splendor.

Sheba may have been a nation in southern Arabia or it could have been in Ethiopia. Wherever the Queen had traveled from, she was a foreign ruler intent on meeting Solomon. According to the accounts in the Bible, the Queen was astonished that God had so richly blessed Israel through Solomon's reign. She offered a generous gift of gold along with large quantities of spices and jewels.

She exclaimed to the king, "Everything I heard in my country about your achievements and wisdom is true! I didn't believe what was said until I arrived here and saw it with my own eyes. In fact, I had not heard the half of your great wisdom! It is far beyond what I was told."

2 Chronicles 9:5-6 NLT

What was the blessing and what was the danger of having such great fame?

Answer: she heard of Solomon's wisdom and wealth

MARCH 28

EHUD'S SWORD

While Ehud escaped, what did King Eglon's servants think the king must have been doing?

King Eglon of Moab harassed God's people, so God raised up a left-handed Benjamite named Ehud. Ehud made a sword with two edges and strapped it to his right thigh under his cloak. He went as a representative of Israel to offer a tribute to Eglon, who was a very fat man. After presenting the tribute he asked if he could share a secret message with the king. Pleased, the king dismissed everyone and they went to Eglon's cool room up on the roof. The book of Judges says that Ehud reached out with his left hand and took the sword from his right thigh and thrust it into Eglon's belly. Gruesomely, the hilt of the sword also went in after the blade, and the fat closed over the blade. Ehud didn't bother removing the sword and left the room and locked the doors.

King Eglon's attendants waited for quite some time assuming the king was relieving himself. It wasn't until after Ehud escaped and rallied the armies of Israel that the Moabites discovered their king dead.

When he had left, the king's servants came and looked, and behold, the doors of the roof chamber were locked; and they said, "Undoubtedly he is relieving himself in the cool room."

JUDGES 3:24 NASB

Why do you think the Bible includes gruesome details in their historical stories? What would you think about the Bible if it didn't include these sorts of details?

Answer: relieving himself in the cool room

CUPBEARER'S REQUEST

Which cupbearer wanted to rebuild Jerusalem's walls?

Nehemiah was a Jew serving faithfully as the cupbearer to the Persian king, Artaxerxes, in the capital of Susa. Day after day, Nehemiah served the king and tested the food and drink, putting his life on the line again and again. Some guests from Judah visited the capital, and Nehemiah inquired about the state of Jerusalem. The men informed him that the remnant of the survivors there were in great distress and that the walls of the city were in ruin. Nehemiah fasted and prayed that God would give him an opportunity to regather some of the scattered tribes of Israel and form a team to go back to rebuild.

Soon, the king noticed that Nehemiah seemed sad. When Artaxerxes asked, Nehemiah humbly shared what he had been told about the condition of his home town of Jerusalem. Nehemiah then boldly requested that the king let him organize a crew and give them safe passage to rebuild Jerusalem. The king granted his request as we learn from Nehemiah's own words, "because the good hand of my God was on me."

Then I said to the king, "If it pleases the king, and if your servant has found favor before you, I request that you send me to Judah, to the city of my fathers' tombs, that I may rebuild it."

Nehemiah 2:5 NASB

How does Nehemiah's authenticity help him accomplish what God had put on his heart?

Answer: Nehemiah

MARCH 30

MORDECAI'S COUSIN

Who was Mordecai's cousin?

Mordecai was a child of the Exile. His father, Jair, had been taken captive from Jerusalem during the reign of King Nebuchadnezzar. In city of Susa, Persian king, Ahasuerus, was looking for a new queen. A contest was established to select one from young women all over the empire.

Mordecai raised his orphaned cousin, Hadassah, as if she was his own daughter. She was known as Esther, and she was exceedingly beautiful in form and face. During the contest for the position of queen, she was taken into the king's court and entered into the elaborate pageantry meant to please the king. Esther kept her Jewish heritage a secret and Mordecai did what he could to advise and protect her. Eventually, Esther was chosen by the king and eventually needed to use her position to rescue the Jewish people from genocide.

He was the guardian to Hadassah, that is Esther, his uncle's daughter, for she had no father or mother. Now the young woman was beautiful of form and face, and when her father and her mother died, Mordecai took her as his own daughter.

ESTHER 2:7 NASB

How do you think Esther felt when she was entered in the elaborate pageantry?

Answer: Esther

MARCH 31

BLESSED ARE THE MEEK

What does Jesus say that the meek will be blessed with?

The meekest human ever was Jesus Christ. He had all authority in heaven and on earth, and yet he assumed the nature of a servant. He created everything from galaxies to stars, oceans to fields, and bears to hummingbirds, yet he walked humbly as part of his own creation. He tolerated conceited leaders and arrogant followers with patience. He repressed any sense of self-entitlement and embraced a position of compassion.

Jesus came to lose his life, not gain it. Jesus came to serve, not to be served. Jesus came to defend others, not himself. Jesus came to give a voice for the voiceless and not demand what he rightfully deserved. And in doing so, Jesus elevated the status of the truly meek, his mere creations who recognize their need for a shepherd, to share with him in all that he made.

"Blessed are the meek,
for they will inherit the earth."

MATTHEW 5:5 NIV

If Jesus humbled himself, how could we not do the same today?

Answer: they will inherit the earth

APRIL

APRIL 1

CLOSE FELLOWSHIP

How old was Enoch when he "disappeared?"

Enoch was 365 years old when he disappeared. Considering his ancestors lived until they were into their tenth century, Enoch's life was relatively brief. His father, Jared, lived to be 962 years old. His son, Methusaleh, lived to be 969 years old. In other words, his son and father are the two oldest people to have ever lived. Enoch's lifespan, however, was six hundred years less than theirs. There seems to be an interesting reason for Enoch's relatively abbreviated life. It appears from a comment in the fifth chapter of Genesis that God himself chose to shorten Enoch's life on earth. The reason for doing so, it seems, was that Enoch "walked faithfully with God."

By Enoch's time, people were becoming more corrupt. The earth was a very sinful place. Soon Noah, who also "walked in close fellowship with God," would lead a small remnant of six people by way of the great judgment of the flood. Sin brought the consequences of sin to every human. Yet Enoch was specifically spared the sting of death because he had found life through a deep relationship with God.

Enoch walked faithfully with God;
then he was no more, because God took him away.

GENESIS 5:24 NIV

How is your relationship with God today? Would you say you are walking in close fellowship with him?

Answer: 365 years old

CONVERSATION WITH JESUS

During the transfiguration, who appeared to speak with Jesus?

Peter, James, and John were invited to accompany Jesus to the top of a high mountain. When they arrived, Jesus "was transfigured before them." His face and clothes took on a heavenly brilliance. To the disciples' bewilderment, Moses and Elijah appeared and spoke with Jesus. Peter eagerly interrupted the conversation to suggest that they set up tents for everyone. While he was still speaking, a bright cloud covered them and a voice said, "This is My beloved Son, with whom I am well pleased; listen to Him!" (Matthew 17:6) The disciples fell to the ground terrified at the sound of the voice. But Jesus gently touched them and encouraged them to get up.

The significance of this event is immense. The glory of Jesus is unveiled. Moses, who represents the Law, and Elijah, who represents the prophets, affirm Jesus's fulfillment of all of the Scriptures. God's voice echoes the one that spoke at Jesus' baptism which revealed Jesus' identity and purpose. And the three disciples were the invited witnesses of it all.

He was transfigured before them; and His face shone like the sun, and His garments became as white as light. And behold, Moses and Elijah appeared to them, talking with Him.

MATTHEW 17:2-3 NASB

Why did Jesus let the three disciples experience this moment?

Answer: Moses and Elijah

APRIL 3

THE FIRST DEACONS

How many deacons did the apostles choose to help them lead the first church in Jerusalem?

The early church was growing so fast that the disciples couldn't keep up. There was a congregation of thousands, all were eager to share meals, possessions, and personal care. But some tensions were emerging with the increasing numbers of people and the diversity of the movement. When some Greek widows were being overlooked in the daily distribution of food, they realized that they had some holes in their management plan. Few of the apostles had backgrounds that lent to large-scale organizational leadership (e.g., fisherman and zealots). They simply needed help.

They selected seven qualified men who enabled the church to continue to serve people and spread the good news of Jesus. One of the men, Stephen, was singled out as being full of faith and of the Holy Spirit. He performed great wonders and signs among the people of Jerusalem and spoke boldly about Jesus.

> Select from among you seven men of good reputation, full of the Spirit and of wisdom, whom we may put in charge of this task. But we will devote ourselves to prayer and to the ministry of the word.
>
> Acts 6:3-4 NASB

God provides a network of gifted people to lead his church. In what ways do you see God using your gifts to help in the work of ministry?

Answer: seven

APRIL 4

HELPING PHILIP

Who came to help Philip during his ministry in Samaria?

After the execution of Stephen in Jerusalem, his friend and coworker, Philip, escaped to the region of Samaria. Despite the violent wave of persecution that had begun against the early church, Philip "began proclaiming Christ" to the Samaritans. God blessed Philip's message, and the Samaritans saw him perform many miracles as he preached. The people seemed very receptive to the good news, and they believed. Even a sorcerer named Simon paid attention and believed.

When the apostles who were still in Jerusalem heard about the incredible reception to the gospel in Samaria, they sent Peter and John, who went and prayed for the people to receive the Holy Spirit.

When the apostles in Jerusalem heard that Samaria had received the word of God, they sent them Peter and John, who came down and prayed for them that they would receive the Holy Spirit.

Acts 8:14-15 NASB

Jesus spent considerable time cultivating the hearts of Samaria. How do you think his conversations at the well and the parables about the Samaritans prepared them for Philip's message?

Answer: Peter

APRIL 5

PLANT OR PEOPLE

What destroyed the plant that had given Jonah shade?

Jonah was mad at God. He had been tasked with telling his enemies in Nineveh about God's truth. The problem Jonah had with this job is that he knew God was merciful and compassionate and filled with unfailing love. He knew that God would forgive the Ninevites for their wickedness if the people turned from their sins. So when the people of Nineveh did repent, Jonah became so deeply frustrated that he wanted to die.

Outside the city, God caused a leafy plant to grow and provide shade for Jonah. But then God sent a worm to destroy the plant. The sun beat down on Jonah's head, causing him to great physical distress. And again, Jonah grew angry with God and wanted to die. God's point was that Jonah cared more about the plant than he cared about the people.

God designated a worm when dawn came the next day,
and it attacked the plant and it withered.

JONAH 4:7 NASB

Are there things you care about more than the people around you?

Answer: a worm

WOMEN OF THE CROSS

What were the names of the four women who stayed at the cross while Jesus was crucified?

It is a remarkable thing that the multitudes of people that had flocked around Jesus for the last few years of his life scattered at his trial and crucifixion. Only a few followers remained at the cross. John tells us in his Gospel that four women stayed with Jesus to the bitter end. They included Jesus' own mother, Jesus' aunt, another woman named Mary, the wife of a man named Clopas, and Jesus' close follower, Mary Magdalene. Their resiliency was certainly only matched by their grief.

When Jesus saw his mother, his heart broke. How devastating this had to be for her. While he hung on the cross, Jesus also saw his beloved disciple, John. Referring to John, Jesus said to his mother, "Woman, behold, your son!" Likewise, he said to John, "Behold, your mother!" We are given a note in the passage that tells us John took Mary into his own household to care for her.

Beside the cross of Jesus stood His mother, His mother's sister, Mary the wife of Clopas, and Mary Magdalene.

John 19:25 NASB

What feeling does John 19:25 produce in you?

Answer: Jesus' mother, his aunt, Clopas's wife, Mary Magdalene

NINTH COMMANDMENT

What is the ninth of the Ten Commandments?

Proverbs 6:16-19 says that bearing false witness is one of the seven things God hates. He detests arrogant eyes, lying tongues, hands that murder, hearts that plot evil, feet that race to do wrong, the false witness against others, and a person who sows discord in a family. It was the false witness of many people that led to Jesus' crucifixion. He was accused of blaspheming God when in fact he was God in the flesh. He was accused of being in alignment with Satan. He was accused of sinning on the Sabbath, of defiling the religious system, and of colluding against the state.

Jesus, in contrast, urged his followers to be true witnesses of his good news. He wants his people to tell others what they have seen and heard. He wants people to give an accurate testimony about what he has done on the cross and how he cares for people.

"You shall not give false testimony against your neighbor."

Exodus 20:16 NIV

Why would someone bear false witness against another?

Answer: you shall not give false testimony

PIERCED SIDE

What happened when Jesus' side was pierced with the soldier's spear?

The Romans were expert executioners. The technique of crucifixion maximized both pain and effectiveness. They would spread the criminal, who may have already been beaten severely, across two wooden beams, nailing their wrists and feet to the cross. They would hoist the cross into a vertical position that caused the criminal's weight to strain painfully against the spikes. Unable to lift up, the criminal's body would slowly suffocate in excruciating agony.

At times, Roman soldiers were ordered to speed up the process of death. They would break the legs of the criminal, causing them to suffocate more quickly. In order to finish the execution before the Sabbath began, the Roman soldiers broke the legs of the two men who were crucified next to Jesus. When they got to Jesus, they discovered he was already dead, so they did not break his legs. One of the soldiers pierced his side with a spear and blood and water poured out, proving his death. It is likely that the intense trauma of the flogging and crucifixion had caused fluids to gather around or in Jesus' lungs.

One of the soldiers pierced His side with a spear,
and immediately blood and water came out.

John 19:34 NASB

Why would Jesus allow himself to go through such agony?

Answer: blood and water came out

BE A BELIEVER

After the resurrection, which disciple doubted Jesus was alive?

Thomas had not seen what the other disciples had seen. They were telling him about how Jesus was alive and had appeared to them. The night of the resurrection, Jesus stood among them while they were hiding in a room with the doors shut. They were afraid of the leaders who crucified Jesus, but rejoiced when they saw him. He spoke to them that night and commissioned them to tell others about him. He breathed on them and told them to receive the Holy Spirit and forgive people of their sins. But Thomas was not with them that night. And he was struggling to comprehend all they were telling him.

Eight days later Jesus appeared to the disciples again. This time Thomas was there. He then told Thomas to place his finger in his nail scars and in his side. He encouraged Thomas to "not continue in disbelief, but be a believer." Thomas cried out, "My Lord and my God!" (John 20:26-28)

The other disciples were saying to him, "We have seen the Lord!" But he said to them, "Unless I see in His hands the imprint of the nails, and put my finger into the place of the nails, and put my hand into His side, I will not believe."

JOHN 20:25 NASB

Would you say your faith is more like Thomas' faith before he sees the risen Jesus, or after?

Answer: Thomas

WHY JOHN WROTE

Why did John write what he did in his book?

John ends his Gospel account wanting everyone to know that there was so much else he could have added. "Jesus also did many other things," John wrote, "If they were written in detail, I expect that even the world itself would not contain the books that would be written" (21:25). There were so many more miracles, so many other teachings, so many other interactions, so many more moments.

But John also wanted everyone to know that the reason he wrote this book and included the content that he did was so people would "believe that Jesus is the Christ, the Son of God." John wanted people to believe in Jesus because then they would have life in His name.

Many other signs Jesus also performed in the presence of the disciples, which are not written in this book; but these have been written so that you may believe that Jesus is the Christ, the Son of God; and that by believing you may have life in His name.

John 20:30-31 NASB

What are some of the sections of the Gospel of John that were specifically selected so that you might know that Jesus is the Christ?

Answer: so you would believe that Jesus is the Christ

APRIL 11

NEVER DYING RUMOR

Which disciple did people think might never die?

After the resurrection, Jesus asked Peter to join him on a walk along the shore of the Sea of Galilee. He asked Peter three times whether Peter loved him. Each time Peter responded that he did. And with each answer, Jesus instructed him to shepherd his sheep. After the third time, Jesus added some detail to what this would mean for Peter in following Jesus. He described to Peter by what kind of death he would have. Christian historians indicate that Peter may have been crucified in Rome.

Peter was understandably troubled by this conversation, so he looked around and saw John behind them. Peter couldn't stop himself from asking an awkward question about what it was going to cost John to follow Jesus. "What about him, Lord?" he said. Jesus, undistracted, simply told Peter, "If I want him to remain alive until I return, what is that to you? As for you, follow me" (John 21:22). John shares personally that this conversation sparked a rumor that he would not die.

> This account went out among the brothers, that that disciple would not die; yet Jesus did not say to him that he would not die, but only, "If I want him to remain until I come, what is that to you?"
>
> John 21:23 NASB

Would it be easier to follow Jesus wholeheartedly if you knew what would happen or if you didn't know?

Answer: John

BETHANY FRIENDS

Who were Jesus' three friends in Bethany?

Jesus had several people who followed him who weren't listed among the twelve disciples. There was a group of seventy-two people that he commissioned to preach in his name (Luke 10:1). There was Matthais and Joseph (Barsabbas) who were considered when Judas had to be replaced as one of the twelve; Matthais was chosen. Present at the crucifixion were his mother, his aunt, another Mary, the wife of Clopas, and Mary Magdalene. Other followers included Joseph of Arimathea, Nicodemus, Salome, Joanna, and many more.

Three of his dearest friends were Mary, Martha, and their brother Lazarus. They appear fairly regularly in the Gospels. These three lived in Bethany, near Jerusalem. Jesus would stop there on his journeys to Jerusalem and often stay while he was in the holy city. Martha liked to serve, while Mary would prefer to sit and listen to Jesus' teaching (Luke 10:38-42). Mary once poured expensive oil on Jesus' feet and wiped it with her hair (John 12:1-8). Of course, they are best known because of the events of John 11, where Jesus raised his friend Lazarus back from the dead.

A certain man was sick: Lazarus of Bethany,
the village of Mary and her sister Martha.

John 11:1 NASB

When you read John 11, what kind of friendship does it seem these three had with Jesus?

Answer: Mary, Martha, and Lazarus

APRIL 13

LIVING WATER

Jesus asked someone to draw water from the well for him.
Who was it?

The disciples were clearly uncomfortable when Jesus stopped in Samaria to get a drink. Samaritans were the undesirables, having complicated ethnic and religious roots extending back hundreds of years. Jesus and his disciples came to the Samaritan village of Sychar near a historic site where Jacob had given his son, Joseph, a field. According to John, it was also the home of a watering hole known as Jacob's Well. Tired from his long walk, Jesus sat down by the well and began a conversation with a woman who had come to draw water.

Jesus asked her to give him a drink. The woman was surprised because Jewish men refused to have anything to do with Samaritans, especially the women. "If only you knew the gift God has for you and who were speaking to," Jesus continued, "you would ask me, and I would give you living water" (John 4:10). The conversation they had changed the Samaritan woman's life. Afterward she went back to her town and told everyone about Jesus.

A woman of Samaria came to draw water.
Jesus said to her, "Give Me a drink."

JOHN 4:7 NASB

If you could have a conversation with Jesus at your local coffee shop, what do you think he would want to talk about?

Answer: the Samaritan woman

APRIL 14

FIRST TO THE TOMB

Who won the race to the empty tomb, Peter or John?

What else were the two disciples supposed to do? When Mary Magdalene came running back from the tomb, they had no choice but to run to it. Mary told them that the tomb was empty and that she couldn't find Jesus' body. That was impossible! The body had been laid in the tomb, embalmed and wrapped. The tomb had a massive bolder placed over the entrance and then it was sealed shut. The Romans had placed soldiers outside the tomb to guard it.

So they ran. John was younger and faster. But when he got there he stopped at the entrance and looked in. He saw the linen wrappings lying there, but couldn't bring himself to take another step. Peter arrived next and went right inside. His brash and bold demeanor led him straight into the crypt. He also noticed the linen wrappings, as well as the cloth that had covered Jesus' head. It was folded and lying apart from the other wrappings. John struck up the courage to join Peter inside the empty tomb—and he saw and believed that Jesus had risen from the dead.

The two were running together; and the other disciple ran ahead, faster than Peter, and came to the tomb first; and he stooped to look in, and saw the linen wrappings lying there; however he did not go in. So Simon Peter also came, following him, and he entered the tomb.

John 20:5-6 NASB

Who was the first witness of the empty tomb? Why is that significant?

Answer: John, but Peter was the first to enter the tomb

APRIL 15

BEST DECISION

FINISH THIS VERSE

Trust in the LORD with all your heart
And do not lean on _______ _______ _______.
In all your ways acknowledge Him,
And He will _______ _______ _______ _______.

There is no better decision in life than to choose to trust God. It is pointless to lean on our own understanding when he is ready to offer perfect guidance, wisdom, and discernment for every possible circumstance. God created us to walk with him and to seek him for all we need. He created us to acknowledge his presence so that we can walk the right paths throughout the seasons of life.

God did not create us to be half-hearted, apathetic, or self-centered in the decisions we make. Instead, he wired us to be whole-heartedly trustful and devotionally intentional in what he has called us to do. When we are, he promises to direct our steps and reveal his way.

Trust in the LORD with all your heart
And do not lean on your own understanding.
In all your ways acknowledge Him,
And He will make your paths straight.

PROVERBS 3:5-6 NASB

What situation in your life today do you need to entrust to God?

Answer: your own understanding; make your paths straight

THE PROMISED LAND

What did God say the Promised Land would be flowing with?

God wanted Israel to be set apart from other nations so they could be a light to world. He wanted them to represent what it looked like to be in a right relationship with the one true God. "Do not live according to the customs of the people" around you, he commanded. The other nations did things that were detestable to him.

God promised that if Israel followed his instructions, the land he was giving them would overflow with abundance. It would be a land flowing with milk and honey. This was true literally since the land was capable of sustaining successful agriculture and livestock farming including the bees for honey and the cattle for milk. It was also true figuratively since the land provided sweetness and joy in its provision for sustenance and life.

"I have promised you, 'You will possess their land because I will give it to you as your possession—a land flowing with milk and honey.' I am the LORD your God, who has set you apart from all other people."

LEVITICUS 20:24 NLT

In the generations following the time of today's verse, why did Israel sometimes flourish and sometimes struggle to survive in the Promised Land?

Answer: milk and honey

HIDE A LAMP

What does Jesus say a person should not put a lamp under?

Jesus calls his followers the light of the world. Just like a town built on a hill cannot be hidden from sight, neither can God's people be hidden. The light of their good deeds shines brightly in a darkened, sinful world. People are drawn to the safety and warmth of the community of God's gathered people. People want to benefit from the productivity and peacefulness that occurs in the light. For in the darkness is chaos and danger. At night, Jesus declares, is when the thief comes to steal.

So why would anyone try to hide their light? If they did, the light would go out. No one, Jesus says, would put their lamp under a bowl. To do so simply doesn't make sense. So neither should God's people hide the light of the good news of God's kingdom.

"Neither do people light a lamp and put it under a bowl. Instead they put it on its stand, and it gives light to everyone in the house."

Matthew 5:15 NIV

How can you shine the light of your faith in Jesus today?

Answer: a bowl

CARRYING OUR SIN

What animal symbolically took the people's sin and carried it into the wilderness?

A. The scapegoat
B. The beast of burden
C. The sheep in wolf's clothing
D. The leviathon

A scapegoat is an animal used by the Levitical priests in ancient Israel as a symbol of atonement for the people's sins. We learn in the book of Leviticus that the high priest would select a goat by choosing lots and trusting God to provide. Once a goat was chosen, the high priest would lay both of his hands on the goat's head and confess over it all the wickedness, rebellion, and sins of the people of Israel, and in so doing, transfer the people's sins to the head of the goat. A designated man would then drive the goat into the wilderness. Significantly and symbolically, the goat would carry all the people's sins upon itself.

John the Baptist called everyone's attention to Jesus as the scapegoat. He proclaimed that Jesus takes away the sins of the world (John 1:29). The sins of the world were transferred to Jesus and carried away through his perfect sacrifice.

The other goat, the scapegoat chosen by lot to be sent away, will be kept alive, standing before the LORD. When it is sent away to Azazel in the wilderness, the people will be purified and made right with the LORD.

LEVITICUS 16:10 NLT

How can you show your gratitude to Jesus for taking your wickedness upon his shoulders and offering you forgiveness for sin?

Answer: A) the scapegoat

FIRST FIVE BOOKS

What are the first five books of the Bible called?

One of the last things Moses did in his life was encourage his protégé, Joshua, to meditate on the book of the law. Moses was referring to what Jews came to call the *Torah,* which is Hebrew for "teaching," "instruction," or "directives." In academic circles, these five books are often called the *Pentateuch*, meaning "five books," or "five scrolls."

The book of the law is made up of Genesis, Exodus, Leviticus, Numbers, and Deuteronomy. These five books account for twenty percent of the words in the Old Testament. They tell the story of the foundations of creation, sin, and God's plan to redeem a covenant relationship with mankind through the people of Israel. These books are filled with instructions—for example, the Ten Commandments—and also with the adventurous accounts of God's people through the generations of Abraham to Moses. This laid the groundwork for the future Messiah.

Keep this Book of the Law always on your lips; meditate on it day and night, so that you may be careful to do everything written in it. Then you will be prosperous and successful.

JOSHUA 1:8 NLT

Jesus later claimed that he is the fulfillment of everything written in the book of the law (Matthew 5:17, Luke 24:27). How can that be?

Answer: the book of the law, the Torah, or the Pentateuch

APRIL 20

MAN FROM NAIN

In the village of Nain, what did Jesus do to raise the young man back to life?

When Jesus was coming into the village of Nain, a funeral procession was coming out. Luke reported that a young man had died, and that he was the only son of a widow. A large crowd was mourning with her.

Luke said that when Jesus saw her, his heart overflowed with compassion. As the procession continued, Jesus approached the woman and encouraged her. Then he touched the coffin. When everyone stopped, Jesus told the dead young man to get up. Immediately the boy sat up and began to talk! Jesus, in his compassion, gave him back to his mother.

He walked over to the coffin and touched it, and the bearers stopped. "Young man," he said, "I tell you, get up." Then the dead boy sat up and began to talk! And Jesus gave him back to his mother.

Luke 7:14-15 NLT

What do you learn about Jesus from this encounter? What draws you to him? What overwhelms you about him?

Answer: he touched the coffin and told the boy to get up

WHAT MAN LIVES ON

Jesus said that, "Man shall not live on _______ alone."

A. an island
B. bread
C. money
D. earth

After Jesus spent forty days and nights fasting and praying, Satan tempted him and said, "If you are the Son of God, tell these stones to become bread." The idea of simply turning stones to food must have been an appealing idea. But Jesus responded with a resilient rejection of Satan's taunt, as we are told in today's Scripture verse.

Jesus was referring to Deuteronomy 8:3 when Moses informed Israel that God "humbled you, causing you to hunger, and then feeding you with manna, which neither you nor your ancestors had known, to teach you that man does not live on bread alone but on every word that comes from the mouth of the Lord." The people learned over the years that manna alone did not sustain them as they tried to make their way to the Promised Land. They needed to hunger and thirst for God's Word, and to rely on him for everything.

"It is written: 'Man shall not live on bread alone,
but on every word that comes from the mouth of God.'"

MATTHEW 4:4 NIV

What do you hunger for more than anything else?

Answer: bread

LISTENING TO CRITICISM

TRUE OR FALSE
The Bible says it is better to be criticized by a wise person than to be praised by a fool.

Assessing ourselves with the opinions of fools will lead us wayward. Their words will build a false sense of security and corrupt the foundation of our lives. Foolish praise puffs up our egos and diminishes discernment. Foolish affirmations drown out the ability to assess and hear the truth. It blurs the ability to see blind spots.

It is healthy to listen to wise counsel. At the end of Psalm 139, David asks God to search him, to test him, and to point out anything in him that offends God. King Solomon points out in Proverbs 15 that if you reject discipline, you only harm yourself, but if you listen to correction, you grow in understanding. Heeding constructive criticism, Solomon says, makes a person feel at home among the wise..

Better to be criticized by a wise person
than to be praised by a fool.
Ecclesiastes 7:5 NLT

What wise criticism do you need to regard in your own life today?

Answer: true

PARTRIDGE HUNT

Who said that he was only a flea, but was being hunted as if he were a partridge?

King Saul had lost his way, so God anointed the young shepherd, David, as the next king. He gave David great successes against Goliath and other enemies of Israel. David's fame grew and he became more popular than Saul. Saul's jealousy became so embroiled that he gathered his armies and used his riches to hunt David down. David lost everything and had to flee for his life. He hid in caves and tried to defend those close to him.

At one point, David snuck into Saul's military camp with a fellow warrior, Abishai. They got right up next to Saul while he was asleep. Abishai wanted David to kill Saul right there, but David refused to strike his king. He chose to trust in the Lord's plan. Instead, they took Saul's spear and a jug of water that were next to Saul's head and went back to their own camp. In the morning, David called out to Saul from across the valley and held up the spear and water jug. Saul was embarrassed and emotionally moved by David's mercy. He gave David a blessing and promised to stop pursuing him any further.

"Let not my blood fall to the earth away from the presence of the LORD, for the king of Israel has come out to seek a single flea like one who hunts a partridge in the mountains."

1 SAMUEL 26:20 ESV

How did David have the strength to resist taking revenge on Saul?

Answer: David

JACOB'S FINAL YEARS

Where did Jacob live for the last seventeen years of his life?

Jacob spent most of his life near the land that his grandfather, Abraham, had been given. But when a severe famine struck the land later, he asked his sons to seek help from the overseeing ruler in Egypt, the second most powerful in command of the empire. His sons traveled to Egypt and begged for mercy from the man who turned out to be their long-lost brother, Joseph. After several alarming interactions, Joseph eventually asked his brothers to bring their father to live in prosperity and peace with him. So Jacob left the land that God had promised him and his descendants to go to Egypt. He trusted God even if he didn't understand. God had rescued Joseph from the grave, had elevated him to a position of powerful authority, and was giving his family the opportunity to grow and to prosper.

Eventually the descendants of Jacob who was also called Israel, would multiply to around a million people, and through a dramatic exodus, would eventually return home to the land of their fathers, Abraham, Isaac, and Jacob.

Israel settled in the land of Egypt, in the region of Goshen. They acquired property in it and became fruitful and very numerous. Now Jacob lived in the land of Egypt 17 years, and his life span was 147 years.

GENESIS 47:27-28 CSB

What do you think Joseph understood of God's long-range plans when he saw his brothers asking for help?

Answer: Egypt

SAMSON'S NAZIRITE VOW

Samson's Nazirite vow at birth meant that
he could never ______ ______ ______.

One of the most compelling themes in the story of Samson is the tension around whether or not he was going to fulfill his vow. An angel told his mother that she would give birth to a son who would deliver Israel from the grip of the Philistines. As a sign of his calling, God required Samson to be Nazirite from birth. The Bible introduces the Nazirite vow in Numbers 6; a Nazirite is separated from others in order to be fully consecrated to God. The vow was established as a voluntary personal decision for a limited season of time for a special occasion. The sign of the vow was that hair wasn't cut during its duration.

In Samson's case, it would seem that God himself had selected him to be fully consecrated for the entirety of his life. But Samson struggled to personally accept the vow and he failed to protect the symbol of his vow, his long hair.

"You will conceive and give birth to a son, and no razor shall come upon his head, for the boy shall be a Nazirite to God from the womb; and he will begin to save Israel from the hands of the Philistines."

JUDGES 13:5 NASB

In what ways have you voluntarily set yourself apart for God?

Answer: cut his hair

APRIL 26

FIRST HUSBAND

What was the name of Bathsheba's first husband?

One of the saddest chapters in the Bible is 2 Samuel 11. King David had grown lazy and stayed home while his armies went to battle. While walking out on the roof of his palace, he looked across the city and noticed a beautiful woman named Bathsheba. He learned that she was the wife of Uriah, one of his captains who was at war. He sent messengers to bring her to him, and he slept with her.

When David found out Bathsheba was pregnant, he called Uriah back from war and told him to go home to his wife. Uriah slept with the king's palace guard, however, because his fellow soldiers were still on the battlefield. David ordered Uriah to the front lines when he returned to battle and had the rest of the army withdraw, which resulted in Uriah's death. David took Bathsheba as his wife and she gave birth to a son. The chapter ends with a remarkably sad statement: "The Lord was displeased with what David had done."

He sent someone to find out who she was, and he was told, "She is Bathsheba, the daughter of Eliam and the wife of Uriah the Hittite."

2 Samuel 11:3 NLT

David was known as a man after God's own heart. How does a person like David lose their faithfulness?

Answer: Uriah

AUTHOR OF PROVERBS

TRUE OR FALSE
King Lemuel wrote several of the Proverbs in the Bible.

King Lemuel is a somewhat unknown figure in the Bible. Some have speculated this was a pseudonym for Solomon. Others have suggested he may have been King Hezekiah or another wise king in Judah's history. The only reference to Lemuel is in Proverbs 31 where he is cited as the author of at least nine verses. Proverbs says that his mother taught him several wise lessons.

She counseled him that as he, the king, he should not waste his strength on women or wine. Both can ruin a king's character and judgment, she explained. But she also counseled him to rule righteously. For instance, he should "speak up for those who can't speak for themselves." He should, "ensure justice for those being crushed." It was the king's calling, to "speak up for the poor and helpless and see that they get justice" (vv. 8-9). These proverbs weren't meant for only a king, however, so they were collected and shared in the Bible's book of wisdom. We can truly be grateful for the wisdom from King Lemuel's mother as well as the king for writing down her words for all generations.

The sayings of King Lemuel contain this message,
which his mother taught him.
O my son, O son of my womb,
O son of my vows,
do not waste your strength on women,
on those who ruin kings.

Proverbs 31:1-3 NLT

Which of Lemuel's proverbs (31:1-9) is most meaningful to you?

Answer: true

MIGHTY HAVE FALLEN

TRUE OR FALSE

The phrase, "How the mighty have fallen," comes from the Bible.

There are many phrases people believe come from the Bible but aren't actually found anywhere in it. For instance, many people have heard that the Bible says, "God helps those who help themselves." That is not in the Bible. Some claim that the phrase, "Cleanliness is next to godliness," comes from the Bible. It doesn't.

But what about the phrase "Oh, how the mighty have fallen?" This phrase has been used in stories, shows, movies and speeches in popular culture. It is a three-thousand-year-old phrase used by King David to cry over the deaths of King Saul and his son, Jonathan. He used the phrase three times in a song of lament. David took Jonathan's death especially hard because his strong and faithful friend had been slain.

"How the mighty have fallen
in the midst of the battle!"

2 Samuel 1:25 NASB

What does the phrase "how the mighty have fallen" teach us about God's plans for humanity through history?

Answer: true

ZACCHAEUS' TREE

What kind of tree did Zacchaeus climb so that he could see Jesus?

Jesus was coming through Jericho at the time of today's biblical account. The crowds gathered along the roads to see the man who might be the Messiah. Zacchaeus, however, was a man of small stature, and was struggling to see over the backs and shoulders of everyone. Zacchaeus was also a tax collector, shunned among his own people in those days because he used questionable methods to take money from the Jews in order to support the oppressive Roman Empire. So no one in the crowd was likely to assist this small, notorious man that day.

Zacchaeus noticed a sycamore tree along the road. These long-living trees have a thick, knotty trunk with large branches capable of holding a person's weight. The branches can easily stretch over the road, which would have given Zacchaeus a considerable vantage point to see Jesus and his disciples entering into town. And when Jesus came to that spot, he noticed Zacchaeus and invited himself over for dinner. The encounter changed Zacchaeus's life forever.

He ran on ahead and climbed up a sycamore tree to see Him, because He was about to pass through that way.

Luke 19:4 NASB

What did Jesus mean when he said in reference to Zacchaeus, "For the Son of Man has come to seek and to save that which was lost" (Luke 19:10)?

Answer: a sycamore tree

HUNGER AND THIRST

Why does Jesus say those who hunger and thirst for righteousness will be blessed?

Jesus hungered and thirsted for justice. It is the reason he came. He deliberately walked among people whose lives had been ravaged by sin. He hated that people were pushed down and overrun when he had created the world to live in the peace of God. His vision for the world did not include oppression and violence. In one of the most famous and countercultural messages the world has ever heard, Sermon on the Mount, Jesus made it clear that God values human life, and he expects people to fight for those whose lives have been stolen.

Do our hearts break over the wrongs that are committed against the innocent? Do our souls cry for those whose voices have been taken from them? If so, we are in good company. For God's heart breaks over the sins and imbalances of this world. God cries out for those whom he created with dignity but have lost their voices.

"Blessed are those who hunger and thirst for righteousness, for they will be filled."

Matthew 5:6 NIV

Can you serve or support an organization or a church which defends those who have been wronged?

Answer: because they will be filled

MAY

THE FIRST SCOUT

The first bird that Noah released from the ark was a _______.

A. raven
B. quail
C. dove
D. sparrow

After the rains started and the flood waters rose, it would be a full year before Noah and his family would stand again on dry land. Forty days into the flood, Noah hoped for signs of land, so he sent out a raven. It must have been disheartening to see the raven fly back and forth without success. Noah later sent out a dove to see if the waters had receded. This bird couldn't find anywhere to perch either. Eventually, after many more attempts over many more days, the dove was able to bring back an olive leaf, indicating that the flood had receded, and vegetation was growing once more.

The story of these scout birds reveals the inner struggle of faithfulness. It was by no means an easy task to build the ark, to board a remnant of animals and humans inside of it, to weather the storms, and to wait months before beginning again on land. Yet Noah practiced a resilience of faith that refused to quit on the promises of God. As a result, he was credited with righteousness, and humanity was saved.

After forty days Noah opened a window he had made in the ark and sent out a raven, and it kept flying back and forth until the water had dried up from the earth.

GENESIS 8:6-7 NIV

What tests of faith are you experiencing today? What resilience of faithfulness do you need?

Answer: A) raven

MAY 2

MOTHER-IN-LAW

Which disciple had a mother-in-law who was healed by Jesus?

In the fishing town of Capernaum on the Sea of Galilee, Jesus had asked Simon and his brother Andrew to become his disciples. At once, they left their nets and followed him. After being joined by two other fisherman, also brothers, named James and John, Jesus taught in the local synagogue and cast a demon out of a tormented man. The people were amazed and asked, "Who is this?" News about Jesus began to spread quickly.

When they left the synagogue, Jesus and his four new disciples went to Simon and Andrew's house. Simon's mother-in-law was sick with a fever. Jesus took her hand and helped her up. Her fever left her, and she began to serve them. It wasn't long before the whole town had gathered at the house looking for Jesus so they could be healed.

Simon's mother-in-law was in bed with a fever, and they immediately told Jesus about her. So he went to her, took her hand and helped her up. The fever left her and she began to wait on them.

MARK 1:30-31 NIV

If you had been that in the town of Capernaum that day, what kind of things might you have heard about Jesus?

Answer: Simon Peter

HONEY FROM A LION

Who ate honey out of a lion's carcass?

Samson shared a riddle with the young men who had gathered at his wedding party; "Out of the one who eats came something to eat; out of the strong came something sweet". Samson waged that they wouldn't be able to solve the riddle within seven days.

What the young men didn't know is the riddle had come from Samson's recent experience when he was traveling to see his bride. On his way to Timnah to see her, a lion attacked him. Samson killed the lion with his bare hands but told no one what he had done. Later, on his return trip home, he noticed that a swarm of bees had made a hive in the lion's carcass. So, Samson scooped out some honey with his bare hands and shared it with his parents.

He scooped some of the honey into his hands and ate it along the way. He also gave some to his father and mother, and they ate it. But he didn't tell them he had taken the honey from the carcass of the lion.

JUDGES 14:9 NLT

Samson didn't do anything in a typical fashion. Why do you think God put up with Samson's eccentric and wild personality?

Answer: Samson

FIFTH DAY

What did God make on the fifth day of Creation?

The first chapter of the Bible says that God created the world in six days. On the fifth day he said, "Let the waters teem with swarms of living creatures, and let birds fly above the earth in the open expanse of the heavens" (v. 20). The oceans and the skies became the open expanses for God's creativity. The variety and ingenuity of his creations was unbounded. He made larger-than-a-house-sized sea creatures and small, deep-sea oddities; he made soaring eagles and tiny hummingbirds; he brought to life flocks of migrators and tropical beauties.

Then he commissioned them each to be fruitful and multiply, and fill the waters in the seas, and let birds multiply on the earth. Before he gave the same command to humanity, he assigned the abundance of animal life on the planet. The day after he created humans, he instructed them to govern over the fish of the sea and the birds of the sky.

God created the great sea creatures and every living creature that moves, with which the waters swarmed, according to their kind, and every winged bird according to its kind; and God saw that it was good.

Genesis 1:21 NASB

Which of God's sea or sky creatures is most marvelous to you?

Answer: sea creatures and winged creatures in the air

MAY 5

AUTHORITY TO SERVE

Jesus knew the Father had put all things under his power, so what did he do?

One of the most world-changing truths about Jesus is that on the night before his crucifixion, and even though he had all authority in heaven and earth, he chose to serve people. He could have demanded allegiance. He could have forced people into submission. He could have revealed his full glory and wiped sinful humanity off the face of the planet. But he served. In fact, John tells us that he deliberately took off his outer garment and wrapped a servant's towel around his waist. He took the effort to get a basin of water and he went from person to person washing their feet.

All twenty-four feet of the disciples were washed by the Master. Judas would betray him and he received a foot washing. Jesus washed the feet of Peter, who would deny him. Jesus washed the feet of those who claimed to love him yet would run away the night of his trial and beating. Jesus became obedient rather than demanding obedience. And he became obedient even to death on a cross. He took off his outer garment of glory, so we might be lifted up.

Jesus knew that the Father had put all things under his power, and that he had come from God and was returning to God; so he got up from the meal, took off his outer clothing, and wrapped a towel around his waist. After that, he poured water into a basin and began to wash his disciples' feet, drying them with the towel that was wrapped around him.

John 13:3-5 NIV

Read Philippians 2:1-11. What about Jesus' servant heart is impacting you the most right now?

Answer: washed his disciples' feet

MAY 6

COVERING UP

What kind of leaves did Adam and Eve use to cover up their nakedness?

Adam and Eve gave into temptation and ate from the one tree God had forbidden them—the tree of the knowledge of good and evil. Until then they knew only good. They enjoyed creation and their responsibilities. They enjoyed their walks with God and with one another. But sin had opened their eyes and souls to the knowledge of evil when they ate from the forbidden tree.

They were awakened to thoughts and ideas and concepts that frightened them. Instead of seeing themselves through the eyes of God, they now saw themselves through obscured lenses, a fractured image of who they were created to be. When they had once been pure and innocent, they were now complicated and confused. Suddenly they realized they were naked. This had not been an issue before, but the door had been opened to disparaging self-image and dysfunctional relationships. They found some fig leaves, sewed them together, and hid from themselves, from each other, and from God.

The eyes of both of them were opened, and they realized they were naked; so they sewed fig leaves together and made coverings for themselves.

Genesis 3:7 NIV

Sin covers up. Innocence leads to freedom. How does God work in our lives to lead us back to innocence?

Answer: fig leaves

SIXTH COMMANDMENT

What is the sixth of the Ten Commandments?

The sixth, seventh, and eighth commandments are short and to the point. They are a quick list of clear behavioral expectations: You shall not murder, commit adultery, or steal. They form a social contract for basic functioning of society. But angry and selfish and confused people can do remarkably violent things. God knew that people needed a road map that clearly marked out the boundaries. God pointed out the obvious: it is wrong to murder. Taking another person's life unlawfully, whether premeditated or careless, is sinful.

It is perhaps ironic that God chose Moses to deliver the Ten Commandments to the people of Israel. Moses himself had not upheld these commandments during his lifetime. In fact, Moses was a murderer. Over forty years earlier he killed an Egyptian soldier and fled to Midian to escape his own execution. It must have been humbling for Moses to present the all too obvious, but all too disregarded, commandments of God to the world.

"You shall not murder."

Exodus 20:13 NIV

How does Jesus later expand the definition of murder in Matthew 5:21-22?

Answer: you shall not murder

MAY 8

FACE DOWN

What was the name of the pagan god that fell on its face in front of the ark of the covenant?

The Philistines were feeling confident. They captured the ark of the covenant from the Israelites, which was the most sacred item in Israel, associated with God's presence. Anytime Israel carried the ark into battle, the Israelites slaughtered their enemies. But in the time of Samuel, the priestly leaders of Israel became corrupt and compromised their covenant with God. On the occasion noted in today's verse, God allowed the Philistines to rout the Israelite army and to capture the ark.

With overconfidence, the Philistines placed God's ark of the covenant in the temple of their god, Dagon. The next day the Philistines found Dagon's statue toppled onto its face and prostrate to the ark. They set the statue back up, only to find it on its face again the next day; but this second time, Dagon's head and hands were broken off. God unleashed plagues on the Philistines that day, which continued until they voluntarily chose to send the ark back to the Israelites.

The following morning when they rose, there was Dagon, fallen on his face on the ground before the ark of the LORD! His head and hands had been broken off and were lying on the threshold; only his body remained.

1 SAMUEL 5:4 NIV

Even when we are unfaithful, does God stop being God?

Answer: Dagon

QUARRELS IN CHURCH

In his letter to the Philippians, who does Paul ask to quit quarreling?

Paul's letter to the Philippians is one of the most encouraging books in the Bible. He began the letter praising the believers in Philippi. He says, "I thank my God every time I remember you," and told them that he always prayed with joy for them (1:3-4). Their partnership with him in spreading the gospel was always a tremendous boost of encouragement for Paul, whether he was in prison or traveling around the Roman Empire. He rejoiced because he knew the Philippians were faithful to Jesus and supportive of him.

There is a brief moment in the letter that gives insight into one relationship that was struggling. Paul heard that two people in the church of Philippi were quarreling. These women have contended by my side in the cause of the gospel. Please, he asks the church, help them be of the same mind in the Lord.

I plead with Euodia and I plead with Syntyche
to be of the same mind in the LORD.

PHILIPPIANS 4:2 NIV

Why is it so important for Christians to be united in Jesus and not fall into quarreling?

Answer: Euodia and Syntyche

PEOPLE OF NINEVEH

How many peple lived in Nineveh during the time of Jonah?

Nineveh was a significant Assyrian city in what is now northern Iraq. According to the book of Jonah, it had over a hundred and twenty thousand people and was the political center of the empire's trade and military endeavors. It was a powerful city, but corrupt. God asked Jonah, "Shouldn't I feel sorry for such a great city?"

Jonah struggled with God's compassion. Nineveh was the home of his enemies. He believed they should be destroyed, not offered a chance to repent. But he knew that God desires that no one should perish (2 Peter 3:9). He knew that God wanted him to share God's message with the city because he wanted to save the people of Nineveh instead of annihilating them. The book of Jonah ends with the question posed in today's verse. We do not know Jonah's response.

"Should I not also have compassion on Nineveh, the great city in which there are more than 120,000 people, who do not know the difference between their right hand and their left, as well as many animals?"

Jonah 4:11 NASB

How many people live around you? Should God not also have compassion on them?

Answer: more than one hundred and twenty thousand

MAY 11

RESCUING MOSES

How did Moses' mother save him when he was a baby?

A Levite couple lived during the time of the Egyptian enslavement of the Israelites. Despite the oppressive conditions, Israel was growing in numbers and Pharaoh was concerned about their power. He ordered that every Hebrew boy that was born had to be thrown into the Nile. When the couple gave birth to a boy, they hid him for three months. When they could no longer hide him, the boy's mother put him in a waterproof basket and placed it among the reeds along the Nile riverbank. The boy's sister followed the basket down the river to see what would happen to her brother.

Pharaoh's daughter was bathing at the river. She saw the basket and asked her servants to retrieve it. Her heart broke for the boy, and she decided to care for him as her own. The baby's sister found a local Hebrew woman—who happened to be the boy's mother—to nurse him for Pharaoh's daughter. She named him *Moses* which is like the Hebrew word for "drawing out."

When she could hide him no longer, she got a papyrus basket for him and coated it with tar and pitch. Then she placed the child in it and put it among the reeds along the bank of the Nile.

Exodus 2:3 NIV

What are the significant foundations of Moses' early life in light of what happened later in his life?

Answer: she hid him in a basket and put him in the river

MAY 12

ON THE WALL

What did King Belshazzar of Babylon see on the wall before he died?

While the king of Babylon and his guests partied and praised their metal, wooden, and stone gods, a human hand appeared. It stretched out its fingers and began to write on the wall. The king paled and became faint. He summoned his best astrologers and diviners but none of them could interpret the mysterious writing. The queen told him about a man who served his father, King Nebuchadnezzar. This man was wiser than all of his father's magicians and prophets. So Belshazzar summoned Daniel.

Daniel confronted Belshazzar and told him that he had failed to humble himself to the Most High God. Because he worshipped idols, God sent the hand that wrote, *"Mene, Mene, Tekel, Parsin"* on the palace wall. Daniel informed Belshazzar that the message meant the king's days were numbered, that he was guilty of injustice, and that his kingdom would be divided by the Medes and Persians. That very night, Belshazzar was slain, and Darius the Mede took over the kingdom.

Suddenly the fingers of a human hand appeared and wrote on the plaster of the wall, near the lampstand in the royal palace. The king watched the hand as it wrote. His face turned pale and he was so frightened that his legs became weak and his knees were knocking.

DANIEL 5:5-6 NIV

Is there anything that you worship besides the Most High God?

Answer: a hand writing a message

MAY 13

WRESTLING WITH GOD

What was the wrestling nickname given to Jacob?

A. Socket
B. Manasseh
C. Jake
D. Israel

Genesis 32 tells us that one night, when Jacob was alone, a man wrestled with him through the night until daybreak. Finally, the man touched the socket of Jacob's hip so that his hip was wrenched. The man told Jacob that his name would be known from that point on as Israel. The name *Israel* means "wrestles with God." Jacob realized then that he had seen God face-to-face, and yet his life had been spared.

God invited the nation of Israel to have a unique, special relationship as his covenantal partner, each engaging the other in the activity of life, each contending with the other and offering mutual commitment. Whenever Israel ignored their calling, or refused to wrestle with their faith, or walked away from engaging with God, they failed to help humanity overcome the tension of reconciling with God and failed to take advantage of the privileged opportunity to interact with him on personal terms.

> The man said, "Your name will no longer be Jacob, but Israel, because you have struggled with God and with humans and have overcome."
>
> Genesis 32:28 NIV

Would you say you wrestle with God, or do you avoid engaging with God in a effort to bypass the tensions in your life?

Answer: D) Israel

OLD BROTHERS

Who was older, Moses or his brother Aaron?

Moses and Aaron were not young when they confronted Pharaoh on behalf of the Hebrews; Moses was eighty years old, and Aaron was eighty-three. They had each already lived a lifetime. It could be said that Moses had already squeezed two lifetimes into his eighty years; he spent half his life as a prince in Egypt, living in Pharaoh's household. The other half of his life he was a Midian shepherd, married to Zipporah, Jethro's daughter.

Despite their age, God had a dramatic ministry for both of these men. He called them to trust the rest of their lives to his greater plan. He chose them to go with his authority to Pharaoh, the most powerful man on the planet. They were to speak on his behalf and to prophecy in his name. They worked wonders, pronounced judgments, and implemented his laws. He chose them to rescue a nation that would eventually rescue the whole world.

Moses was eighty years old and Aaron eighty-three,
when they spoke to Pharaoh.

Exodus 7:7 NASB

How old are you? Answer: Never too old to be used by God. How do you see God using you right now?

Answer: Aaron was three years older than Moses

MAY 15

ROD AND STAFF

FINISH THIS VERSE

Even though I walk through the valley of the

__________ __________ __________,

I fear no evil, for ________ ________ ________ ________.

Your rod and Your staff, they ________ ________.

No matter what difficulties we face in life, God promises to be with us. The key is that we seek after him and recognize his guidance. When we, like sheep, wander away from our Good Shepherd, we lose our safety and our blessings. But when we follow the directive presence of our Savior, he makes us lie down in green pastures, leads us beside quiet waters, and restores our souls.

Our Good Shepherd lavishes us with attention by preparing our daily food and anointing our heads. By choosing to dwell with him, his love overwhelms us with goodness and lovingkindness. If evil is the absence or rejection of God, then comfort is the presence and acceptance of him.

Even though I walk through the valley of the shadow of death,
I fear no evil, for You are with me;
Your rod and Your staff, they comfort me.

Psalm 23:4 NASB

How can you put your fears aside and rest in God's protective arms?

Answer: shadow of death; You are with me; comfort me

FEEDING ELIJAH

Who fed Elijah by the brook?

King Ahab was an evil king. As a result, God declared through the prophet, Elijah, that there would be no dew nor rain for years (v. 1). Then he told Elijah to travel eastward and hide by the brook Cherith, which was east of the Jordan River. During the drought, he wanted Elijah to be able to have drinking water.

God also provided food for Elijah in a curious way. He commanded the ravens to provide food for him. Every morning and evening the ravens brought him bread and meat. So, Elijah obeyed God and settled next to the brook.

The ravens brought him bread and meat in the morning and bread and meat in the evening, and he would drink from the brook.

1 Kings 17:6 NASB

What might be the reason God wanted Elijah to go through this experience?

Answer: ravens

MAY 17

THE SOWER

In Jesus' parable of the farmer who sowed seed, on what four areas did the seed fall?

Jesus' famous parable of the sower reveals the ways in which people receive the message about the kingdom of God. Sometimes people aren't receptive and the evil one comes and snatches away what was sown. Or people receive the good news with joy but don't let it take root, so it withers away. Other times, people let God's truth get choked out by the worries and responsibilities in life.

Jesus explained to his disciples that the best soil was in the hearts of those who let their lives be fertile ground for God's Word to grow and produce an abundant crop.

"As he was scattering the seed, some fell along the path, and the birds came and ate it up. Some fell on rocky places, where it did not have much soil. It sprang up quickly, because the soil was shallow. But when the sun came up, the plants were scorched, and they withered because they had no root. Other seed fell among thorns, which grew up and choked the plants. Still other seed fell on good soil, where it produced a crop—a hundred, sixty or thirty times what was sown."

MATTHEW 13:4-8 NIV

How can you cultivate abundant faith in your life?

Answer: on the path, in rocky places, among thorns, on good soil

SAFELY SEALED

Who closed the door to Noah's Ark when the floods came?

After Noah built the ark and loaded it with the animals, it began to rain. As the Bible describes the event: "In the six hundredth year of Noah's life, in the second month, on the seventeenth day of the month, on that day all the fountains of the great deep burst open, and the floodgates of the sky were opened" (Genesis 7:11). And it rained for the next forty days and forty nights.

A vessel of any size would have struggled to remain afloat during such a cataclysmic storm. The ark was enormous, filled with every kind of animal, Noah's family, and supplies for them all. Holes in the hull, leaks in the seams, cracks in the boards, or broken rivets could have caused a catastrophic end for this vessel. But God had given Noah intricate instructions for the construction plans, and Noah had followed them closely. When it was time to enter the ark before the floodgates were opened, the Bible tells us that God himself closed the door behind Noah. His seal was sufficient to keep the ark and all of its inhabitants safe.

Those that entered, male and female of all flesh, entered as God had commanded him; and the Lord closed the door behind him.

Genesis 7:16 NASB

What does the partnership between Noah and God reveal to you about how God wants to work in your life?

Answer: God

MAY 19

SHORTEST VERSE

What is the shortest verse in the Bible?

There is a debate about which verse is the shortest one in the Bible. Most people assume the winner is John 11:35: "Jesus wept." Those two words and nine English letters are sufficient to give that verse the reigning title. However, in the original Greek, 1 Thessalonians 5:16 could claim top spot. Its two words, "Rejoice always," contain only fourteen Greek letters compared to the sixteen Greek letters of John 11:35. But it seems that Job 3:2, with two words and six English letters may be the shortest verse. Job 3:2 is a verse that results from an odd numbering system that led into Job's discourse. "He said," is short enough to earn the top spot for shortest verse.

It is probably worth mentioning that if we want to be sticklers for the original languages, 1 Chronicles 1:25 wins it all. It lists the names of three people in a genealogy—Eber, Peleg, Reu—and is made up twelve English letters, but only nine Hebrew letters, compared to thirteen Hebrew letters for Job 3:2.

He said.

Job 3:2 NIV

Pick one of the verses mentioned above and read it in its context. What do these verses reveal about God's ultimate plan to have relationship with us?

Answer: Job 3:2

MAY 20

TWELVE–YEAR OLD GIRL

Whose twelve-year-old daughter did Jesus raise to life?

Luke 8 is a dramatic chapter. Many women who were followers of Jesus are mentioned by name. Jesus tells his famous parables about a farmer scattering seed and a lamp hidden under a bushel. He makes a controversial comment about who his true family is. And he fell asleep in a boat during a fierce storm. When his disciples woke Jesus up, he simply told the winds and waves to be still, and they were. Then Jesus healed a possessed man and sent the demons into a herd of pigs who plunged into the lake and drowned.

The chapter is capped off when Jesus crossed the lake and large crowds awaited him. Jairus, the local synagogue leader, fell at Jesus' feet and begged him to save his daughter. At that same moment, a woman touched Jesus' robe and was healed of her serious long-term illness. While Jesus was responding to her, a messenger from Jairus' house said that his daughter had died. Jesus told Jairus not to be afraid, but to have faith. His daughter would be healed.

Jesus took her by the hand and said in a loud voice,
"My child, get up!"
LUKE 8:54 NLT

In what areas of your life does Jesus tell you, "Don't be afraid?" From what you know of Jesus, do you believe him?

Answer: Jairus

HARVEST WORKER

FINISH THIS VERSE

"The harvest is ________, but the workers are ________."

Jesus traveled throughout the towns and villages around the Sea of Galilee. He taught in synagogues and homes, announcing the good news about kingdom. He healed people of diseases and illnesses. Matthew said that when Jesus saw the crowds, he had compassion on them because they were like a sheep without a shepherd. Then Jesus turned to his disciples and said, "The harvest is great, but the workers are few." He urged them to pray to God who had authority over the harvest to send more workers into his fields.

There are so many people who are confused and seek a shepherd. They need to know Jesus rather than turning to other voices or influences. Jesus turns to us now and asks us to pray for more workers for the harvest.

He said to his disciples,
"The harvest is great,
but the workers are few.

MATTHEW 9:37 NLT

How are you a harvest worker?

Answer: great; few

PASSOVER AND PENTECOST

The Jewish celebration of Pentecost is how many days after the Passover?

Passover and Pentecost are important biblical celebrations. The Old Testament event of the Passover marks when God passed over the Israelites to save them from the plague of the death of the firstborn sons. It is God's actions that rescued his people from their enslavement and began their exodus toward the Promised Land. The New Testament event of Pentecost was an important marker of God's provision for Israel after the Passover. Seven weeks after the Passover, God's people celebrated Shavuot, which is Hebrew for seven weeks, or Pentecost, which is Greek for fifty days, as a festival of first fruits. Israel would offer a sacrificial tithe of the initial harvest to God as an expression of gratitude for what had been done and for what is to come.

Jesus was crucified on the Passover as the sacrificial lamb who rescues humanity. Seven weeks later, the Holy Spirit came at Pentecost as a reminder of what God had done and to propel the church forward for what was to come.

> When the day of Pentecost came, they were all together in one place. Suddenly a sound like the blowing of a violent wind came from heaven and filled the whole house where they were sitting.
>
> ACTS 2:1-2 NIV

How does having a better understanding of the major Jewish festivals of the Old Testament help you understand the New Testament?

Answer: fifty

PROVIDED SACRIFICE

What animal did God provide for Abraham so he woudn't sacrifice his son Isaac?

God promised Abraham he would become the father of many nations. But there was a significant issue with this promise. Abraham and his wife, Sarah, were very old and they did not yet have children. Eventually, however, God enabled Sarah to give birth to Isaac, who would be the one through whom he would bless the whole world.

Then God asked Abraham to do the unthinkable—Abraham was to sacrifice his son, Isaac as an offering to God. Abraham, certainly overcome with emotion, obeyed God. He walked his son up to the altar, trusting that God would provide the lamb for a burnt offering. Abraham believed that God would send a worthy sacrifice so that his own son would be spared. As Abraham was about to follow through with the sacrifice, God stopped him and provided a ram instead. Abraham called that place, "The Lord will provide."

Abraham lifted up his eyes and looked, and behold, behind him was a ram, caught in a thicket by his horns. And Abraham went and took the ram and offered it up as a burnt offering instead of his son.

Genesis 22:13 ESV

How does this event foreshadow the sacrifice of Jesus on the cross?

Answer: a ram

MAY 24

PROPHETIC BLESSING

Before he died, Jacob blessed his sons. Which of his sons received the following blessing? "The scepter will not depart from _______, nor the ruler's staff from his descendants, until the coming of the one to whom it belongs, the one whom all nations will honor?

Among Jacob's final words was a prophetic blessing for his son, Judah. Jacob, who also went by the name Israel, offered sacred words for each of his sons prior to his death. To Judah, Jacob declared that a royal rule would always be associated with him. Throughout the generations to come, Jacob declared that a ruling authority would forever be present. Furthermore, he predicted that a descendant of Judah's would be honored throughout the nations. He suggested that this descendant would be the one to whom the ruling scepter and staff actually belonged.

It is difficult not to see Jesus in this blessing. King David came through the lineage of Judah. Jesus was in the line of David. Jesus would be called the King of kings, Lord of lords, and Prince of Peace, with authority over everything in heaven and earth.

The scepter will not depart from Judah,
nor the ruler's staff from his descendants,
until the coming of the one to whom it belongs,
the one whom all nations will honor.

GENESIS 49:10 NLT

What do you think Jacob understood from God's promises to him that the whole world would be blessed by one of his descendants?

Answer: Judah

MAY 25

FAMOUS WEDDING WORDS

Who said, "Where you go, I will go. Your people shall be my people, and your God, my God?"

The words of today's verse have been delivered at countless weddings, yet they were not originally devotional words for a new couple. Instead, they were shared from a widowed Moabite woman to her widowed Jewish mother-in-law. Ruth had married one of Naomi's sons. During a famine, Naomi's husband died, and then both her sons died. Naomi heard that God was providing food for people back in her hometown of Bethlehem, so she planned a return. She encouraged her sons' wives to stay in Moab and look for new husbands, but Ruth clung to Naomi and declared that she would never forsake her.

Because of her resilient dedication to Naomi, Ruth emigrated to Bethlehem where she met an honorable man named Boaz. Eventually, he took her as his bride. They gave birth to a boy named Obed, who became the father of Jesse, who became the father of a man named David.

Ruth said, "Do not plead with me to leave you or to turn back from following you; for where you go, I will go, and where you sleep, I will sleep. Your people shall be my people, and your God, my God."

RUTH 1:16 NASB

How does knowing the significant background of these words deepen your understanding of the story of King David?

Answer: Ruth to Naomi (her mother-in-law)

MAY 26

DAVID'S CONFESSION

Who confronted David about his sin with Bathsheba?

After David had an affair with Bathsheba and arranged for the death of her husband, God sent Nathan the prophet to confront him. Nathan told David a story about a rich man and a poor man. In the story, the rich man owned lots of livestock while the poor man had only one lamb who grew up with his children. One day a guest arrived at the rich man's house, but instead of killing an animal from his own flock, he took the poor man's lamb and slaughtered it for their dinner.

David was enraged by this story and declared that the rich man needed to pay compensation to the poor man. At that point, Nathan declared, "You are that man!" He explained how David murdered Uriah and stole his wife. David was deeply convicted by Nathan's words and immediately confessed his sins. Many scholars think that David wrote Psalm 51 in response to Nathan's confrontation.

Nathan said to David, "You are that man!
The Lord, the God of Israel, says:
I anointed you king of Israel
and saved you from the power of Saul."

2 Samuel 12:7 NLT

According to 1 John 1:9, what happens when you confess your sin to God?

Answer: Nathan, the prophet

VERBAL MEASUREMENT

TRUE OR FALSE
According to Proverbs, a truly wise person uses a lot of words.

Those who are wise control their tongues. Fewer words make them more impactful in the temperament of the wise. In fact, even fools look sensible when they learn to measure the usage of their words. The Bible frequently points out that fools rush to speak; "You must all be quick to listen, slow to speak, and slow to get angry" (James 1:19). If we could control our tongues, we could also control ourselves in every other way. The writer of Psalm 141:3 begs God to take control of his mouth.

Paul encourages those who follow Jesus to avoid corrupt speech and invest in building people up (Ephesians 4:29). He told the Colossians to let their words be gracious and seasoned with salt (4:6). A wise tongue, Proverbs 12:18 teaches, brings healing, while foolish words damage both speaker and hearer. Wise words edify and encourage everyone with ears to hear.

A truly wise person uses few words;
a person with understanding is even-tempered.
Even fools are thought wise if they keep silent,
and discerning if they hold their tongues.
Proverbs 17:27-28 NLT

Challenge yourself to speak less today and trust God more in your conversations.

Answer: false

EARNING A NICKNAME

What was Barnabas' original name?

The earliest church in Jerusalem was growing quickly. People were being added to the fellowship of believers every day and the city was taking notice. One of the reasons for the rapid growth is noted in Acts 4. Even though there was an emerging tension of persecution for following Jesus, all of the believers were one in heart and mind. They shared everything they had with one another so that there was no one needy among them. The disciples of Jesus spoke openly about his resurrection, and God's grace was powerfully at work in them all. People were even selling their properties so the money earned from the sales could be distributed to impoverished people.

One of those who sold their property was a Levite man from Cyprus named Joseph. He earned the nickname Barnabas because he was such an encourager. Barnabas soon became a central figure in the book of Acts. He was known as the one who accepted and advocated for others (e.g., Paul and John Mark) and who supported the missionary endeavors to the Gentiles.

Joseph, a Levite from Cyprus, whom the apostles called Barnabas (which means "son of encouragement"), sold a field he owned and brought the money and put it at the apostles' feet.

Acts 4:36-37 NIV

If you were to earn a nickname for the way you interacted with others, what might your nickname be?

Answer: Joseph

MARTYRED FOR JESUS

Who was the first of the twelve disciples to be martyred?

James and John were two of the first people to follow Jesus. They left their fishing business in the Sea of Galilee and dedicated their lives to him. They saw Jesus perform miracles, cast out demons, and claim to be the Son of God. They saw Jesus teach the multitudes, challenge the religious class, and usher in God's kingdom. They saw Jesus walk on water, calm the storm, and raise Lazarus from the dead. They also saw Jesus die on the cross.

Then they saw him alive in the flesh again. They saw his Holy Spirit fall on the believers and turn Jerusalem upside down. They saw all of their friends scattered after Stephen was murdered and Saul led a harsh persecution against them. Then they saw Saul's life transformed by his encounter with Jesus. They saw Peter boldly share the gospel with a Roman centurion's family and heard his bold claim that the message of Jesus was for all people everywhere. And they saw Barnabas go to Antioch in Syria to begin the greatest mission movement in the history of the world. But then King Herod arrested James and had him executed with a sword.

It was about this time that King Herod arrested some who belonged to the church, intending to persecute them. He had James, the brother of John, put to death with the sword.

Acts 12:1-2 NIV

When they dropped their nets all those years ago, what do you think James and John expected to happen by choosing to follow Jesus?

Answer: James, the brother of John

JOSHUA'S DAD

What was the name of Joshua's dad?

A. Priest
B. Pastor
C. Nun
D. Monk

As a young man, Joshua became the protégé of Moses. God chose Joshua in the early years of the exodus to eventually succeed Moses as Israel's leader. Joshua had a powerful faith in God and excellent leadership skills. By the time Israel entered the Promised Land, he commanded the nation of Israel with as much authority and power as Moses had during the years in the dessert.

Joshua had to begin somewhere. We get the picture from Numbers 11 that Joshua saw the world in the typical justice lens of a passionate young man. His father had been from the tribe of Ephraim. Nun, which simply meant "fish," would have been a slave in Egypt, knowing the harsh conditions exacted by Pharaoh upon the Hebrews. Nun had named his son Hoshea, meaning "salvation," evidencing a deep faith that God would deliver his people. Moses then changed his name slightly to Yehoshua, which means "God is my salvation."

Joshua son of Nun, who had been Moses' aide since youth, spoke up and said, "Moses, my Lord, stop them!"

Numbers 11:28 NIV

Considering Joshua and his father, why is it important to leave a spiritual legacy for the next generations?

Answer: C) Nun

THE MERCIFUL

Why did Jesus say the merciful are blessed?

God loves mercy. He sent his one and only Son so that humans could be given mercy. Mercy is not weakness, even if the world wrongly defines it to mean a lack of courage. In fact, mercy can be only granted by someone who has enough power to enact judgment. Mercy can only be dispensed by someone who deserves to demand vengeance or consequences. And mercy can only be given if the person in power is able to pay the cost. Ultimately, mercy recognizes that God is in control, and it acknowledges that the person who deserves judgment is both a fellow child of God and in need of restoration.

Merciful people chose a path of salvation for others. It is the path God chooses. But it is also a path of personal sacrifice, absorbing the consequences of the other person's actions. Mercy doesn't dictate a person's future; it simply opens it up.

"Blessed are the merciful,
for they will be shown mercy."
MATTHEW 5:7 NIV

Would those who depend upon you or interact with you say that you are merciful?

Answer: because they will be shown mercy

JUNE

JUNE 1

PAUL'S CREDENTIALS

What Jewish tribe does the apostle Paul come from?

In terms of religious pedigree, Paul's credentials were impressive. He called himself a Hebrew of Hebrews. He was from a kingly tribe, Benjamin. This was the tribe of the first Israelite king, Saul. From birth, Paul says he was faultless in keeping the regulations of Judaism. And in terms of instruction of the Torah and religious rules of Israel, Paul became an enforcer. He was a Pharisee of renown, feared for his zealous hatred of those who followed Jesus. Paul had a lot to be confident about.

And yet, he wrote, "whatever were gains to me I now consider loss for the sake of Christ" (Philippians 3:7). Compared to knowing Jesus, everything else, Paul said, was a loss. Nothing rivals the value of having life in Christ.

If someone else thinks they have reasons to put confidence in the flesh, I have more: circumcised on the eighth day, of the people of Israel, of the tribe of Benjamin, a Hebrew of Hebrews; in regard to the law, a Pharisee; as for zeal, persecuting the church; as for righteousness based on the law, faultless.

PHILIPPIANS 3:4-6 NIV

What have you gained by following Jesus?

Answer: Benjamin

FIRST GREAT CATCH

Where was Jesus standing when he told Simon to put out into deep water and let down his nets for a catch?

The first recorded miraculous catch of fish that Jesus performed happened while he was in Simon Peter's boat. The crowds around Jesus had become so large that he got into Simon's fishing boat and began to teach from a little way offshore. When he finished teaching, he turned to Simon and told him to go out into deeper water and cast his nets for a catch.

At first, Simon hesitated, explaining that they had been fishing all night long and had caught nothing. Simon and his brother, Andrew, must have been exhausted. Yet something about being in the presence of Jesus while he was teaching had stirred Simon. He responded, "But at your word I will let down the nets" (Luke 5:5). When they cast their nets, such a large number of fish were caught that their nets began to break. They had to get help from another boat, which also began to sink due to the abundant catch. When they got to land, Simon and the others left everything and followed Jesus.

Getting into one of the boats, which was Simon's, he asked him to put out a little from the land. And he sat down and taught the people from the boat. And when he had finished speaking, he said to Simon, "Put out into the deep and let down your nets for a catch."

Luke 5:3-4 ESV

After the biggest catch of his fishing career, why do you think Simon Peter left his business?

Answer: in Simon's boat

JUNE 3

LONGEST PRAYER

Of all the recorded prayers in the Bible, who is it that prays the longest?

The prayer in Nehemiah 9:5-38 is thirty-four verses long and contains over twelve hundred words in English. King Solomon prays in 1 Kings 8:23-53 and that is a close second place with over a thousand words. The longest recorded prayer in the New Testament is John 17, where Jesus prays for his disciples with over six hundred words.

The book of Nehemiah is packed with ten recorded prayers. Central to Nehemiah's purpose was to reestablish and revitalize Jerusalem. It was also pivotal to him to explain the direct relationship with God that his people had previously enjoyed. Nehemiah invited all of the people of Israel to join him in reading the Scriptures for one quarter of a day, and then to confess their sins for another quarter of a day. Then Nehemiah invited them to turn to God in a prayer of praise. He wanted to emphasize the remembrance of God's past actions, an understanding of sin, and a promise to return to a covenant with God.

"You are the Lord, you alone. You have made heaven, the heaven of heavens, with all their host, the earth and all that is on it, the seas and all that is in them; and you preserve all of them; and the host of heaven worships you.

Nehemiah 9:6 ESV

Why is it important to have times when we spend a long time in prayer?

Answer: Nehemiah

JUNE 4

SECOND DAY

What did God make on the second day of creation?

The first chapter of the Bible tells us that God created the world in six days. On the second day of creation, God seems to have created the atmosphere, with oceans of waters covering the earth and clouds covering the skies. Genesis tells us that God called the expanse *heaven*.

It is in the midst of the waters that God would place humanity on the sixth day. It would become the unspoiled environment for humans to live and flourish. The perfect combination of nitrogen and oxygen and other gases gave humanity a home that is unique in the whole universe. God was establishing a special place among the galaxies that would house his most precious creation, people created in his image.

> Then God said, "Let there be an expanse in the midst of the waters, and let it separate the waters from the waters." God made the expanse, and separated the waters that were below the expanse from the waters that were above the expanse; and it was so. God called the expanse "heaven." And there was evening and there was morning, a second day.
>
> GENESIS 1:6-8 NASB

Considering all of the universe, what is the uniqueness of the earth's atmosphere?

Answer: an expanse between the waters

JABEZ'S PRAYER

What three things did Jabez ask for in his prayer to God?

A. Increased land
B. Abundance of children
C. Blessing
D. Protection from pain

In the middle of a number of chapters containing almost nothing but genealogical records in the book of 1 Chronicles, there is an interesting and seemingly out-of-place commentary. Most readers of the Bible may skim or skip through these first nine chapters, considering them not really important or not spiritually inspiring. So, it is easy to miss the random note inserted into the genealogical record of the tribe of Judah next to a man named Jabez.

Jabez's name meant "pain." His mother called him that when he was born because of how painful her labor had been. But when he was older, Jabez prayed that the God would keep him from harm, so that he wouldn't experience pain. "Bless me," Jabez prays, "and enlarge my border." Jabez asked that God's hand would be with him.

> Jabez was more honorable than his brothers; and his mother called his name Jabez, saying, "Because I bore him in pain." Jabez called upon the God of Israel, saying, "Oh that you would bless me and enlarge my border, and that your hand might be with me, and that you would keep me from harm so that it might not bring me pain!" And God granted what he asked.
>
> 1 Chronicles 4:9-10 ESV

How is Jabez's prayer a simple and yet profound template of prayer for your own life?

Answer: A, C, and D

GONG SHOW

Paul said that he would be a noisy gong or a clanging cymbal if he didn't have what?

Paul was a gifted speaker. He impressed people constantly with his explanations of Scripture, his skills of debate, and his eloquence with deep philosophical truths. But even if he spoke in the tongues of men and of angels, all of his articulation and persuasive arguments would be worthless if he did not love others. In fact, Paul said that without a love for people, his message about Jesus would be offensive. Any preaching of the good news would sound more like an annoying crash of a gong or the clanging of cymbals in the ears of those who could hear.

The message of Jesus Christ is so compelling because it is lived out more than it is argued. The truth about Jesus is heard, yes, but even more so, it is seen. The gospel of Jesus is demonstrated through the transformed lives of those who walk in the Spirit. The love of God causes people to overflow with patience, kindness, and humility. It stirs a hunger for truth that grows an attractive, not repellent, resilient inner strength and hope for others.

If I speak in the tongues of men and of angels, but have not love,
I am a noisy gong or a clanging cymbal.

1 Corinthians 13:1 ESV

Would you say that the words of your faith in Jesus are backed up with a loving heart and resultant actions?

Answer: love

JUNE 7

SECOND COMMANDMENT

What is the second of the Ten Commandments?

Mankind was created in the image of God. But since sin entered the scene, mankind has been trying to create gods in humanity's image. Throughout history, mankind has attempted to use the materials of God's creation to create gods. Ridiculously, mankind has then assigned a value of worth and worship to these inanimate idols, often constructing entire systems of ritual and superstition to the vacant images.

God is very clear. He told his people that they must not bow down to them or worship them, for he was their jealous God who would not tolerate their affection for other gods. Such sin, he said, would have ramifications for generations to come. However, he promised to lavish unfailing love for a thousand generations on those who loved him and obeyed his commandments.

"You must not make for yourself an idol of any kind or an image of anything in the heavens or on the earth or in the sea."

EXODUS 20:4 NLT

Is there anything in your life that you have placed in a position of worship besides God?

Answer: you shall not make for yourself an idol of any kind

JUNE 8

BROTHERS AND FATHERS

What brothers were the fathers of the first herdsman and the first musicians?

The Bible tells us that in the early days of humanity, Cain settled east of Eden in the land of Nod, which is the Hebrew term for "wandering." Over time, Cain's descendants developed skillsets that began to organize how mankind would operate in the world.

One of Cain's great-great grandchildren was Lamech. Lamech married a woman named Adah who gave birth to two sons. One, named Jabal, became the father of nomadic shepherds who lived in tents and cared for livestock. The other, named Jubal, became the father of musicians, specifically of stringed and piped instruments. Lamech also bore another son, named Tubal-cain, to another wife named Zillah. Tubal-cain became the father of people who forged tools of bronze and iron.

Adah bore Jabal; he was the father of those who dwell in tents and have livestock. His brother's name was Jubal; he was the father of all those who play the lyre and pipe.

GENESIS 4:20-21 ESV

Why does the Bible share with us these particular beginnings of humankind? What is God inviting us to notice through these details?

Answer: Jabal and Jubal

JUNE 9

THE OLD TESTAMENT

What passage of Scripture did Jesus read out loud in the synagogue?

Jesus went home to Nazareth. He began his ministry and went into the synagogue on the Sabbath day. In front of the congregation on that particular day, he was asked to read from the scroll of Isaiah. He read a section from chapter sixty-one. It was a passage about the Messiah, using first-person language and from the perspective of the Servant of God. It was a first-person explanation about why the Messiah was sent and what he was supposed to do. "The Spirit of the Lord has anointed me to proclaim good news to the poor, release for captives, sight for the blind, freedom for the oppressed, and to proclaim the year of the Lord's favor," Jesus read.

Luke tells us that Jesus then rolled up the scroll and gave it back to the synagogue attendant. He sat down to elaborate on the reading. He said, "Today this Scripture has been fulfilled in your hearing" (Luke 4:21).

The scroll of the prophet Isaiah was given to him. He unrolled the scroll and found the place where it was written,
"The Spirit of the Lord is upon me,
because he has anointed me
to proclaim good news to the poor.

Luke 4:17-18 ESV

What statement was Jesus making at the start of his ministry by the reading of this passage?

Answer: Isaiah 61

JUNE 10

GLORY OF GOD

FINISH THIS VERSE

Let the words of my _______ and the meditation of my _______ be acceptable in your sight, O Lord, my rock and my redeemer.

Psalm 19 is a beautiful psalm about the glory of God which is evident both in the heavens of creation and in his laws. The speech of praise that the skies pour forth is constant. And the testimony that goes out from God's law is always good.

Likewise, the words of the mouth and the meditation of my heart, the psalmist says, should be acceptable in the sight of the Lord. In other words, how could I not imitate the same sort of praise reflected in the heavens and in the commandments? How could I do anything that fails to reveal his joy? How could I not speak with purity and truth? How could I not think on things that are good and admirable and praiseworthy?

Let the words of my mouth and the meditation of my heart
be acceptable in your sight,
O Lord, my rock and my redeemer.

Psalm 19:14 ESV

How can your words and heart be acceptable to the Lord today?

Answer: mouth; heart

JESUS IS

Paul told the Colossians that Jesus is the _______ _______ of the invisible God.

Jesus Christ is God in the flesh. Paul said that Jesus created everything, including the things we can see and the things we can't. He holds all of creation together. He is the head of the church, and he is supreme over everything living and dead. Jesus, Paul said, is the first in everything.

Philippians 2:6-8 articulated that Jesus, being in his very nature God, made himself nothing and became human in order to die on the cross. John 1:1 says that Jesus was with God and was God. John 1:3 says that he created everything. John 1:14 says that he became flesh and made his dwelling among us. John 1:18 says that no one had ever seen God but Jesus—who is himself God and has made him known.

Christ is the visible image of the invisible God. He existed before anything was created and is supreme over all creation, for through him God created everything in the heavenly realms and on earth.

Colossians 1:15-16 NLT

How great is Jesus?

Answer: visible image

HALL OF FAITH

TRUE OR FALSE
Samson is included in the list in Hebrews 11 of people from the Old Testament who had great faith in God?

Hebrews 11 is a hall of fame—or faith—for the Bible. "Faith shows the reality of what we hope for" (v. 1), the writer of Hebrews says. Abel, the son of Adam and Eve, is cited for his righteous offering. Enoch is highlighted for walking closely with God. Noah is included for building the ark. Abraham and Sarah and Isaac and Jacob are all emphasized repeatedly for the roles they played. Joseph stands out for his consistent faithfulness. Moses, of course, is given special recognition. And many others are included that we would all agree represent individuals of proven faithfulness.

There are several in this great cloud of witnesses who perhaps seem out of place. For instance, there's Rahab the Canaanite prostitute, and Barak, who seemed to trust Deborah more than he trusted God. There's also Gideon who tested God repeatedly. Jephthah, despite his questionable track record is listed. Even Samson, the womanizing, compromised judge, is included. Yet it is not their greatness that Hebrews 11 highlights, but God's greatness. All it takes for these individuals is faith in God for a hall-of-faith-worthy inclusion.

How much more do I need to say? It would take too long to recount the stories of the faith of Gideon, Barak, Samson, Jephthah, David, Samuel, and all the prophets.

HEBREWS 11:32 NLT

Read Hebrews 11. What does this chapter have to say about your own life of faith in God?

Answer: true

KING OF SALEM

Abraham gave a tithe to which king of Salem?

Hebrews 7 calls Melchizedek a priest of God Most High. He was the king of Salem, which means king of peace. He first appears in the Bible in Genesis 14, blessing Abraham (then called Abram) and praising "God Most High, Creator of heaven and earth" (v. 19). Abraham offered a tithe to Melchizedek as God's representative in the area that became known as Jeru-salem. Hundreds of years later, in Psalm 110, David references Melchizedek. He was a priest and a king who had the ability to judge and rule nations as well as to represent the people before God.

The book of Hebrews teaches us that Jesus Christ is a high priest in the order of Melchizedek. This means Jesus is worthy to rule the world with justice and peace and he is worthy to be God's eternal representative to people of all nations.

Abraham took a tenth of all he had captured in battle and gave it to Melchizedek. The name Melchizedek means "king of justice," and king of Salem means "king of peace."

HEBREWS 7:2 NLT

What do you notice about the way the Old and New Testament work together through the life of Melchizedek?

Answer: Melchizedek

WRITER OF HEBREWS

TRUE OR FALSE
Timothy is mentioned in the book of Hebrews, but Paul is not.

Interestingly, scholars are not sure who wrote the book of Hebrews. They are certain that the writer knew Timothy since he and his circumstances are mentioned near the end of the book. Throughout Christian history, the book has often been attributed to Paul's authorship because it contains weighty theological arguments that require extensive comprehension of the Jewish religious system as well as the Old Testament. But Paul is never mentioned by name and the book has many words, phrases, and themes that are not present in Paul's other writings. Some scholars suggest that the book of Hebrews was authored by Barnabas who was a Levite and a mentor for Paul as well as a missional leader in the early church. Other scholars suggest that it was written by Apollos, one of the early missionary leaders of the church and an excellent defender of theological truths.

No matter who wrote the book, Hebrews makes it very clear that Jesus is the author and perfecter of our faith (12:2). He is the fulfillment of everything set forth in the Old Testament, and he is the sustainer of our walk with God today.

You should know that our brother Timothy has been released,
with whom I shall see you if he comes soon.

Hebrews 13:23 ESV

In your opinion, which three verses in the book of Hebrews articulate the great work that Jesus has done?

Answer: true

JUNE 15

QUALIFIED OR NOT

FINISH THIS VERSE

"Go and make ________ of all the ________, baptizing them in the name of the Father and the Son and the Holy Spirit."

After his resurrection, Jesus gave his followers some work to do. He told them that he had all of the authority on heaven and earth, and with that authority he was commissioning them to do an important job. Their job was to make more disciples of all kinds of people all over the world.

Jesus' disciples weren't superstars. In fact, many of them were still riddled with doubt about what was happening. None of them felt qualified to change the world or to represent Jesus perfectly. But they understood it wasn't in their own abilities and power that they were to go into all of the world, but that they would be sharing the good news of Jesus in name of God the Father, the Son, and the Holy Spirit.

"Go and make disciples of all the nations, baptizing them in the name of the Father and the Son and the Holy Spirit."

Matthew 28:19 NLT

Who are you currently helping to follow Jesus?

Answer: disciples; nations

FAITH WITHOUT WORKS

James says that faith without works is _______.

A. worthless
B. ridiculous
C. annoying
D. dead

Each of the potential answers in the multiple-choice question above is theologically correct. Faith without works is worthless, for believing in something that doesn't impact the practice of life has no value in a person's life. Faith without works is ridiculous, for it simply doesn't make sense to believe in something and live a life contrary to that belief. Faith without works is annoying because others grow frustrated that what we say is not consistent with how we live. And, as James teaches, faith without works is dead because it has no pulse.

What is the purpose of believing in Jesus but continuing to live as if he Jesus isn't real? Paul compares such a way of living to a resounding gong or a clanging cymbal (1 Corinthians 13). True faith attaches itself deeply to Christ and is changed by him: renewed in thoughts and transformed in behavior.

In the same way, faith by itself,
if it is not accompanied by action, is dead.

JAMES 2:17 NIV

Would you say that your faith is dead, breathing but sick, alive but inconsistent, or alive and healthy?

Answer: D) dead

THE SEED

Jesus said that the kingdom of heaven is like what kind of seed planted in a field?

Jesus compared the kingdom of heaven to a mustard seed that a man planted in his field. That small mustard seed, though it seems insignificant at first, grows into the largest plant in the garden. The mustard plant grows tall enough and strong enough to become a place of refuge for birds.

The parable has eternal layers of meaning. God himself came to earth in the humblest form as a child in Bethlehem, small and insignificant. Jesus gave up his glory in heaven in order to plant his kingdom on earth. Likewise, when God begins a humble, good work in us, he turns that seed into an abundant crop that blesses others. We are but fragile jars of clay that contain the mighty treasure of God's Holy Spirit. His work in us produces a harvest of joy and mercy, forgiveness and character, perseverance, and hope.

"The kingdom of heaven is like a mustard seed, which a man took and planted in his field. Though it is the smallest of all seeds, yet when it grows, it is the largest of garden plants and becomes a tree, so that the birds come and perch in its branches."

MATTHEW 13:31-32 NIV

What seemingly small prayer could you request of God right now that could produce dramatic results in your life?

Answer: a mustard seed

JUNE 18

FOR THE UNRIGHTEOUS

When the Bible says that "the righteous for the unrighteous" suffered for sins, who is it referring to?

We did not deserve to be offered salvation through Jesus. We earned an eternal death because of our rebellion against a holy God. Yet God in his mercy, came to our rescue. He took the consequences of our sin upon himself, dying on the cross, cleansing us of our unrighteousness. He then conquered the grave and rose to life, inviting us to stand alive with him for all of eternity.

Peter teaches that this is the message of truth shared in the practice of baptism. That which was dead in sin is made alive in Christ. That which was wrong in us, is made righteous in Christ. That which we would have suffered, was suffered by Christ. And Jesus did this so that we might be in the presence of God.

Christ also suffered once for sins, the righteous for the unrighteous, to bring you to God. He was put to death in the body but made alive in the Spirit.

1 Peter 3:18 NIV

How can you praise God today for his work of salvation through Jesus Christ on the cross?

Answer: Jesus Christ

SHORTEST BOOK

What book of the Bible has the fewest number of verses?

Trying to determine which book of the Bible is the shortest is a bit of challenge. The winner of the contest for the book with the least number of words is 3 John, with 219 words. The contest for the least number of chapters results in a five-way tie between Obadiah, Philemon, 2 John, 3 John, and Jude, each with just one chapter. But the winner of the contest for the book with the least number of verses is 2 John, with thirteen (3 John has fourteen, by the way).

The reason that John, as he told his readers, wrote so little in his second epistle is that he intended to speak to them in person. His letter is heart-warming and faith-warning. Writing a letter was valuable in terms of its encouragement and admonition, but even more impactful would be seeing them face to face. John longed to be with others who continued to walk in the truth of Jesus Christ despite tremendous opposition.

I have much to write to you, but I do not want to use paper and ink. Instead, I hope to visit you and talk with you face to face, so that our joy may be complete.

2 John 12 NIV

Take a couple of minutes to read the thirteen verses of 2 John. What stands out to you from John's message?

Answer: Second John

JUNE 20

A CLOSE FRIEND

Jesus raised one of his closest friends, who had died, back to life. What was his friend's name?

Jesus received a serious message from Mary and Martha, two sisters who were very close to Jesus. They sent word that their brother, Jesus's dear friend, was sick. When he received this distressing news, he informed his disciples that the sickness would not end in death. For some reason, however, Jesus didn't hurry to save him. Instead, Jesus waited a couple of days to get on the road. Strangely, on the way to Bethany, Jesus told his disciples flatly, that his friend was dead.

By the time they arrived in Bethany, he had already been dead for four days. Jesus saw the sisters grieving deeply. And Jesus saw the tomb. He was overcome with anger and sadness, and he wept visibly. He ordered that the tomb stone be rolled away, despite the horrible stench that would come from the tomb. Then he shouted, "Lazarus, come out!"

> Jesus shouted, "Lazarus, come out!" And the dead man came out, his hands and feet bound in graveclothes, his face wrapped in a headcloth. Jesus told them, "Unwrap him and let him go!"
>
> John 11:43-44 NLT

John 11:45 informs us that many people who saw this believed in Jesus. What would your reaction have been that day?

Answer: Lazarus

JUNE 21

PERSPECTIVE

Peter said that a day to God is like _______ _______ _______,
and a thousand years is like _______ _______.

Even believers in the early church wondered about God's timing. When was Jesus going to return? Why hasn't he ushered in his kingdom yet? Why is God letting us be persecuted? How long will this continue?

Don't overlook a simple, yet mind-boggling truth, Peter urges. Our concept of time isn't anything like God's concept of time. We tend to forget that God created time for our sake. We exist within the confines of days and seasons and years. God merely spoke that construct into being. Peter argues, "The Lord is not slow to fulfill his promise as some count slowness, but is patient toward you, not willing that any should perish" (2 Peter 3:9). When the day of the Lord arrives, he assures us, it will be like a thief in the night. We won't know it's coming. Peter urges us to be diligent in faithfulness. And in the meantime to grow in the grace and knowledge of Jesus Christ.

Do not forget this one thing, dear friends: With the Lord a day is like a thousand years, and a thousand years are like a day.

2 PETER 3:8 NIV

Do you ever wonder why God seems to be slow in a response you are expecting? How does this verse help put some perspective on our concept of time?

Answer: a thousand years; a day

BOOK OF JUDE

TRUE OR FALSE
The book of Jude has no references to the Old Testament.

Jude started his letter by referring to himself as the brother of James who was the brother of Jesus. It perhaps was in humility that Jude was more comfortable calling himself James' brother rather than Jesus' brother. It was certainly in the power of his calling for Jude to travel the world and share the good news about Jesus and confront people with his truth. That Jude so deeply embraced Jesus as his Lord is a testimony to the resurrection and remarkable transforming work of the Holy Spirit in his life.

Even though it is only one chapter, the book of Jude talks about Egypt, Sodom and Gomorrah, the archangel Michael, Moses, Cain, Balaam, Korah, and Enoch. It is power-packed with references to the Old Testament as well as some unfamiliar stories lost in Jewish history and apocryphal legends. Jude does not shy away from challenging the sins of history that threatened the early church in his day. "Keep yourselves in the love of God," he urged. "Save others by snatching them out of the fire." God will keep you from stumbling (vv. 22-24).

Woe to them! They have taken the way of Cain;
they have rushed for profit into Balaam's error;
they have been destroyed in Korah's rebellion.

JUDE 11 NIV

Take a moment to read straight through the twenty-five verses of the book of Jude. What message does God want you to notice as you read this punchy little book?

Answer: false

TALKING DONKEY

Who was riding the donkey that talked?

Balaam was incredibly stubborn. He flirted with allegiances between God and the enemies of God. He refused to follow the Lord completely and played a political game to benefit himself. In response, God became angry and sent an angel to block Balaam's progress with the enemies. The donkey that Balaam was riding saw the angel of the Lord in front of them with a sword drawn. The donkey lurched and went off the trail into the field. Balaam struck the donkey and tried to turn it back to the road, but the donkey resisted and ended up crushing Balaam's foot against a wall. In the struggle, Balaam hit the donkey again and again.

When Balaam drew his sword and threatened to kill the donkey, God opened the mouth of the donkey and allowed it to confront Balaam. Then he opened the eyes of Balaam to show him the angel standing in the road. Balaam fell to his face in fear. The angel advocated for the righteousness of the donkey and judged the sinfulness of Balaam.

The donkey said to Balaam, "Am I not your donkey,
on which you have ridden all your life long to this day?
Is it my habit to treat you this way?" And he said, "No."

NUMBERS 22:30 ESV

What does this remarkable story reveal to you about the stubbornness of humans?

Answer: Balaam

JUNE 24

IMPORTANT BURIAL SITE

Who was the first person to die in Egypt but to be buried in Israel?

Before Jacob died in Egypt, he requested that his bones be buried back in the caves of Machpelah, near Mamre in Canaan, in the Promised Land where his grandfather, Abraham, and grandmother, Sarah, had been buried. It was also the burial site of his parents, Isaac and Rebekah, and of Jacob's wife, Leah.

Upon his father's death, Joseph had his father embalmed with all the privileges of a wealthy Egyptian ruler, and then he relayed his desires to Pharaoh. Pharaoh encouraged Joseph and his whole family to travel along with a formidable entourage of important Egyptian officials back to their home region. With the Canaanites of the land watching with awe, this large and powerful delegation buried Jacob.

Pharaoh agreed to Joseph's request.
"Go and bury your father, as he made you promise," he said.

GENESIS 50:6 NLT

Who was the second person who died in Egypt and was buried in Israel? Joseph. Why is this significant?

Answer: Jacob

JUNE 25

SAMUEL'S MOTHER

Who was Samuel's mother?

Hannah was not able to have a baby with her husband Elkanah. She prayed earnestly about this. She vowed to dedicate him to God if only she could give birth to a son. One time, she prayed so fervently, in fact, that the high priest, Eli, noticed her. He saw that her lips were moving but there was no sound coming out of her mouth. He concluded that she must have been drunk. But when he chastised her for drinking, she shared that she was simply distressed over not being able to have a child. Eli blessed her and prayed that God would let Hannah find favor with him and grant her request.

Hannah brought her son, Samuel, to Eli and asked that Samuel be raised in presence of God. "As long as he lives," Hannah said, "he is lent to the Lord." Eli agreed and took the child. Eventually this child would begin hearing from God directly, leading God's people to freedom from their enemies, and setting up the future kings of Israel.

In due time Hannah conceived and bore a son, and she called his name Samuel, for she said, "I have asked for him from the Lord."

1 Samuel 2:20 ESV

When was the last time you prayed earnestly for something?

Answer: Hannah

SOLOMON'S REQUEST

What did Solomon ask the LORD to give him?

A. Fame
B. Wealth
C. Long life
D. Wisdom

When Solomon became king of Israel, he told God that he wanted to govern the people well. He asked for wisdom to handle the responsibilities and decisions of his position. God was so pleased by Solomon's request that he lavished Solomon with unparalleled insight and knowledge. God said to him, "Because you have asked for wisdom in governing my people with justice and have not asked for a long life or wealth or the death of your enemies—I will give you what you asked for! I will give you a wise and understanding heart such as no one else has had or ever will have!" (1 Kings 3:11-12)

Then God gave Solomon even more. He said, "And I will also give you what you did not ask for—riches and fame! No other king in all the world will be compared to you for the rest of your life! And if you follow me and obey my decrees and my commands as your father, David, did, I will give you a long life." (vv. 13-14)

The LORD was pleased that Solomon had asked for wisdom.

1 KINGS 3:10 NLT

What will you ask God for today?

Answer: D) wisdom

MAYBE AGUR

TRUE OR FALSE

One of the authors of the book of Proverbs is Agur son of Jakeh.

Proverbs 30 contains a collection of wisdom sayings from a man named Agur, son of Jakeh. Scholars are not sure who this man was or what he did for a living. Some have speculated that this is another pseudonym for Solomon, similar to how he likely used "teacher" for the book of Ecclesiastes. Others even wonder if Agur's name, which means "gathered," refers to the collection of sayings rather than an actual individual. Likewise, the names of Ithiel and Ucal, to whom this section of proverbs is directed, are not known in history. Many have wondered if their names should be translated into their meanings of "feeling weary" and "consumed."

Whatever the case, this collection of personal proverbs is profoundly vulnerable. "I am more stupid than any man," the writer says. "I have not mastered human wisdom and don't know God" (v. 3). If Agur is comparing himself to God, this harsh self-assessment makes sense.

The words of Agur the son of Jakeh, the pronouncement.
The man declares to Ithiel, to Ithiel and Ucal:
I am certainly more stupid than any man,
And I do not have the understanding of a man.

Proverbs 30:1-2 NASB

Agur wonders if he can know God and what his name might be. "You know him and have seen him," Jesus says later in John 14:7. How do Jesus' words fit with Agur's proverbs?

Answer: true (maybe)

JUNE 28

THE COPPERSMITH

What was the name of the coppersmith who did Paul much harm?

Paul missed Timothy. He was nearing the end of his imprisonment in Rome and also the end of his life. He was able to have guests and was working hard to orchestrate disciple-makers from his arrested situation in Rome. But he was lonely. Second Timothy 4 gives a revealing look into the old apostle's own need for pastoral care.

Alexander the coppersmith hurt Paul deeply in some way, having strongly opposed the gospel. Demas had flat out deserted him, and it seems he also abandoned the faith. Crescens had gone to encourage the believers in Galatia; Titus was on a mission to Dalmatia. Paul sent Tychicus to Ephesus. "Only Luke is with me," he told Timothy. "At my first defense no one came to stand by me," he shared. "Do your best to come to me quickly." And please, he urged, "get Mark and bring him with you, for he is useful to me for ministry."

Alexander the coppersmith did me great harm;
the Lord will repay him according to his deeds.
Beware of him yourself, for he strongly opposed our message.

2 Timothy 4:14-15 esv

Who do you have that stands by you in your faith through every circumstance?

Answer: Alexander

JUNE 29

TIMOTHY'S MENTOR

Who was Timothy's mentor as a pastor?

Paul was a great mentor for Timothy. He invited Timothy on his missionary journeys and gave him important responsibilities. He cared about Timothy's family. He spoke well of him to others. And he took extensive, deliberate efforts to equip Timothy with all the skills and expertise he would need to be a primary leader in the growing movement of the early church. Stemming from his own extensive religious training, Paul taught Timothy practical instructions to organize a local church and to live according to the ways of God. Paul also gave Timothy a seminary-level education on theology and biblical foundations.

Paul's sound doctrinal teaching enabled Timothy to remain resilient as a pastor. Scripture, Paul instructed, is useful for all of the skills that Timothy would need to shepherd people in faith and to lead a church. The servant of God can be thoroughly equipped for every good work of ministry. Scripture derives from God and spurs people to do God's good work.

As for you, continue in what you have learned and have become convinced of, because you know those from whom you learned it, and how from infancy you have known the Holy Scriptures, which are able to make you wise for salvation through faith in Christ Jesus.

2 Timothy 3:14-15 NIV

Who has been a mentor of faith in your own life?

Answer: Paul

JUNE 30

PURE IN HEART

Why did Jesus say the pure in heart are blessed?

Those who are pure create a refreshing scandal in this world. Their simple trust in God and childlike desire to care for others is counter-cultural. Their uncorrupted perspective is alarmingly innocent. But their integrity gives them a strength that allows them to live free from the guilt of being in debt to others.

To be pure doesn't mean we are inexperienced, ignorant, or naive. The world might mock purity, calling it backward, weird, or uncool, but that is merely because the world doesn't understand it. The world can't conceive of the eternal survival power of purity because it only knows corruption. Those who are pure in heart can see things that are obscure to the corrupted heart. Purity begins in the nature of a person's character when the focus is upon God, not upon themselves. Purity then extends into a person's everyday actions. Purity opens the eyes of a person's soul to see Jesus face-to-face. The people with such purity see Jesus at work as he tackles sin with the unexpected weaponry of a clean heart.

"Blessed are the pure in heart,
for they will see God."

Matthew 5:8 NIV

What aspects of your life reflect God's?

Answer: because they will see God

JULY

THE MEDIATOR

When Paul tells Timothy that there is only one mediator, who was he referring to?

Paul urged Timothy to pray for all people, especially for kings and those in authority, in order to allow the followers of Jesus to live peaceful and quiet lives in all godliness and holiness. The reason for petitioning and praying and requesting this from God was twofold. First, it is good, and pleases God. Second, God wants all people to be saved and to come a knowledge of the truth. After all, Paul argued, Jesus has made this possible, so we should all pray!

Jesus himself mediates. He deliberately gave himself as a ransom so people would be saved and know God. Therefore, Paul urges, people everywhere should lift up holy hands without anger (vv. 6-8). Whether or not a believer is mindful of their actions impacts whether or not the gospel is spread. God wants his people to be intentional participants in his mission.

There is one God, and there is one mediator between God and men, the man Christ Jesus, who gave himself as a ransom for all, which is the testimony given at the proper time.

1 Timothy 2:5 ESV

With Paul's heart, how can you pray to God our Savior today?

Answer: Jesus

GREAT AUTHORITY

How many men carried the paralyzed man who was let down through the roof?

The crowds around Jesus had grown thick, and people were struggling to get close to him. When he returned to Capernaum where several of his disciples lived, news spread quickly that he was home. The house where he was staying became packed with guests, and no one could get close to the door. But there were four men who desperately wanted to get their paralyzed friend to Jesus. They cut a hole through the roof and lowered their friend on his mat right in front of Jesus.

Seeing their faith, Jesus forgave the sins of the paralyzed man. The religious leaders who were in the house were furious because that was blasphemy—only God could forgive sins! Jesus knew what the angry leaders were thinking, so he asked them if it would be easier to tell the man his sins were forgiven or to tell him to get up and walk. To prove who he was and what kind of authority he had, Jesus turned to the paralyzed man and told him to stand up, pick up his mat, and go home. At once the man jumped up and walked.

Soon the house where he was staying was so packed with visitors that there was no more room, even outside the door. While he was preaching God's word to them, four men arrived carrying a paralyzed man on a mat.

MARK 2:2-3 NLT

What does Jesus reveal about himself in this event?

Answer: four

LONG JUDGMENT

About one hundred years after Jonah preached in Nineveh, which prophet gave another announcement to the city?

God gave Nineveh a chance to turn away from their wickedness and toward him. He sent a reluctant prophet named Jonah to warn the city of the destruction that would befall them unless they repented. The leaders and people of the city listened to Jonah and turned to God, much to Jonah's dismay. But true repentance seemed to have died in the following generations. One hundred years after Jonah's mission, God told the prophet Nahum to speak a significant pronouncement against the city. For the entirety of his three chapters, Nahum poetically described the apocalyptic collapse of the Assyrian capital.

"The Lord is good," Nahum writes, "But with an overwhelming flood He will make a complete end of its site" (1:7-8). Their evil hurt so many people. The empire which had once wreaked havoc across the Middle East would soon be overrun. It was time for their judgment.

The pronouncement of Nineveh.
The book of the vision of Nahum the Elkoshite:
A jealous and avenging God is the LORD;
The LORD is avenging and wrathful.
The LORD takes vengeance on His adversaries,
And He reserves wrath for His enemies.

NAHUM 1:1-2 NASB

Does it encourage or discourage you that God works his will across generations and throughout the span of history?

Answer: Nahum

THIRD DAY

What did God make on the third day?

The first chapter of the Bible tells us that God created the world in six days. On the third day, God made dry land to separate the waters which he called "seas," and vegetation on the land. God intended the land to be fertile and productive. He made the earth so that it would grow life on its surface. He spoke fruitfulness into his creation. He said, "Let there be vegetation," with plants that yield seeds and trees that bear fruit. God saw that this was good.

This DNA of the planet later becomes the natural illustration for God's people. God wants his people to naturally overflow with abundant life. God wants his people to have fertile soil in their hearts for his kingdom to produce the fruit of the Spirit and to spread the seeds of his good news.

God said, "Let the waters below the heavens be gathered into one place, and let the dry land appear"; and it was so. And God called the dry land "earth," and the gathering of the waters He called "seas"; and God saw that it was good. Then God said, "Let the earth sprout vegetation, plants yielding seed, and fruit trees on the earth bearing fruit according to their kind with seed in them"; and it was so.

GENESIS 1:9-11 NASB

How does your own life of faith reflect the natural abundance of the third day of creation?

Answer: dry land and vegetation

THESSALONIAN EXAMPLE

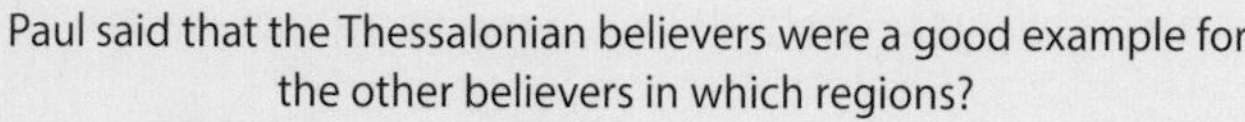

Paul said that the Thessalonian believers were a good example for the other believers in which regions?

A. Macedonia and Achaia
B. Judea and Samaria
C. Sodom and Gomorrah
D. Babylon and Rome

In the early years of the growing church, Christians in one city often became encouragers to Christians in other cities. The word would get out from one city to the next that followers of Jesus were standing firm in their faith despite persecution, hardships, or temptations. When Paul and Silas first went to Thessalonica, many people in the synagogue listened and were persuaded to join them. This upset some people who started a riot. They attacked the house of a man named Jason, searching for Paul and Silas to drag them out to be stoned. Instead, they dragged Jason and some other believers to stand before the city council. "They are guilty of treason against Caesar," the troublemakers accused, "for they profess allegiance to another king, named Jesus" (Acts 17:1-7).

Jason and the others did not give up their faith. In fact, Paul was impressed and encouraged with their deep conviction in Jesus. This impacted other believers in other cities as they heard news of their faithfulness.

> You became imitators of us and of the Lord, for you received the word in much affliction, with the joy of the Holy Spirit, so that you became an example to all the believers in Macedonia and in Achaia.
>
> 1 Thessalonians 1:6-7 ESV

If people outside your church community heard about your faith, what would they hear?

Answer: A) Macedonia and Achaia

JULY 6

ARMOR OF GOD

Which of the following was not included in the armor of God in the sixth chapter of Ephesians?

A. Belt
B. Shoes
C. Shield
D. Spear

Our struggle is not against flesh and blood. It is spiritual. There are powers and forces in this dark world that are intent on attacking those who follow God. Protect yourself, Paul urges, with the armor which God has supplied you.

For attacks that cause confusion, gird yourself with a belt of truth. For attacks of immorality, protect the purity of your heart with a breastplate of righteousness. For attacks of hostility, ready your feet to swiftly respond in defensive peace. For all attacks on your soul, use the shield of faith which will block any evil. Wear a helmet of salvation to firm up your mind. And always carry the Word of God which is sharp and cuts through any deception.

Stand firm then, with the belt of truth buckled around your waist, with the breastplate of righteousness in place, and with your feet fitted with the readiness that comes from the gospel of peace. In addition to all this, take up the shield of faith, with which you can extinguish all the flaming arrows of the evil one. Take the helmet of salvation and the sword of the Spirit, which is the word of God.

Ephesians 6:14-17 NIV

In what part of your faith do you feel most guarded, and in what part do you feel most vulnerable?

Answer: D) Spear

TENTH COMMANDMENT

What is the tenth of the Ten Commandments?

Proverbs 14:30 teaches that jealousy is like cancer in the bones. Jealousy eats away at the soul. It ruins contentment. It distracts the heart. It disrupts the pursuit of prioritizing God's kingdom above all else. It corrupts the thoughts and focus of the mind. It places a wedge between relationships. It unravels the functioning of society.

Love, we are taught in 1 Corinthians 13:4, does not envy. Love does not pursue selfish ambition. Love prioritizes the betterment of others. Love is patient and kind. Love finds contentment in any situation. Rather than dwelling on what is lacking, love dwells on what God has provided and the opportunities to be present with others. Love frees the heart from a bondage in which people are addicted to needing what other people have.

"You shall not covet your neighbor's house. You shall not covet your neighbor's wife, or his male or female servant, his ox or donkey, or anything that belongs to your neighbor."

Exodus 20:17 NIV

What jealous desires might you be holding on to today?

Answer: you shall not covet

GOD'S HANDIWORK

As God's handiwork, what does Paul tell the Ephesians we were created to do?

As followers of Jesus, we are meant to do good things. But please note, it is not because we do good things that we have earned the right to follow Jesus. "It is by grace you have been saved," Paul wrote to the Ephesians. It is "not from yourselves, it is the gift of God—not by works, so that no one can boast" (2:8-9).

We are not our own handiwork; we are God's handiwork. He made each of us into a masterpiece, but masterpieces with admirable purposes. We have a function, a calling. We have been commissioned by the Artist himself. It is his good work that has made us; it is his good work instilled within us, and it is his good work that will naturally produce good works from us. This was his plan for you all along.

We are God's handiwork, created in Christ Jesus to do good works, which God prepared in advance for us to do.

Ephesians 2:10 NIV

What good work that would glorify God are you resisting today?

Answer: good works

FRUIT OF THE SPIRIT

Name at least five of the nine fruits of the Spirit.

The fruit produced in someone's life is directly related to what they have rooted themselves into in the first place. If someone has planted themselves into poor soil with shallow roots, they will struggle to access living water and nutrients, and they will produce a poor crop. If, on the other hand, someone has planted themselves in fertile soil with ever-deepening roots, accessing living water and nutrients, they will yield an abundant harvest.

Whenever someone roots into Jesus, they tap into all of the unlimited resources and attributes of Christ. It is in him that the follower of Jesus is able to stand firm. And it is in Jesus that the believer overflows with the qualities of God. The fruit of the Spirit are the features of Jesus evidenced in the life of one being changed by God. The unending well of Jesus produces a life overflowing with love and joy and peace and all of the other life-giving characteristics of Jesus.

The Holy Spirit produces this kind of fruit in our lives: love, joy, peace, patience, kindness, goodness, faithfulness, gentleness, and self-control. There is no law against these things!

GALATIANS 5:22-23 NLT

Which of the fruits of the Spirit do you most lack? Take time to pray and to root yourself into Jesus, asking him to produce those fruits in your life today.

Answer: read Galatians 5:22-23

JULY 10

PAUL IN JERUSALEM

The first time Paul went back to Jerusalem after becoming a Christian, which two apostles did he meet there?

Paul revealed a lot about himself through his letters to believers. In the book of Galatians, he unpacks his previous way of life as a strict adherent to Judaism and his zealous persecution of the church. The followers of Jesus in Jerusalem were terrified of him. But on his way to Damascus, when Jesus was revealed to him, and the calling to preach to the Gentiles was given to him, he retreated to spend time with God. In fact, he waited three years to go back to Jerusalem.

There was trepidation amongst the believers in Jerusalem when he did go back. But Peter embraced him and had Paul stay with him. James, the brother of Jesus, also met with Paul. These were important meetings to confirm that Paul had, in fact, been changed and called to preach to the Gentiles. After that he went to Syria and Cilicia where they were glad to meet the man who formerly persecuted the church and was now preaching the faith he once tried to destroy.

Three years later I went to Jerusalem to get to know Peter, and I stayed with him for fifteen days. The only other apostle I met at that time was James, the Lord's brother. I declare before God that what I am writing to you is not a lie.

GALATIANS 1:18-20 NLT

If you had been Peter or James, how might you have received Paul when he came back to Jerusalem three years after killing Stephen and persecuting the church there?

Answer: Peter, and James the brother of Jesus

THORN IN THE FLESH

Who said that they had a thorn in the flesh?

A. Samson
B. Paul
C. Moses
D. Daniel

From an earthly point of view, Paul had a lot of reasons to be arrogant. Before knowing Jesus, he was a prominent Pharisee who kept the Jewish laws faultlessly and enforced them fervently. After being transformed by Jesus, he poured that same drive into his mission to spread the gospel from Israel to Rome. Along the way he had profound encounters with God and dynamic experiences in ministry. As a man, he would be tempted to boast about his accomplishments. But as a man impacted by Jesus, he only wanted to boast about his weaknesses.

To keep him from becoming prideful, Paul said that he was afflicted with a regular thorn in the flesh. Paul called this experience of torment a messenger of Satan. On three specific occasions, he cried to the Lord to remove this thorn. But God told him, "My grace is sufficient for you, for my power is made perfect in weakness" (2 Corinthians 12:9).

Because of the extraordinary greatness of the revelations, for this reason, to keep me from exalting myself, there was given to me a thorn in the flesh, a messenger of Satan to torment me—to keep me from exalting myself!

2 Corinthians 12:7 NASB

How can God's power be made more perfect in your weaknesses today?

Answer: B) Paul

JULY 12

COMMISSIONED

When Jesus sent his disciples out two by two, what did he tell them to do if a town refused to welcome them?

Jesus wanted to empower his disciples to spread the good news about his kingdom. He called his twelve disciples together and commissioned them to go in groups of two throughout the region, to teach people and show them God's power. He gave them authority to cast out evil spirits and told them to rely on kind people to host them and care for them. He instructed them to teach a message of repentance of sins and to encourage people to turn to God. He didn't want them to take anything with them except the clothes they were wearing, a walking stick, and their sandals. If, however, a town refused to welcome them, they were to shake the dust off their feet as they left to show those people that they were left to their own fate.

The disciples eagerly went out and were amazed that they had the ability to cast out demons and to heal people. They were able to minister to many people, anointing them with olive oil. Later, after his resurrection, Jesus commissioned his followers again to do a similar rescue mission but on a grander scale. He told them they would be his witnesses, ministering to people everywhere from Jerusalem to Judea to Samaria and to the ends of the earth.

"If any place refuses to welcome you or listen to you, shake its dust from your feet as you leave to show that you have abandoned those people to their fate."

MARK 6:11 NLT

The goal of the mission was to urge people to repent of their sins and to turn to God. What then is the symbolic meaning of having the disciples shake the dust off their feet?

Answer: shake the dust from their feet as they left the town

JULY 13

THE IDOL

What did Aaron make out of the people's gold while Moses was on Mount Sinai?

Early in the exodus wandering, the people of Israel struggled to trust Moses or God. Even after the plagues, even after crossing the Red Sea, even after the manna and the quail, even after the pillar of fire, and the water from the rock, the people still wavered in their commitment.

While Moses was on Mount Sinai receiving the commandments from God, the people grew impatient. They pressured Aaron, the older brother of Moses and Israel's priest, to make gods to go before them. Aaron collected all the gold earrings from the nation and fashioned them into an idol in the shape of a calf. He launched a festival to sacrifice to the gods in front of the calf. God ordered Moses, who had Joshua with him, to go down and confront the corrupt people of Israel. They had quickly turned their backs on their one true God and had returned to worshipping pagan idols as they had done in Egypt.

He took what they handed him and made it into an idol cast in the shape of a calf, fashioning it with a tool. Then they said, "These are your gods, Israel, who brought you up out of Egypt."

Exodus 32:4 NIV

How quickly do you swing back and forth between your focus on God and your pursuit of other things?

Answer: a golden calf

JULY 14

FRAGILE JARS OF CLAY

Paul says that the light of Christ shining within us is like fragile clay jars containing what?

The light of Jesus shines from within us. The very One who created the light to shine in the darkness has made his light shine from within our hearts. This is powerful. We always carry around in our body the death of Jesus, Paul wrote to the Corinthian church. God's power is great even if we ourselves are fragile.

Being persecuted for our faith, though it may hurt, does not mean we are abandoned for Jesus is with us. Being confused by the difficulties of life, though troubling, does not leave us in despair for God's Spirit is in us. Being struck down by the forces of the world, though it may be frightening, does not destroy us for the Good Shepherd calls our name and carries us home. Even if we are hard pressed on every side, we will not be crushed. We do not lose heart, for our eternal glory outweighs any momentary troubles. Because of this treasure, because of the light shining in our hearts, we fix our eyes on what is unseen and eternal.

We now have this light shining in our hearts, but we ourselves are like fragile clay jars containing this great treasure. This makes it clear that our great power is from God, not from ourselves.

2 Corinthians 4:7 NLT

How does God's light in you empower you to face everything that happens?

Answer: a great treasure

ONE WAY

FINISH THIS VERSE

Jesus told him, "I am the _______, the _______, and the _______. No one can come to the Father except through me."

Jesus told his followers very clearly that there is only one way for people to approach God the Father—through him! In other words, there are not many ways to heaven. There are not multiple avenues leading to God. There are not lists of religious preferences or human practices that permit people to find their way to heaven or develop their own truths.

The one and only way to receive forgiveness from sin and to have a relationship with God is through the death and resurrection of Jesus Christ. It is by believing in him that people are saved. Jesus came to earth to rescue and redeem us. He died on the cross to pay for the consequences of our sins. He rose from the grave to conquer death and offer us new life. God so loved the world that he sent his one and only Son so that whoever believes in him will not perish but have eternal life (John 3:16).

Jesus told him, "I am the way, the truth, and the life.
No one can come to the Father except through me."

JOHN 14:6 NLT

Do you know Jesus as your Lord and Savior?

Answer: way; truth; life

JULY 16

WITNESSES

According to Paul's letter to the Corinthians, how many people saw the Resurrected Jesus?

After the resurrection, Jesus didn't only appear before Mary in the garden and his disciples. Paul shared with the Corinthian church that he was also seen by hundreds of people at one time. Paul goes on to say that at the time of the writing of this letter, most of those five hundred people were still alive. He added that Jesus also then appeared to James, the brother of Jesus, and all of the apostles. Last, Jesus appeared to Paul.

Paul recognized that he had been given an undeserved privilege to meet Jesus face to face. His calling to share the gospel of Jesus throughout the world was humbling to him. He was, in his estimation, the least of the apostles and did not even deserve to be called an apostle. It was only by God's grace that Paul had been given the chance to know salvation through Jesus.

He was buried, and he was raised from the dead on the third day, just as the Scriptures said. He was seen by Peter and then by the Twelve. After that, he was seen by more than 500 of his followers at one time, most of whom are still alive, though some have died.

1 Corinthians 15:4-6 NLT

If you could talk to one of the eyewitnesses of the resurrected Jesus, what questions would you ask them?

Answer: over five hundred

THE GREATEST

Who did Jesus say was the greatest in the kingdom of heaven?

All authority in heaven and earth has been given to Jesus. He is the King of kings and the Lord of lords, the Alpha and the Omega. Angels worship him, and all the nations of the earth bow their knees to him. Still, his disciples dared to ask who was the greatest in the kingdom of heaven.

Instead of demanding their allegiance as he had every right to do, Jesus directed their attention to a child. He instructed them to become like little children, innocent and dependent, small and humble. Unless they did so, they wouldn't even get into the kingdom of heaven. If, however, they were willing to humble themselves like a small child, they would be considered the greatest. Elsewhere, Jesus taught that the first will be last and the last will be first (Matthew 20:16). This is the posture Jesus took.

"Whoever takes the lowly position of this child
is the greatest in the kingdom of heaven."
MATTHEW 18:4 NIV

What can you do today to depend on God and serve others?

Answer: whoever takes the position of a child

WRITING ROMANS

What was the name of the man who wrote down Paul's words in the letter to the Romans?

Tertius had a front row seat, as well as pen and quill, to the greatest theological argument ever written. Paul wrote God's revealed story and Tertius heard it even before the Romans did. This letter contains the essentials of how humanity is redeemed through the death and resurrection of Jesus Christ. Tertius was the scribe who got to write it all down. Paul dictated about the most instrumental person in human history, and Tertius was the skilled person privileged to record it.

Because this book was actually a long letter to the Christians living in Rome, it contained a lot of greetings. Almost forty people are mentioned by name in the last chapter of Romans. One of those names is Tertius. It's almost like he slipped a quick hello into the text while Paul was mentioning all the other people who would be receiving the letter.

I, Tertius, the one writing this letter for Paul,
send my greetings, too, as one of the Lord's followers.

Romans 16:22 NLT

What are some of the verses in the book of Romans that you think Tertius might have found the most inspiring?

Answer: Tertius

JULY 19

LONGEST CHAPTER

What is the longest chapter of the Bible?

Psalm 119 is the longest chapter of any book in the Bible, coming in at 176 verses. This single chapter is longer than several of the smaller books of the Bible. It contains twenty-two stanzas with eight verses in each. Each stanza begins with one of the twenty-two letters of the Hebrew alphabet, all in order, and each verse in each stanza starts with that Hebrew letter.

Some of the most famous verses of the Bible come from this chapter, such as "I have hidden your word in my heart that I might not sin against you" (v. 11) and "Your word is a lamp for my feet, a light on my path" (v. 105). The entire chapter is a deliberate and elaborate love song for God's instructions. There is a repeated desire to study and learn his law and an understanding that pursuing his teaching leads to a deeper relationship with him. As a result, life is better.

Because I love your commands
more than gold, more than pure gold,
and because I consider all your precepts right,
I hate every wrong path.

Psalm 119:127-128 NIV

What verse from Psalm 119 will you memorize this week?

Answer: Psalm 119

TWO NAMES

Peter raised a woman to life who had two names. What were her two names?

In the early days of the Church, Peter travelled around to different towns in Judea, Galilee, and Samaria sharing the good news about Jesus. Once when he went to the town of Lydda, he healed a man named Aeneas who had been paralyzed for eight years. While Peter was there, some believers in the nearby town of Joppa sent two men who begged him to come immediately.

Peter went with the two men and was led into the upper room of a house in Joppa. The room was filled with women weeping for a woman named Tabitha, who was also known as Dorcas in Greek. She had become ill and died. Peter learned that Tabitha had been kind and helped the poor. The grieving women showed Peter the coats and other clothes that Dorcas had made for them. Peter asked them all to leave the room, then he knelt, prayed, and told Tabitha to get up.

Peter asked them all to leave the room; then he knelt and prayed. Turning to the body he said, "Get up, Tabitha." And she opened her eyes! When she saw Peter, she sat up!

Acts 9:40 NLT

Peter stayed in Joppa for quite some time after this event. If you had lived there, would you have tried to talk with Peter? If so, what would you have asked him?

Answer: Tabitha and Dorcas

NOT ASHAMED

In the first chapter of Romans, what does Paul say he is not ashamed of?

By the time he wrote his letter to the Romans, Paul had boldly preached the gospel of Jesus to Jews and Gentiles. Paul traveled from Israel to Syria, Crete, Asia Minor, Greece and then to Macedonia. He had been jailed and harassed, chased out of cities, and beaten until almost dead. He saw lives transformed and people healed, but the movement spread, and cities turned upside down.

Paul longed to see the believers in the great city of Rome. He prayed for the opportunity to visit so he could see the growing church there. He had been through much, and he longed to be at the growing strategic center of the worldwide movement of the Christianity. He had a great sense of obligation to preach the good news. Nothing could stop him, for he was confident in the gospel of Jesus.

I am not ashamed of the gospel, because it is the power of God that brings salvation to everyone who believes: first to the Jew, then to the Gentile.

Romans 1:16 NIV

Do you have a sense of obligation about being part of spread of the gospel of Jesus Christ?

Answer: the gospel

JULY 22

END OF ACTS

TRUE OR FALSE

There are twenty-nine chapters of the book of Acts.

The book of Acts ends with an unfinished story. Paul is under house arrest in Rome awaiting a trial with Caesar. He was arrested in Jerusalem for preaching about Jesus and spent considerable time in prison arguing his case before being sent by armed guard to Rome. Along the way, he was shipwrecked for three months in Malta before being transported by another ship to Rome. Besides having an armed guard, he seemed to have a significant amount of freedom in his private lodging, hosting streams of guests. He was still able to boldly proclaim the kingdom of God and teach people regularly about Jesus. No one tried to stop him because he was already arrested and awaiting trial.

The book of Acts ends with Paul hosting people and spreading the gospel. There is no attempt to explain what happened after this. We can't be sure of Paul's fate, though there are some historical accounts that usually involve his execution for preaching about Jesus as God. But the point of the book of Acts was never Paul's story. Rather, it focused on planting the seeds of the message; it told the story of the power of Jesus Christ taking root and spreading from Jerusalem to the ends of the earth.

For two whole years Paul stayed there in his own rented house and welcomed all who came to see him. He proclaimed the kingdom of God and taught about the Lord Jesus Christ—with all boldness and without hindrance!

Acts 28:30-31 NIV

What inspires you about the to-be-continued style of the end of the book of Acts?

Answer: false; there are twenty-eight chapters

CROWING ROOSTER

Before the rooster crowed, what did Peter claim about his relationship with Jesus?

In one of the saddest verses of the Bible, Peter declared to random people that he wasn't associated with Jesus. Peter blatantly denied knowing Jesus three separate times, the man he dedicated his life to for three years, the man he proclaimed as the Christ, the man he promised he would die for. Peter completely turned his back on Jesus.

"You were with Jesus" (Matthew 26:69) said a slave woman to Peter in the courtyard near where Jesus was being beaten. "I don't know what you're talking about," Peter exclaimed. "You were with Jesus of Nazareth" (v. 71) another slave woman pointed out. "I don't know the man," Peter stated. "We can tell by the way you talk that you're one of his followers," some bystanders argued. That's when Peter began to curse and swear and flat out reject that he knew Jesus. Then the rooster crowed, precisely as Jesus had predicted it would (v. 34).

Then he began to curse and swear,
"I do not know the man!"
And immediately a rooster crowed.

Matthew 26:74 NASB

When faced with the public opportunity to be identified as a follower of Jesus, how would you respond?

Answer: that he didn't know him

JULY 24

EMBALMING PROCESS

How long did the embalming process for Jacob's body take?

Upon his death, Joseph's father, Jacob, was treated to a burial process worthy of an Egyptian ruler. Because Joseph was the second in command for all of Israel, his father was given royal treatment. Joseph ordered his own specialized physicians to embalm his father's body, a process which involved removing the organs and drying the body. The series of procedures took forty days. Afterwards, Egypt mourned the death of Joseph's father for seventy days.

Jacob requested that his bones be brought back to his homeland to be buried next to his grandfather, Abraham; his father, Isaac; and his wife, Leah. Joseph took an impressive assembly with him for the funeral. It included his own extended family and many Egyptian officials. The embalming process would have kept Jacob's body preserved for the significant journey.

Joseph told the physicians who served him to embalm his father's body; so Jacob was embalmed. The embalming process took the usual forty days. And the Egyptians mourned his death for seventy days.

Genesis 50:2-3 NLT

Why is it significant that Jacob, who was also called Israel, wanted his bones buried back in the land of Abraham, his grandfather?

Answer: forty days

JULY 25

SAMUEL HEARD

When Samuel was a boy, God began calling to him. But who did Samuel think was speaking at first?

It is a sad commentary that in the days of Samuel, the word of the Lord was uncommon. The people of Israel were pursuing other gods and behaving in ways that were evil in the sight of the Lord. When Samuel heard someone calling his name in the middle of the night, he simply assumed it was Eli, the high priest who was raising him.

After hearing his name being called and responding, "Here I am!" to Eli three times, the high priest realized that something special was happening. He understood that God was calling for Samuel. Eli must have remembered the vibrant prayers of Samuel's mother, Hannah, and he must have recognized the vibrant spirit of faith inherent in the boy. Eli then instructed Samuel to respond differently the next time. He instructed Samuel to respond, "Speak, Lord, for your servant is listening."

Then the LORD called Samuel, and he said, "Here I am!" and ran to Eli and said, "Here I am, for you called me." But he said, "I did not call; lie down again." So he went and lay down.

1 SAMUEL 3:4-5 ESV

Would you recognize the voice of the Lord calling you?

Answer: Eli

JULY 26

TEMPLE CONSTRUCTION

How many years were there between Isreal leaving slavery in Egypt and the building of the Temple in Jerusalem?

For nearly five hundred years, God had presided with Israel in the tabernacle which was a tent structure used for hundreds of years as a mobile facility. Moses led the people through the exodus in the desert and had established Israel's laws. Joshua led the people into the conquest of the Promised Land which had been given to their ancestor, Abraham. The judges were raised up to rescue God's people from their sin and from the oppression in the land. Samuel anointed Saul to reign and begin unifying Israel into one nation. David established a kingdom and envisioned a permanent place of worship for God to dwell with his people. Solomon's primary goal early in his reign, then, became the construction of this impressive building—the temple.

As long as Solomon and Israel were sincere in following God, he promised to dwell with his people. It took 480 years between the time of their rescue from slavery in Egypt until the beginning of the construction of the temple. It took another thirteen years to complete the project. But it took less than one generation before Solomon and all of Israel with him had compromised their commitment to the Lord.

It was in midspring, in the month of Ziv, during the fourth year of Solomon's reign, that he began to construct the Temple of the LORD. This was 480 years after the people of Israel were rescued from their slavery in the land of Egypt.

1 KINGS 6:1 NLT

What long-lasting goals do you have for your life? Do they honor the Lord? Will you stay committed to him more than to your goals?

Answer: four hundred and eighty years

HONEST WEIGHT

Which is heavier according to the book of Proverbs:
a stone or resentment?

Dishonest scales were an issue for the Israelites. When the country established the laws for their nation, having pure and honest scales was a priority. Using the same scale to measure different items became one of the most important factors displaying integrity. Traders who wanted to cheat their customers were prone to manipulating one scale used for buying and one another scale for selling, each calibrated to the trader's benefit (e.g., Deuteronomy 25, Leviticus 19).

The book of Proverbs encourages people to take a fair, honest measurement of themselves compared to other things. For instance, the verse today suggests that people understand the true heaviness of the resentment that is caused by reckless conduct. A large stone might seem like it would be heavy, and a large pile of sand might seem weighty, but if we measure them fairly against the burdens in people's lives caused by foolish behavior, they are lighter. A fool weighs people down with the complications and resentments that stem from their provocations.

A stone is heavy and sand is weighty,
but the resentment caused by a fool is even heavier.

Proverbs 27:3 NLT

Fairly assess the weight you've put on others through your own foolish conduct and take some time to pray about how God may want you to respond.

Answer: resentment

WHAT CHILD

What child was this talking about? "There the child grew up healthy and strong. He was filled with wisdom, and God's favor was on him."

After dedicating their baby in the temple and fulfilling all the requirements of the religious laws, Mary and Joseph made their way back to settle in their own town of Nazareth, in Galilee which is in northern Israel. There they raised Jesus. He grew in stature and in wisdom. Luke notes that the grace of God was on him. His parents were faithful to follow God's instructions for keeping the celebrations of the Jewish faith. They traveled to Jerusalem every year for the festival of the Passover.

When he was twelve years old, Jesus stayed in the temple courts, sitting amongst the religious teachers and listening and speaking with them. Luke tells us that everyone who heard him was amazed at his understanding and his answers. As the years went on in Nazareth, Jesus was obedient to his parents. Mary treasured all of these things in her heart.

The child grew and became strong;
he was filled with wisdom,
and the grace of God was on him.

Luke 2:40 NIV

What interests you the most about Jesus' upbringing?

Answer: Jesus

THE PRODIGAL'S JOB

After leaving home, what job did the prodigal son take?

The prodigal son began to realize he made a mistake. In a rash decision, he had demanded his inheritance, effectively saying to his father, "I wish you were dead." He then took his money and belongings and moved to a distant land where he squandered everything he had in wild living. He began to starve when a famine hit. Broke and desperate, he got a job feeding a farmer's pigs. The young man was hungry; even the pods he was feeding the pigs looked appetizing.

That's when he came to his senses. He realized that even his dad's hired workers had more than enough food and he was starving. He decided to go back home and apologize to his father, which he did, saying, "I have sinned against heaven and against you. I am no longer worthy to be called your son. Please take me on as a hired servant" (Luke 15:18-19).

He went and hired himself out to one of the citizens of that country, who sent him into his fields to feed pigs. And he was longing to be fed with the pods that the pigs ate, and no one gave him anything.

Luke 15:15-16 ESV

Why do people sometimes have to go through prodigal moments in life like this?

Answer: feeding pigs

STANDARDS

FINISH THIS VERSE

All have _______ and fall short of the _______ of God.

God has a standard of holiness. It is not so much of a bar to reach as it is a whole state of being. It is pure and perfect, righteous and good. It is just and honest, loving and altruistic. No person has ever kept that standard. Everyone has corrupted and fractured their state of being. Everyone has complicated their lives with impurity and imperfection, unrighteousness and evil. Everyone has committed injustice and dishonest acts; they have harbored hatred and feelings of selfishness.

And yet, in God's standard of holiness, is his incredible, beautiful desire for no one to perish. God, in a perfect outpouring of mercy, took the penalty of our sins and made us right in his sight.

All have sinned and fall short of the glory of God,
and all are justified freely by his grace
through the redemption that came by Christ Jesus.

Romans 3:23-24 NIV

What response to God is stirring within your soul?

Answer: sinned; glory

BLESSED PEACEMAKERS

Why does Jesus say the peacemakers are blessed?

Millions of people throughout history have given their lives so peace would be possible. There has been a long war in the world waged against peace. There are powers and movements in which the only goal is the deterioration of peace. Peace is not passive. It doesn't happen by accident. Peace is the intentional push into the fray of hostility. Peace is accomplished through incredible personal strain and sacrifice.

Peace is what Jesus is. He is the initiator of shalom, God's whole peace. He pushes into the darkness and shines a great light. At first the battle seems overwhelming. In fact, his effort cost him his life. But it is a cost he decided was worth the outcome. Peace. When people embrace him, and when they choose to become peacemakers themselves, all of heaven celebrates.

"Blessed are the peacemakers,
for they will be called children of God."

MATTHEW 5:9 NIV

How might God want you to make peace today?

Answer: because they will be called children of God

AUGUST

ONE AND ONE

FINISH THIS VERSE

Adam's one sin brings _______ for everyone, but Christ's one act of righteousness brings a right relationship with God and _______ _______ for everyone.

Paul taught in the book of Romans that when Adam sinned, sin entered the world and brought death to everyone. Everyone since has sinned against God. Adam, in his sin, represented the sinfulness of all humankind. But Jesus represents God's gracious gift to humankind. Adam's sin was powerful enough to affect every human, but Christ's free gift is even more powerful to overcome sin.

Everyone who received death through the one man, Adam, receives the gift of life through Jesus. In theological language, Jesus is the "second Adam" who restores the righteousness of humanity. He offers a reset of the human condition by giving us right standing with God, resulting in eternal life.

Adam's one sin brings condemnation for everyone,
but Christ's one act of righteousness brings a right
relationship with God and new life for everyone.

ROMANS 5:18 NLT

If someone asked you how Adam and Jesus are connected in the Bible, what would you say?

Answer: condemnation; new life

TIME FOR A WALK

What time of the night did Jesus come to his disciples walking on the water?

Jesus wanted some time alone to pray. He had been teaching and healing masses of people throughout northern Israel, and he had fed five thousand men plus their families. To get some focused time alone, he sent his disciples across the Sea of Galilee while he went up into the hills by himself to pray.

But late that night he could see that the disciples were struggling to remain afloat against some strong winds and the large waves washing over their boat. About three o'clock in the morning, Jesus went out to them, walking on the water. The disciples thought he was a ghost and were terrified. But Jesus called out to them, "Don't be afraid! Take courage! I am here!" Then he climbed into their boat. The disciples were overwhelmed with amazement; they had trouble understanding the significance of this moment.

He saw that they were in serious trouble, rowing hard and struggling against the wind and waves. About three o'clock in the morning Jesus came toward them, walking on the water. He intended to go past them, but when they saw him walking on the water, they cried out in terror, thinking he was a ghost.

Mark 6:48-49 NLT

Even after being a part of this momentous miracle, why was it difficult for the disciples to fully absorb who Jesus was?

Answer: about three o'clock in the morning

AUGUST 3

INNER STRUGGLE

TRUE OR FALSE
Paul said in Romans 7, "I know that nothing good lives in me."

It surprises people sometimes to learn that Paul struggled with sin. Like the rest of humanity, he struggled to do what was right. But Paul was always honest and transparent about himself in his writings. His rawness is refreshing in how much it reveals and is relevant. It seems that Paul is writing directly to humans in every era.

In Romans 7, Paul was especially vulnerable. He shared how frustrated he was with the fact that he struggled with his sinful nature. He confessed that he sinned by the actions he did and didn't do. He had sins that he committed and good that he omitted. "What a miserable person I am!" he exclaims. "Who will free me from this life that is dominated by sin and death?" (v. 24) The answer is in Jesus Christ (v. 25).

I know that nothing good lives in me, that is, in my sinful nature. I want to do what is right, but I can't. I want to do what is good, but I don't. I don't want to do what is wrong, but I do it anyway.

Romans 7:18-19 NLT

How can you be more vulnerable today?

Answer: true

FIRST DAY

What did God make on the first day of Creation?

The first chapter of the Bible tells us that God created the world in six days. On the first day of creation, God simply said, "Let there be light," and there was light. He spoke it into being. So powerful was God's creative power that he merely had to say what he wanted to create, and it was created. This was the pattern for the following five days of creation as well. "God said," was the common refrain.

God's Word from the first page of the Bible becomes the basis by which all things are made. John's gospel later describes this: "In the beginning was the Word… Through him all things were made… In him was life, and that life was the light of all mankind… The Word became flesh and made his dwelling among us" (John 1:1-14).

God said, "Let there be light"; and there was light. God saw that the light was good; and God separated the light from the darkness. God called the light "day," and the darkness He called "night."
And there was evening and there was morning, one day.

GENESIS 1:3-5 NASB

How does the Bible say Jesus was present and involved in Genesis 1?

Answer: light

AUGUST 5

FREEDOM POWER

FINISH THIS VERSE
There is no _______ for those who belong to Christ Jesus.

The power of the Holy Spirit to free us is greater than the power of sin to keep us captive. Let this life-giving truth overwhelm us today. Let this freeing gift from God lift our souls. Let the good news of Jesus Christ reach deeply into our hearts, open locked doors, and unclasp chains. Let our fears be calmed and our hurts be healed. Let our loneliness be met by the eternally close relationship God offers us. Let our ears hear him call our names and invite us to walk with him.

Let our minds be aligned with God's perspective, so it doesn't betray us again. Let God's thoughts for us, for our days, become the filter for our opinions and decisions. Let his Word be in our mouths. In Jesus, we are not controlled by our sinful nature. We are controlled by the Spirit. Christ lives in us today. His Spirit takes up residence in our lives.

There is no condemnation
for those who belong to Christ Jesus.

ROMANS 8:1 NLT

How do you see the Holy Spirit working in your life?

Answer: condemnation

WHO WILL CONDEMN

In Romans 8, who does Paul say will condemn us?

A. Satan
B. Ourselves
C. Pharisees
D. No one

If Jesus gave his life for us, can anyone speak any condemnation against us? Isn't Jesus' work on the cross strong enough to overcome any accusation of sin? Isn't Jesus' blood shed for us enough to overcome any accusation of unworthiness? Isn't Jesus' prayer, "Father, forgive them," enough to overcome our worst choices? Isn't Jesus' last breath enough to overcome Satan's greatest schemes? Isn't Jesus' resurrected breath enough to overcome any attempt to destroy our souls?

Jesus died for us. He took our sins to the cross. He buried our sins in the grave. He rose to life and left our sins behind, still in that grave. Our sin is gone. Jesus fought for us. He defended us. He took our place. Who can condemn us any longer?

Who dares accuse us whom God has chosen for his own? No one—for God himself has given us right standing with himself. Who then will condemn us? No one—for Christ Jesus died for us and was raised to life for us, and he is sitting in the place of honor at God's right hand, pleading for us.

Romans 8:33-34 NLT

Who do you think speaks condemnation over you? What can you do about that?

Answer: D) no one

AUGUST 7

THIRD COMMANDMENT

What is the third of the Ten Commandments?

Each one of the Ten Commandments is frequently broken in our world. Culture is filled with the worship of other gods and the pursuit of selfish idols. People rarely keep the Sabbath. People regularly commit murder and adultery. Our world is rampant with theft, lies, and lust. Keeping the Sabbath is perhaps the most ignored command, but maybe the most egregiously disregarded commandment is the third: You shall not misuse the name of the Lord your God.

People frequently use God's name as an expletive, often combining it with vulgar and profane words. People also use God's name thoughtlessly, assigning his name to events or activities without any consideration for his reputation or authority. Speaking on his behalf is a big deal, and it should be done with the greatest measure of caution, carefully regarding his holiness. God takes this seriously. He states in today's verse, "For the Lord will not hold anyone guiltless who misuses his name."

"You shall not misuse the name of the LORD your God,
for the LORD will not hold anyone guiltless who misuses his name.

EXODUS 20:7 NIV

How attentive are you to the way you use God's name?

Answer: you shall not misuse the name of the Lord

AUGUST 8

WHAT SEPARATES

According to Paul, what can separate us from Christ's love?

A. Idols
B. Nothing
C. Unintentional sin
D. Powers of hell

Is Jesus strong enough to hold us? Do we think that the storms of life are stronger than he is? Do we think there is anything in all of heaven or earth which can overcome Jesus' power? Are demons stronger than him? Can hell contain him? Can the grave keep him captive? Can fears immobilize him? Do we think there is anything that can pry his arms open from holding us? Do we think he will tire and grow weak? Do we think he will become disinterested in us? Do we think he will be distracted and forget about us?

There is no thing in all of creation, in the sky above or the earth below, that will ever be able to separate us from the love of God.

I am convinced that nothing can ever separate us from God's love. Neither death nor life, neither angels nor demons, neither our fears for today nor our worries about tomorrow—not even the powers of hell can separate us from God's love. No power in the sky above or in the earth below—indeed, nothing in all creation will ever be able to separate us from the love of God that is revealed in Christ Jesus our Lord.

ROMANS 8:38-39 NLT

What fear do you face today? Pray through Romans 8:38-39 multiple times and let God equip you.

Answer: B) nothing

THE WHOLE STORY

TRUE OR FALSE
Paul said that Christ is God.

The Bible is a whole story. It is not a random collection of unrelated events in human history. It is a cohesive revelation of God's unrelenting pursuit of humanity through creation, struggle and salvation. The Bible is the story of how God himself entered the scene to rescue the people he made and whom he loved. God invited humans to walk with him in a pure relationship, but humanity rebelled.

God commissioned Abraham to become a nation from which the whole world would be rescued. Abraham and his sons became the fathers of the tribes of Israel—the Hebrew people. From this nation came the Messiah who is the Savior of all nations. God himself was born in the flesh as a Jew, living in poverty and oppression in a sinful world. He walked and dined with humans, taught and healed them, and then died for them with a brutal death. His work on the cross was the crux point of the whole story. His outstretched arms and final breath are the central moment in all of history. The Son of God became the Son of Man to bring mankind back into a relationship with God.

Abraham, Isaac, and Jacob are their ancestors, and Christ himself was an Israelite as far as his human nature is concerned. And he is God, the one who rules over everything and is worthy of eternal praise! Amen.

Romans 9:5 NLT

How can you tell the whole story of God in a few sentences?

Answer: true

AUGUST 10

VOLUNTARY GENEROSITY

FINISH THIS VERSE

I urge you, brothers and sisters, in view of God's mercy, to offer your bodies as a _______ _______, holy and pleasing to God—this is your true and proper worship.

Because Jesus offered himself as a living sacrifice on our behalf, can we not offer ourselves as a living sacrifice for him? When we think of all Jesus voluntarily gave up for us, how can we not freely give everything we have to the glory of God? How can we not dedicate our pursuits today to him? How can we continue to live for our own gain? How can we prioritize ourselves above others? How can we not take on a servant's heart? How can we care so little for the interests of our neighbors? How can we go on living self-centered lives?

When we consider all that God has done for us, we have no other proper response than to offer ourselves as holy and pleasing to God. This becomes our everything.

I urge you, brothers and sisters, in view of God's mercy, to offer your bodies as a living sacrifice, holy and pleasing to God—this is your true and proper worship.

ROMANS 12:1 NIV

How can you life a life that is holy and pleasing to God?

Answer: living sacrifice

AUGUST 11

HOW TO BE SAVED

TRUE OR FALSE
The Bible says you can be saved if you do enough good works which please God.

No matter how many good things we do, that will not dictate whether or not we will be in right standing with God in eternity. The Bible says that if we openly declare that Jesus is Lord and believe in our hearts that God raised Jesus from the dead, we will be saved. That's it. Simple. Believe in Jesus and say so. That's all it takes. The good work has already been done by Jesus on the cross and from the grave. Why should we need to do any more good works to try to be saved? Was his death and resurrection not sufficient for us?

Paul quotes the prophet Joel when he says, "Everyone who calls on the name of the Lord will be saved" (Romans 10:13; Joel 2:32; Acts 2:21). We must confess with our minds and with our mouths that Jesus did the work for us. We need to quit trying to earn our way into heaven and accept the free gift God has for us.

If you openly declare that Jesus is Lord and believe in your heart that God raised him from the dead, you will be saved.

ROMANS 10:9 NLT

Have you declared that Jesus Christ is Lord? Do you believe in your heart that Jesus was raised from death to life?

Answer: false

REJECTED AT HOME

What was the name of Jesus' hometown which rejected him?

Jesus returned to his hometown of Nazareth with his disciples after a tremendously fruitful time of ministry around the Sea of Galilee. He began to teach in the local synagogue and impressed many of the people there. But his old friends and neighbors couldn't quite grasp his power and authority. They asked one another, "Where did he get all this wisdom?" They scoffed at him: "He's just a carpenter, the Son of Mary." They belittled him: "He's only the brother of James, Joseph, Judas and Simon. And his sisters live right here among us." Mark 6:3 tells us that the people in his hometown were deeply offended and refused to believe in him.

Jesus fully comprehended what they were saying and thinking. He responded to them, "A prophet is honored everywhere except in his own hometown and among his relatives and his own family" (v. 4). Mark informs his readers that Jesus couldn't do any miracles in Nazareth because of their unbelief, except to place his hands on a few people and heal them (v. 5). Mark mentions that Jesus was amazed at their unbelief (v. 6).

Jesus told them, "A prophet is honored everywhere except in his own hometown and among his relatives and his own family."

MARK 6:4 NLT

What would Jesus say about your belief in him today?

Answer: Nazareth

CLOTHE YOURSELF

Paul said that you should clothe yourself in _______.

A. the presence of Christ
B. fig leaves
C. good works
D. sackcloth

Paul urged us to love each other, follow God's commands, and be aware of what is going on around us. Readers of Romans 13:8-14 can feel Paul's sense of urgency. To live for Jesus is a high calling that carries with it great significance. How we live impacts whether or not others will discover life through Jesus by our witness.

Paul begs his readers to remove dirty clothes and put on the shining armor of right living, avoiding all the trappings of wild living that compromise our testimonies. How can quarreling and jealousy, promiscuity and immorality ever reveal that Jesus has freed us from the captivity of unfulfilled lives that chase after momentary pursuits? Instead, Paul urges that we clothe ourselves with the presence of the God.

Instead, clothe yourself with the presence of the Lord Jesus Christ. And don't let yourself think about ways to indulge your evil desires.

Romans 13:14 NLT

What will others notice you wearing today?

Answer: A) the presence of Christ

IN ROME

Which of the following Roman Christians was not included in Paul's greetings in Romans 16?

A. Rufus
B. Narcissus
C. Herodian
D. Alexander

Many people are mentioned in Romans 16. For instance, there is Herodion, whom Paul calls a fellow Jew. Paul also mentioned a man named Narcissus and, ironically perhaps, his whole household. There were sisters named Tryphena and Tryphosa, Persis and Rufus, and Rufus' mom who held a special place in Paul's heart. Each person had their own story and profound faith in Jesus Christ. Paul longed to be with them. The fellowship of believers in Rome changed the world. Within a few short years, the number of ordinary people in the Roman Empire who followed Jesus would threaten the very foundations of Caesar's rule.

He was in Rome at a later time, but he was not included in the book of Romans. Alexander was a coppersmith who deserted Paul in Rome several years after Paul wrote this letter to the Christians in Rome. Read 2 Timothy 4:14-15 for that story.

Greet Herodion, my fellow Jew. Greet the Lord's people from the household of Narcissus. Give my greetings to Tryphena and Tryphosa, the Lord's workers, and to dear Persis, who has worked so hard for the Lord. Greet Rufus, whom the Lord picked out to be his very own; and also his dear mother, who has been a mother to me.

Romans 16:11-13 NLT

Are you a part of a vibrant community of Christians? Why or why not?

Answer: D) Alexander

AUGUST 15

IN THE BEGINNING

FINISH THIS VERSE

In the beginning God ________ ________ ________ ________ ________ ________.

There may be nothing more foundational to the human understanding of the origins of life than to recognize that God created everything. To deny this is to deny his ultimate authority over life itself. The theological idea is that God created *ex nihilo*, which means "out of nothing." God didn't go looking for cosmic ingredients in his laboratory. He didn't need to borrow anything from a neighbor. He didn't enlist the angels to fill a grocery list. No, he didn't need any supplies whatsoever. He didn't need anything at all. He was God.

In the beginning, God created. He did this because he is creative in his very nature. He merely spoke things into being. His Word is living and active. He speaks and light shines in the darkness, water rushes from the springs, and mountains are put into their places. God says the word, and humanity is formed from the dust, in his image, bearing his likeness and character.

In the beginning God created the heavens and the earth.

GENESIS 1:1 NLT

How do you consider the profound creative power of the Word of God in your life?

Answer: created the heavens and the earth

AUGUST 16

GOD QUESTIONED JOB

TRUE OR FALSE

God asked Job if he knew when the wild goats give birth?

The fact that Job survived his conversation with God is a testament to God's mercy. "Where were you when I laid the foundations of the earth?" God challenged, "Who kept the sea inside its boundaries?" "Have you made daylight spread to the ends of the earth?". God tested Job, "But of course you know all of this! For you were born before it was all created, and you are so very experienced!" God continues, "Who sends rain to satisfy the parched ground?" "Can you direct the movement of the stars?" "Do you know the laws of the universe?" "Who provides food for the ravens?" "Do you know when the wild goats give birth?" "Have you given the horse its strength?" "Is it your wisdom that makes the hawk soar?" (v. 26)

For four chapters, God challenges Job with these put-you-in-your-place questions. "Do you still want to argue with the Almighty? You are God's critic, but do you have the answers?" (Read Job 38-41.)

"Do you know when the wild goats give birth?
Have you watched as deer are born in the wild?"

Job 39:1 NLT

Have you ever been critical of God? Read Job 40:3-5 and Job 42:1-6 to see Job's response to God's challenge.

Answer: true

AUGUST 17

TEMPLE TAX

Where did Peter and Jesus get money to pay the temple tax?

Two things are astonishing about the miracle of the coin in the fish's mouth. First, it is remarkable that Jesus would instruct Peter to catch a fish, open its mouth, and pull out a four-drachma coin to pay the tax price for the two of them. This miracle demonstrates how much control Jesus had over creation and over the affairs of humankind. He can orchestrate events whenever and however he designs.

Second, Jesus humbled himself such that he paid the temple tax. In a remarkable posture of submission to the government structures of the day, Jesus was willing to pay a cost for the house of God on the earth. Jesus left his seat of authority in heaven only to have to pay a price for the cost of maintaining the government's expenses in Jerusalem. The kings of the earth ask their servants to pay taxes, he concluded with Peter. Taking the nature of a servant, he paid the tax like everyone else had to.

"So that we may not cause offense, go to the lake and throw out your line. Take the first fish you catch; open its mouth and you will find a four-drachma coin. Take it and give it to them for my tax and yours."

Matthew 17:27 NIV

If Jesus was willing to submit himself to our ridiculous systems, how could we not submit ourselves to him today?

Answer: in the mouth of a fish

DIFFERENT FOCUS

According to 1 Samuel, "People judge by outward appearance, but the Lord looks at _______ _______."

A. the heart
B. your position
C. the future
D. the unseen

The saying says, "Don't judge a book by its cover." We are tempted to assume that it must be a great book because it looks attractive. We believe that person must be a great leader because they are impressive looking. We assign God's calling to someone who looks worthy of such a task.

It is interesting when Isaiah describes the Messiah. He says, "there was nothing beautiful or majestic about his appearance, nothing to attract us to him" (Isaiah 53:2). In fact, Isaiah says, "Many were amazed when they saw him. His face was so disfigured he seemed hardly human, and from his appearance, one would scarcely know he was a man" (52:14). When Samuel was looking for the man who would replace King Saul, he was looking for someone impressive, someone who looked like a king. But God chose a boy, David, who was a man after his heart (1 Samuel 13:14).

> The LORD said to Samuel, "Don't judge by his appearance or height, for I have rejected him. The LORD doesn't see things the way you see them. People judge by outward appearance, but the LORD looks at the heart."
>
> 1 SAMUEL 16:7 NLT

Don't attend as much to how you will appear today as much as you give attention to the condition of your heart with God.

Answer: the heart

SHORTEST CHAPTER

What is the shortest chapter in the Bible?

Two chapters before the longest chapter in the Bible—Psalm 119 with 166 verses—is the shortest chapter of the Bible, Psalm 117, with only two verses. The longest chapter is about loving God's commands; the shortest chapter is about praising God for loving his people so faithfully.

It is time, the writer of Psalm 117 urges, for everyone around the world to praise God because his steadfast love for us is great. How could we not worship him when he has been completely faithful to us? In fact, his faithfulness is eternally enduring. His love for us will never falter nor fail. Praise the Lord!

Praise the Lord, all nations!
Extol him, all peoples!
For great is his steadfast love toward us,
and the faithfulness of the Lord endures forever.
Praise the Lord!

Psalm 117:1-2 ESV

How can you praise God for his love today?

Answer: Psalm 117

A LONG SERMON

Paul raised a young man named Eutychus to life. What was the reason the young man had died?

We all know people who have fallen asleep during a sermon—maybe we have done it ourselves! Today's verse shows us that it's happened over the ages. One night, many people gathered in an upstairs room where Paul was preaching. Acts 20 says that Paul was speaking late into the night and that the room had flickering lamps. A young man named Eutychus grew sleepy and dozed off. He was sitting on a windowsill, however, and fell three stories down to his death.

The moment must have been extremely alarming for everyone. It seemed to have greatly impacted Paul, who hurried down and took Eutychus in his arms. We are told that everyone then went back upstairs and shared communion together and ate, almost as if nothing had happened. We also learn that Eutychus was taken home alive and well, and everyone was greatly relieved.

As Paul spoke on and on, a young man named Eutychus, sitting on the windowsill, became very drowsy. Finally, he fell sound asleep and dropped three stories to his death below. Paul went down, bent over him, and took him into his arms. "Don't worry," he said, "he's alive!"

Acts 20:9-10 NLT

How do you feel about this story?

Answer: he fell asleep and then fell out of a window

PSALM OF REPENTANCE

Which psalm is David's response when he was confronted about his sin with Bathsheba?

King David committed adultery with Bathsheba, and she became pregnant. He tried to hide his sin by arranging for Bathsheba's husband to sleep with her so he would think the baby was his. When that failed, he arranged for the husband to be killed in battle.

Nathan the prophet came to David and confronted him. He told the king a story about a rich man who had large herds of sheep and livestock. He took the only sheep a poor man owned so he could slaughter it for dinner. This story made David very angry. David demanded to know who the rich man was, so punishment could be unleashed on him for doing such a terrible thing. Nathan told David it was him (2 Samuel 12:1-13). As he had done throughout his life, David wrote a psalm to express his deepest grief and pain. What emerged is one of the most gut-wrenching songs of repentance ever written. It is vulnerable, honest, and raw—which is the posture every sinner should take before a holy God.

Have mercy on me, O God,
because of your unfailing love.
Because of your great compassion,
blot out the stain of my sins.
Wash me clean from my guilt.
Purify me from my sin.

Psalm 51:1-2 NLT

Read Psalm 51. What stands out to you about the brokenness of David's heart?

Answer: Psalm 51

SOURCE OF HELP

What is the answer to this question in Psalm 121: "I look up to the mountains—does my help come from there?"

We can search for help from all kinds of places in life. We can abuse substances that dull the emotions and the thinking, yet there's no long-term relief. We can turn to physical pleasures that temporarily trick the mind, but they leave the soul empty. We can take the counsel of people who tell us what we want to hear, but they fail to be insightful or truthful. We can turn to activities to escape life's worries, but we only find momentary distractions. We can turn to disciplines and habits that improve the routine and overall health, only to discover that the body and mind continue to grow older.

When we need help, where can we turn? Psalm 121 says our help comes from God. He's the one who made heaven and earth. He will not let our feet slip. He watches over us while we rest. He will not tire. He is the shade at our right hand, so the heat will not harm us during the day. He will protect us all of our lives, now and forevermore.

I look up to the mountains—
does my help come from there?
My help comes from the Lord,
who made heaven and earth!

Psalm 121:1-2 NLT

What help do you need from God today?

Answer: No, my help comes from the Lord

AUGUST 23

PEOPLE AND SHEEP

In the Bible, people are often called sheep, and Jesus is called our ______ ______.

Perhaps our most common description as God's people is that we are sheep and he is our shepherd. Psalm 23 famously begins, "The Lord is my shepherd." Psalm 100:3 says that we are the sheep of his pasture. It is a sacrificial lamb that is most commonly chosen to represent a person for the forgiveness of sins.

Jesus claims all of this imagery for himself. He refers to himself as the Good Shepherd. He describes the close relationship he has with his sheep who know his voice and trust in him. He teaches how he would do anything to rescue a lost sheep and protect his flock. And Jesus shares that he lays down his life for the sheep. He was the sacrificial lamb. In other words, a good shepherd takes on the nature of his sheep and gives up his life for them.

"I am the good shepherd.
The good shepherd lays down his life for the sheep."

John 10:11 NIV

How has the Good Shepherd provided for you recently?

Answer: Good Shepherd

AUGUST 24

FEMALE JUDGE

What was the name of the only female judge of Israel?

There is a regular cycle in the book of Judges where a generation does evil in God's sight, as a result they cry out to him for rescue, and they are saved by a judge who was raised up by the Lord. One of the best of these judges was a woman named Deborah.

Deborah held meetings with Israel's leaders, made judgements about major decisions or issues, and suggested strategies for war. As a prophetess who spoke on behalf of God, she guided Israel with the word of God. Israel's general, Barak, wouldn't make a move without her. All of Israel trusted her discernment and followed her governance. Israel learned to trust God once again because Deborah was such a consistent and wise leader. Through a dramatic victory against Sisera, the powerful commander of the Canaanite armies, Deborah provided peace in the land for forty years.

Deborah, the wife of Lappidoth,
was a prophet who was judging Israel at that time.

JUDGES 4:4 NLT

How was Deborah a forerunner for the ultimate Judge, Jesus?

Answer: Deborah

AUGUST 25

CONTENTS OF THE ARK

What did God instruct Moses to put inside the ark of the covenant?

The ark of the covenant was an ornamental box that could be carried with long poles by the Levites. God forbade anyone from touching the ark as it represented his presence and power. When the Israelites carried the ark into battle, God would strike down Israel's enemies. Eventually the ark was placed in the inner sanctuary of the temple constructed by Solomon. And in the future, as depicted in the book of Revelation, the ark once again is featured as a significant indication of the Lord's reestablished kingdom.

Through the years, the ark became a sort of safe deposit box for Israel's most sacred relics such as Aaron's budding staff, Moses's writings, and even a pot with manna. But when it was first being constructed, God told Moses to place into it the stone tablets that he had given him with the ten commandments written on them. Doing so signified the seriousness with which God took his covenant with the people of Israel.

"Place inside the Ark the stone tablets inscribed with the terms of the covenant, which I will give to you. Then put the atonement cover on top of the Ark."

Exodus 25:21 NLT

Why was the ark such a significant symbol as Israel was being established as a nation?

Answer: the stone tablets with the Ten Commandments

AUGUST 26

TEMPLE DEDICATION

How many cattle and sheep did Solomon give as a peace offering at the dedication ceremony of the new temple?

A. 2 cattle and 12 sheep
B. 22 cattle and a 120 sheep
C. 220 cattle and 1,200 sheep
D. 22,000 cattle and 120,000 sheep

Almost five hundred years after God's people escaped slavery in Egypt, they were ready for a dramatic celebration. They knew that God had remained faithful to them over the generations, even as Israel had faltered in its own dedication many times. They were thankful that God kept the covenant he had made with Abraham, Isaac, and Jacob, as well as the promises he had made to Moses and Joshua.

The people recognized that God blessed King David and King Solomon by uniting the nation and establishing peace in Zion. They also knew that he was making the temple his dwelling place. They understood that he reigned, offered forgiveness, and held their destiny. They responded with a lavish demonstration of their desire to have peace with God, to live with him, and to walk in his ways. Their outpouring of sacrifices was astonishing. Their offering to God indicated the priority with which they considered their relationship to him.

Solomon offered to the Lord a peace offering of 22,000 cattle and 120,000 sheep and goats. And so the king and all the people of Israel dedicated the Temple of the Lord.

1 Kings 8:63 NLT

What would you be willing to offer to God if you were asked to demonstrate your gratitude for all he had done and your commitment to him?

Answer: D)

FIFTH COMMANDMENT

What is the fifth commandment?

The first four commandments have much to do with our relationships with God the Father. Have no other gods before him. Make no idols for worship. Never misuse his name. And always keep the Sabbath holy.

The other six commandments are concerned with our relationship with others. The first of these, mentioned before the sins of murder, adultery, theft, lying, and jealousy, is the instruction to honor parents. If the people of Israel would honor their mothers and fathers, they would live long, fulfilled lives in the land the Lord was giving them. It seemed significant that God connected a promise to this command only. Living in the land successfully required that people treated their parents with respect. Perhaps the way God's people treated those who went before them, who raised them and taught them about the daily routines of work and love and life, is the key to whether or not a society can function well. Broken homes and broken generations create chaos for a culture.

"Honor your father and your mother, so that you may live long in the land the LORD your God is giving you."

EXODUS 20:12 NIV

How is your relationship with your parents? What can you do to honor them today?

Answer: honor your father and mother

TESTS

The book of Proverbs says that fire tests the purity of silver and gold and God tests _______ _______.

During the time the book of Proverbs was written, Egypt was the world's expert on the refining process for precious metals. Using various combinations of sand and salt while crushing and melting the rocks and minerals, gold and silver could be separated and purified. If the raw gold or silver withstood the tests and their purer forms were able to be concentrated together, these metals could then be melted into molds and shapes for jewels, ornaments, and furnishings. It was a time-consuming process that required considerable manpower and investment.

It could be said that God puts humans through a similar process. Through different applications of pressures and trials, God tests the human heart. His Spirit works to separate us from other impure alloys in order to purify us in his righteousness. He then shapes us into his purposes for works of good service.

Fire tests the purity of silver and gold,
but the LORD tests the heart.

PROVERBS 17:3 NLT

How do you think God will be testing your heart today?

Answer: the heart

AUGUST 29

GOD LOVES YOU

David said in Psalm 139 that the Lord knit him together where?

Psalm 139 helps us understand how valuable a human being truly is. In this psalm, David marveled at how much God loved him. David was overwhelmed as he considered how much God considered him (v. 2). He realized God was always with him in all of his thoughts, all of his activities, and in every place he went. His life was never hidden from God. His whole being was exposed. And God loved him even still.

David thanked the Lord for making him so wonderfully complex! He admired God's workmanship in the secret places, and he was blown away by how God thought of him (vv. 13-17).

You made all the delicate, inner parts of my body
and knit me together in my mother's womb.
Thank you for making me so wonderfully complex!
Your workmanship is marvelous—how well I know it.

Psalm 139:13-14 NLT

Do you know that God made you and he has always loved you?

Answer: in his mother's womb

AUGUST 30

THE LAST PROVERBS

TRUE OR FALSE
The last verses of the book of Proverbs are about "a corrupt husband."

The book of Proverbs is initially addressed to the son of Solomon. The king passed on his best advice and insight to his son, pointing out the difference between wise and foolish living. He instructed his son to avoid harmful people and deceptive women. And he taught his son to pursue the company of faithful people and a wife of integrity.

The book of Proverbs ends with over twenty verses focused on the characteristics of a noble wife. Such a wife will fill her husband with confidence all of his life. She works hard for her family and serves others. She makes good decisions that improve the family's situation, and she cares for her family at any hour. She invites the needy into her home. She prepares her family for hardships and provides a comfortable home. She contributes to her husband's good reputation and blesses her community. She is clothed with strength and dignity, and she gives instructions with kindness.

Charm is deceptive, and beauty does not last;
but a woman who fears the LORD will be greatly praised.
Reward her for all she has done.
Let her deeds publicly declare her praise.

PROVERBS 31:30-31 NLT

Whose character does a person who lives this way ultimately represent?

Answer: false; they are about a noble wife

AUGUST 31

THE PERSECUTED

Why are those who are persecuted because of righteousness blessed?

If we are righteous, it is not likely we are pursuing personal gain. Our concerns do not reflect those of the world; rather, we are concerned with that which concerns God. We see everything differently than people whose eyes are set on worldly lusts, prides, worries, and fears. We filter and view circumstances the way God views things. We feel like strangers in this world; we are citizens of heaven and ambassadors representing God to others. If we are righteous and kindhearted, others may conclude that we conflict with them, and therefore they can develop animosity toward us. We may discover that some people ridicule, challenge, or harass us because our values are set apart from theirs. We can find ourselves at odds with the prevailing culture.

Jesus knew that those who followed in the ways of God were choosing to live contrary to the sinful pressures of the world. He knew they would pay a cost because they were people of the kingdom. And he knew they would inherit eternal life in the heavenly kingdom of God.

"Blessed are those who are persecuted because of righteousness, for theirs is the kingdom of heaven."

MATTHEW 5:10

Would you say you are more a citizen of heaven and that you live by its rules? Or are you more a citizen of the world living according to its rules?

Answer: because theirs is the kingdom of heaven

SEPTEMBER

LOVING ATTRACTION

In the Song of Solomon, the young man compliments his lover, saying that her nose is as fine as what landmark?

If you are looking for something to blush about, read the Song of Solomon. While the book of Judges is alarming in its depiction of violent human behavior, Song of Solomon is shocking in its articulation of sensuality. It is an inside look into the love story between a prince and his bride. Its embarrassing poetry explores romantic tensions and provides an intimate look into the heart-fluttering infatuation of a man and a woman falling in love and growing in physical attraction for one another.

The Song of Solomon also serves as an astonishing parable about God's intimate love for his bride and vice versa. Throughout the Bible God compares his relationship with his people to a marriage that is intimate and loving. He wants to know his bride and wants his bride to know him.

Your neck is as beautiful as an ivory tower.
Your eyes are like the sparkling pools in Heshbon
by the gate of Bath-rabbim.
Your nose is as fine as the tower of Lebanon
overlooking Damascus.

Song of Solomon 7:4 NLT

When Jesus is called the groom and the Church is called his bride, explore how the imagery of an intimate marriage is picked up in the New Testament?

Answer: the tower of Lebanon overlooking Damascus

SEPTEMBER 2

MESSY WORK

Besides putting his own fingers in the man's ears, what else did Jesus do to heal the deaf man with the speech impediment in the town of Sidon?

Often when he healed people, Jesus simply spoke. Sometimes he would touch the person. Sometimes people would touch him. But occasionally he would do things during the healing process that might have made people uncomfortable. Once, Jesus spit straight into the eyes of a blind man. On another occasion, he spat on the ground and made a muddy clay which he put on a man's blind eyes. Jesus didn't avoid the awkwardness of these moments and may have even used discomfort as an opportunity for people to grow in their trust of him.

Mark told us about a man in the northern town of Sidon who was deaf and unable to speak clearly. When Jesus arrived in the town, people begged him to lay hands on the man and heal him. After Jesus put his fingers in the man's ears, he must have surprised everyone when he spit on his fingers and touched the man's tongue. This unclean act would have alarmed any strict religious person of the day. But if they had any concerns, they soon were overwhelmed when Jesus looked to heaven, sighed, and said, "Be opened!". Instantly, the man heard perfectly and spoke clearly.

Jesus led him away from the crowd so they could be alone.
He put his fingers into the man's ears.
Then, spitting on his own fingers, he touched the man's tongue.

MARK 7:33 NLT

Would you be willing to let Jesus the Healer do his work in your life in a way that might make you uncomfortable?

Answer: he spit on his own fingers and put them on the man's tongue

ANOTHER DISCIPLE

Who replaced Judas Iscariot as one of the twelve apostles?

After Jesus' ascension into heaven, his early followers had the huge task in front of them of assuming his ministry. In order to get ready, they needed to appoint another disciple to fill the position which was left vacant when Judas Iscariot betrayed Jesus and died. The disciples wanted to choose someone who had been with them from time Jesus was baptized by John the Baptist and had witnessed Jesus' resurrection.

They nominated two men who had been faithful followers of Jesus. One man was named Joseph but also had two other names he was known by: Barsabbas and Justus. The other man was named Matthias. The process to choose the one who would fill the open position may seem primitive to modern readers, but to the disciples it showed a tremendous trust in the leading of God's Spirit for the mission of the early Church. They cast lots and chose Matthias. We don't know much else about these two men except that they had exhibited a consistent walk with Jesus and were willing to put their lives on the line because of their commitment to him.

Then they cast lots, and Matthias was selected
to become an apostle with the other eleven.

ACTS 1:26 NLT

What does it mean to you to realize that besides the disciples there were other faithful followers of Jesus during his ministry on earth?

Answer: Matthias

SEPTEMBER 4

KING OF THE DEN

Which king sent Daniel into the lion's den?

Darius the Mede was the third king of Babylon after Daniel was taken into captivity. By this time, Daniel had risen in the ranks and had become a trusted advisor to the king, despite his Jewish heritage and his faith in the one true God. During his reign, Darius divided his vast kingdom into a hundred and twenty provinces, and Daniel was to administrate all of them. The king's plans angered his other administrators. They planned to ensnare Daniel and remove him from his high position. They urged Darius to issue a decree that everyone must pray only to Darius or be thrown into the den of lions. The king liked the decree, and he signed it into law.

When Daniel heard about the decree, he continued his daily prayers to God with his window open toward Jerusalem. He was arrested, much to Darius' dismay, and thrown into the lion's den with a stone placed over the mouth of the den. The king sealed the tomb with his own royal seal and returned to his home, ironically, to pray for Daniel.

> At last the king gave orders for Daniel to be arrested
> and thrown into the den of lions. The king said to him,
> "May your God, whom you serve so faithfully, rescue you."
>
> Daniel 6:16 NLT

What is your daily habit of prayer?

Answer: Darius

SEPTEMBER 5

FOURTH DAY

What did God make on the fourth day of Creation?

The first chapter of the Bible tells us that God created the world in six days. On the fourth day God created the sun, the moon, and the stars. These significant celestial bodies were not created until after God created light on the first day, the atmosphere on the second day, and the land and vegetation on the third day. And interestingly, there was evening and there was morning after each of the first three days.

It would seem that God created his own source of light on the first day and created a cycle of dark and light for each day even before he created the instruments of the universe which would define the human understanding of a day. The sun, the moon, and the stars would become the method by which humanity would measure days and years, comprehend seasons, and illustrate the concept of darkness and light. And God saw that this was good.

> Then God said, "Let there be lights in the expanse of the heavens to separate the day from the night, and they shall serve as signs and for seasons, and for days and years; and they shall serve as lights in the expanse of the heavens to give light on the earth"; and it was so. God made the two great lights, the greater light to govern the day, and the lesser light to govern the night; He made the stars also.
>
> Genesis 1:14-16 NASB

What is the most amazing thing to you about the universe God has made?

Answer: sun, moon, and stars

SOOTHING SAUL

What instrument did David play to sooth King Saul?

King Saul compromised his walk with God and began to be tormented by evil spirits. Some of Saul's advisors suggested that a good musician playing the harp might help soothe the troubles of his soul. Saul asked them to find someone. One of Saul's servants suggested the son of a man named Jesse from Bethlehem. The young man was a talented harp player and also a brave warrior. He was wise and handsome, and brought with him the Lord's presence.

King Saul hired David to tend to him. David would play the harp whenever Saul was tormented. Over time, Saul grew to trust and rely upon David for his faithful service. Eventually, David became Saul's armor bearer, responsible for keeping Saul's armor clean and in good repair.

Whenever the tormenting spirit from God troubled Saul,
David would play the harp. Then Saul would feel better,
and the tormenting spirit would go away.

1 Samuel 16:23 NLT

Why do you think God let David spend so much time with King Saul, giving him the opportunity to see this side of his tormented life?

Answer: the harp

SEPTEMBER 7

JOHN THE BAPTIST'S DIET

John the Baptist's diet consisted of:
A. cicadas and oranges
B. locusts and honey
C. lamb and pomegranates
D. manna and fish

John the Baptist was a relative of Jesus who had gone out into the Judean countryside to preach about repentance. The Gospel of Matthew tells us that John the Baptist was prophesied about seven hundred years earlier by the prophet, Isaiah, when he said, "Listen! It's the voice of someone shouting, 'Clear the way through the wilderness for the Lord! Make a straight highway through the wasteland for our God!'" (Isaiah 40:3)

John's dramatic message that tilled the soil for the Messiah was even more emphatic with his grizzly appearance. People may have been drawn to get a glimpse of John as much as to go hear his message. Matthew tells us that people came from all over Judea and the Jordan Valley to see and hear John. John wore clothes made from camel hair and he ate locusts and wild honey. When he spoke, he amazed people with the authority of his call to repent of sin and turn to God. En masse, people's hearts were convicted, and they sought to be baptized in the Jordan River for the forgiveness of sins.

John's clothes were woven from coarse camel hair,
and he wore a leather belt around his waist.
For food he ate locusts and wild honey.

MATTHEW 3:4 NLT

Why do you think God chose John with his strange appearance and behaviors, to be the one to prepare the way for the Messiah?

Answer: B) locusts and honey

ISAIAH'S CONSISTENCY

During the reigns of what kings did Isaiah prophesy?

Isaiah had quite a run as a prophet. He survived the reigns of multiple kings, political upheavals, and violent persecutions. Seven hundred years before Jesus was born, the prophet Isaiah lived in a time where there was rampant abuse of power and a lot of spiritual poverty. Yet, as Isaiah reminded the people, when life is at its darkest and harshest, the light of the world will vividly shine.

Isaiah's name means "the Lord is salvation." His message was considered bad news by those who opposed God. But his message was good news for the poor, hope for the hurting, sight for the blind, and freedom for the oppressed, in the words of Isaiah 61:1–3. Because of this, Isaiah was not always popular with the powerful, ruling classes. He had to persevere through multiple kings, stressful cultural trends, and a lot of adversity. But ultimately, he pointed people to God's plan of deliverance through the coming Messiah.

These are the visions that Isaiah son of Amoz saw concerning Judah and Jerusalem. He saw these visions during the years when Uzziah, Jotham, Ahaz, and Hezekiah were kings of Judah.

Isaiah 1:1 NLT

How does Isaiah's resilient faithfulness through the changes and challenges of culture give you courage to live for Jesus today?

Answer: Uzziah, Jotham, Ahaz, and Hezekiah

SEPTEMBER 9

SUFFERING SERVANT

TRUE OR FALSE
Over seven hundred years before Jesus was born, Isaiah said that the Servant of God would be pierced for our transgressions.

Over seven hundred years before Jesus was born, Isaiah prophesied that the Messiah would be despised and rejected by his own people. He would take up our pain and suffering even while we considered him rejected by God. He would be pierced for our transgressions and crushed for our iniquities. Isaiah proclaimed that the punishment that brought us peace was on him and that by his wounds we are healed.

We are like sheep that have wandered astray, and still God laid our sins on the Suffering Servant. As he was led away to slaughter, he kept his mouth silent just as Isaiah prophesied. He was cut off from the land of the living and assigned a grave with the wicket and with the rich in his death even though he had committed no violence and had no deceit. Isaiah proclaimed that his life would be an offering for sin, but after he had suffered, the Servant of God would see the light of life and be satisfied. He would bear the sin of many and make intercession for the transgressors.

He was pierced for our transgressions,
he was crushed for our iniquities;
the punishment that brought us peace was on him,
and by his wounds we are healed.

Isaiah 53:5 NIV

Where do you see Jesus in Isaiah 53?

Answer: true

HIDDEN IN YOUR HEART

FINISH THIS VERSE

I have hidden your word in my heart, that I might not ______ ______ ______.

The best way to avoid sin and to live a life that pleases God is to hide his Word deep in your heart. This means you read it, study it, think about it, and memorize it. Implanting God's Word in your life will change the way you think about your choices, give you discernment for decisions, and strengthen you for difficulties. It will help you know him better and improve your communication with him through prayer.

Jesus hid Scripture in his heart. When he was tempted by Satan in the desert, he quoted verses from the Bible. When he was challenged and tested, he responded with verses that were embedded in his daily routines. When others sought him for wisdom, he quoted Scripture. When he taught, he walked through the stories and the commands of the Law and the Prophets with authority and clarity. Jesus rested his life in the Word of God.

I have hidden your word in my heart,
that I might not sin against you.

Psalm 119:11 NLT

Memorize this verse today.

Answer: sin against you

SEPTEMBER 11

BRONZE SNAKE

What happened when the poisoned Israelites looked at the bronze snake?

As the Israelites wandered in the wilderness after their exodus from Egypt, they grew impatient. They began to speak against God and against Moses. They began to complain about the manna that God was providing for them every day. Numbers 21 tells us that the Lord sent venomous snakes that bit many of the Israelites. As they lay dying, the people repented and cried out for mercy. God told Moses to fashion a bronze snake and put it on a pole. As people trusted God and looked at the snake, which acted as a symbol of the cause of their trouble and impending death, they would find healing and live.

Later, Jesus claimed, "Just as Moses lifted up the snake in the wilderness, so the Son of Man must be lifted up, that everyone who believes may have eternal life in him" (John 3:14-15). He became the symbol of the sin, the cause of humanity's trouble and death. And as people look to the cross and believe in him, they are healed from their sins and given eternal life.

Moses made a bronze snake and put it up on a pole.
Then when anyone was bitten by a snake
and looked at the bronze snake, they lived.

NUMBERS 21:9 NIV

What do you need healing for in your life today?

Answer: they were healed

SEPTEMBER 12

COLLAPSED WALLS

Without an outright attack, the Israelites knocked down the walls of which city?

As the nation of Israel entered into the Promised Land after forty years of wandering in the wilderness, they encircled the fortified city of Jericho. But rather than attacking the city, the Lord instructed them to march around it once a day for six days. On the seventh day, they were instructed to march around the city seven times and then blow their trumpets and shout.

Israel trusted God with this unconventional warfare. Joshua ordered the priests to carry the ark of the covenant in the marching line with the army, but to remain silent for six days. On the seventh day, after the seventh march around the city, Joshua commanded the army to sound the trumpets and to shout! At the sound, the walls of Jericho collapsed. The army rushed in and took the city. Only Rahab and the people of her house were spared, because earlier she protected two Israelite spies and began to follow God. The news of this radical destruction by Joshua's God spread quickly throughout the land.

When the trumpets sounded, the army shouted, and at the sound of the trumpet, when the men gave a loud shout, the wall collapsed; so everyone charged straight in, and they took the city.

Joshua 6:20 NIV

Why do you think God wanted Israel's first battle in the Promised Land to be conducted this way?

Answer: Jericho

SEPTEMBER 13

LORD OF THE SABBATH

How did Jesus show the Pharisees that he was the Lord of the Sabbath?

Some influential Pharisees were becoming increasingly upset with Jesus. One of the things that most irritated them was that Jesus was willing to heal people on the Sabbath. They believed that there should be no work at all done on the Sabbath day because it had been commanded by God to be a day of rest (Hebrews 4:9-10). They accused Jesus of doing unlawful things. Jesus challenged them to understand what God meant when he told the Israelites, "I desire mercy, not sacrifice" (Hosea 6:6). Alarmingly, Jesus then boldly told them that he himself was the "Lord of the Sabbath."

They began to plot how they might find a reason to kill him. As Jesus came into the synagogue on the Sabbath, they baited him into healing a man with a shriveled hand. Jesus responded, "If any of you has a sheep and it falls into a pit on the Sabbath, will you not take hold of it and lift it out? How much more valuable is a person than a sheep! Therefore, it is lawful to do good on the Sabbath" (Matthew 12:11). He then told the man to stretch out his hand. When the man did so, he found it completely restored.

"The Son of Man is Lord of the Sabbath." Going on from that place, he went into their synagogue, and a man with a shriveled hand was there. Looking for a reason to bring charges against Jesus, they asked him, "Is it lawful to heal on the Sabbath?"

MATTHEW 12:8-10 NIV

Why did the Pharisees want to kill Jesus instead of worship him?

Answer: he healed a man with a shriveled hand on the Sabbath

WAITING A GENERATION

Why did the Lord make Israel wander in the desert for forty years before they could enter the Promised Land?

When Israel left Egypt and came to the edge of the Promised Land, they sent twelve spies to survey the land. Ten of the men returned saying that the nations in the land were filled with giant men who made the Israelites seem like grasshoppers. The other two spies, Joshua and Caleb, disagreed with this assessment, convinced that God had led them to this point and would continue to lead them into the Promised Land. But the people of Israel listened to the majority and complained against Moses and God for bringing them to this point only to die at the hand of the giants in the land (see Numbers 13-14).

God decided to strike the ten unfaithful spies with plagues. He also declared that everyone over the age of twenty (except Joshua and Caleb) would need to pass away before he would let Israel enter the land. It would take forty years before the next generation of Israel would allow God to lead them into the Promised Land.

The LORD's anger burned against Israel and he made them wander in the wilderness forty years, until the whole generation of those who had done evil in his sight was gone.

NUMBERS 32:13 NIV

What does this teach us about God's timeline for his own plans?

Answer: so the generation that had done evil was dead

SEPTEMBER 15

HE IS WITH YOU

FINISH THIS VERSE

"Have I not commanded you? Be strong and _______. Do not be afraid; do not be discouraged, for the Lord your God will be with you _______ _______ _______."

Joshua was about to lead Israel into the Promised Land across the Jordan River. He would do this feat without his powerful mentor, Moses, who had been Israel's leader for forty years. The tasks were daunting. The challenges were overwhelming. The demands were exhausting. And the potential for failure was high.

Before he embarked, he was emboldened by God. God assured Joshua that there was no need to fear. He could be strong and courageous and unafraid because God would be with him throughout the journey. Later, Jesus echoed the same words to his disciples, again and again. He said, "And surely I am with you always, to the very end of the age" (Matthew 28:20).

"Have I not commanded you? Be strong and courageous.
Do not be afraid; do not be discouraged,
for the LORD your God will be with you wherever you go."

JOSHUA 1:9 NIV

How can you remember each day that God is with you?

Answer: courageous; wherever you go

SEPTEMBER 16

PAUL'S PROFESSION

During his missionary travels, what did the apostle Paul do for work to support himself?

A. Carpentry
B. Fishing
C. Shepherding
D. Tentmaking

During a wave of Jewish persecution in Rome, Aquila and his wife Priscilla fled. They made their way to the city of Corinth where they set up their tentmaking business. There they met another Jewish man, a Christian named Paul. Like them, Paul had learned the trade of tent-making. Looking to build their business and make a living in Corinth, they hired Paul and invited him to live with them.

Each Sabbath, they listened to Paul reason in the synagogue with other Jewish people and God-fearing Greek people. When two more passionate Christians named Silas and Timothy also came to Corinth, Paul devoted himself exclusively to preaching and testifying that Jesus was the Messiah. The ever-present witness of these men changed the lives of Aquila and Priscilla forever. They became two of the most influential figures in the spread of Christianity across the Roman Empire as they utilized their business skills to share their faith in Jesus.

Paul went to see them, and because he was a tentmaker as they were, he stayed and worked with them.

Acts 18:1-3 NIV

Read how Paul described this couple in Romans 16:3-5. What does this reveal about the life-changing power of Jesus Christ in the early spread of Christianity?

Answer: D) tentmaking

SEPTEMBER 17

OPENED DOOR

Jesus said the door would be opened to you if you did what?

Jesus wants us to be intentional with him. He wants us to ask him to supply our needs, to seek his kingdom throughout our lives, to knock on his door and find refuge in his home. Jesus promises that if we do these acts of humility and grace, God will come through for us. Ask him for something and he will give it. Seek him, and you will find him. Knock on his door, and he will open it.

The key in these encouraging statements from Jesus is focus. In each case, our focus is to be on God and his kingdom. When Jesus teaches his disciples to pray, he instructs them to first acknowledge God's holiness and then to align with God's will on earth as it is on heaven. It is in this posture of God-before-everything that everything else can be added to our lives. It is when we ask for anything in God's name that he assures us his kingdom is ours.

"I say to you: Ask and it will be given to you; seek and you will find; knock and the door will be opened to you. For everyone who asks receives; the one who seeks finds; and to the one who knocks, the door will be opened."

Luke 11:9-10 NIV

What do you truly need today?

Answer: knock

PILLAR OF SALT

Who was turned into a pillar of salt?

The people in the cities of Sodom and Gomorrah became overrun with sinful practices. When two angels arrived at the house of Abraham's nephew, Lot, a particularly horrific event began to unfold. The men of Sodom threatened perverse and violent acts toward the angels. Lot, in an attempt to spare the angels but clearly struggling with his own sense of morality, responded with an equally egregious option by offering his own daughters to the abusive men. The angels stepped in, thankfully, and blinded the men and ordered Lot and his family to flee the city because God was about to destroy the city.

Lot frantically tried to corral his whole family so they could flee, but they thought he was joking. Finally, he, his daughters, and his wife ran for their lives away from the city. The angels warned them not to flee to the mountains and not to look back at the apocalypse, or they would be caught up in it. As they ran, God rained down sulfur on the entire region, destroying everything. Lot's wife looked back and was turned into a pillar of salt.

> He overthrew those cities and the entire plain, destroying all those living in the cities—and also the vegetation in the land. But Lot's wife looked back, and she became a pillar of salt.
>
> Genesis 19:25-26 NIV

How does confused morality create chaos for a city?

Answer: Lot's wife

SEPTEMBER 19

LONGEST VERSE

What is the longest verse of the Bible?

The ninth verse of the eighth chapter of the book of Esther is often considered to be the longest verse of the Bible. In the English Standard Version, it is made up of eighty words. It contains two sentences, each with multiple phrases and stated points of content.

In context, this verse describes details surrounding laws that were enacted to protect the Jews living in the kingdom of Persia. King Xerxes was angry that one of his leading advisors had been advocating for the genocide of the Jews. It was the king's new wife, Esther, and her uncle, Mordecai, who alerted him to this evil plot. King Xerxes decreed that Jewish people in his land had the right to unite and defend themselves and their property. The day that these new laws took effect became celebrated on the calendar as *Purim*.

The king's scribes were summoned at that time, in the third month, which is the month of Sivan, on the twenty-third day. And an edict was written, according to all that Mordecai commanded concerning the Jews, to the satraps and the governors and the officials of the provinces from India to Ethiopia, 127 provinces, to each province in its own script and to each people in its own language, and also to the Jews in their script and their language.

ESTHER 8:9 ESV

What do you know about the story of the book of Esther? How did God use Esther and Mordecai to rescue the Jewish people?

Answer: Esther 8:9

GREAT CONTEST

How many prophets of Baal did Elijah challenge on Mount Carmel?

The Israelites pretended to be committed to God while worshipping Baal, following the evil practices of King Ahab and Queen Jezebel. Elijah confronted his people and asked, "How long will you waver between two opinions? If the Lord is God, follow him; but if Baal is God, follow him" (1 Kings 18:20). But the people, we are told, said nothing.

Elijah challenged the four-hundred fifty prophets of Baal to a duel. He instructed that two bulls be prepared for sacrifice and each placed on a separate pile of wood. Then the prophets of Baal could call on their god to set fire to the sacrifice. They agreed. They spent all morning calling on Baal, but there was no response. Elijah began to taunt them saying, "Shout louder! Perhaps he is busy, or traveling" (v. 27). They shouted the rest of the day, but there was no fire from Baal. Elijah ordered his altar to be doused with water three times. Then he called to the God of Abraham, Isaac, and Israel. "Let it be known today that you are God in Israel" (v. 36). Then the fire of the Lord fell and burned up the sacrifice and the altar and licked up all of the water.

Then Elijah said to them, "I am the only one of the LORD's prophets left, but Baal has four hundred and fifty prophets.

1 KINGS 18:22 NIV

In terms of how you live out your faith in God, do you waver between two opinions?

Answer: four hundred and fifty

MOSES' WIFE

Who was Moses' wife?

In a moment of anger, Moses killed an Egyptian solider who was beating a Hebrew slave. When Pharaoh learned what Moses had done, he tried to kill him, but Moses fled to the land of Midian across the Red Sea. Moses arrived at a well where the priest of Midian drew water. The priest would send his seven daughters to carry the water and fill the troughs for their flocks. While Moses was at the well, some devious shepherds started harassing the daughters, and Moses chased them away and rescued them. The priest was thankful and invited Moses to stay with them.

In time, Moses became part of the family when he married the priest's daughter, Zipporah. The couple gave birth to a son named Gershom, which sounds like the Hebrew word that means "foreigner." Both Zipporah and her father became important and consistent influences during the monumental tasks that the Lord had ahead for Moses.

Moses accepted the invitation, and he settled there with him.
In time, Reuel gave Moses his daughter Zipporah to be his wife.

Exodus 2:21 NLT

What might it demonstrate about the Lord's plan of salvation for the world that Moses had a non-Jewish wife?

Answer: Zipporah

SEPTEMBER 22

MY THOUGHTS AND YOURS

TRUE OR FALSE
God said that his thoughts are like our thoughts and his ways are like our ways?

Isaiah urged God's people to seek the Lord while he was near. He pleaded with them to turn from their wicked ways so God could have mercy on them ad forgive them. Isaiah knew that forgiveness was possible because of who God was. He was different than the grudge-holding, stubborn people Isaiah dealt with. He pointed out that God is holy, righteous, merciful, and always very good.

"It is the same with my word," said the Lord. "I send it out, and it always produces fruit. It will accomplish all I want it to, and it will prosper everywhere I send it" (Isaiah 55:11). God's thoughts are much richer than ours. And his ways are much better.

"My thoughts are nothing like your thoughts," says the LORD.
"And my ways are far beyond anything you could imagine.
For just as the heavens are higher than the earth,
so my ways are higher than your ways
and my thoughts higher than your thoughts."

ISAIAH 55:8-9 NLT

How might the Lord's thoughts and ways be different than yours?

Answer: false

SEPTEMBER 23

SPARROW PRICE

How much does Jesus say is the price of two sparrows?

God loves the creatures of his great creation. He is aware of every animal from small to large. Jesus teaches that even though people might not think they are important, not even a single common sparrow can fall to the ground without God the Father knowing it and caring about it.

Jesus teaches that we are even more valuable to the Father than an entire flock of sparrows. God loves us more than we can ever fully realize. He knows every single hair on each of our heads. His thoughts of us are "precious" and "outnumber the grains of sand" (Psalm 139:17-18). He knows when we get up and when we fall asleep. He knit us together in our mothers" wombs. He discerns our thoughts and knows our words before we speak. He protects us and shepherds us. He laid down his own life for us.

"What is the price of two sparrows—one copper coin? But not a single sparrow can fall to the ground without your Father knowing it. And the very hairs on your head are all numbered. So don't be afraid; you are more valuable to God than a whole flock of sparrows."

MATTHEW 10:29-31 NLT

How much do you grasp the love of God for you?

Answer: one penny, or one copper coin

FEMALE RESCUER

What did Jael use to kill Sisera while he was sleeping?

The commander of the Canaanite armies, Sisera, ruthlessly oppressed the people of Israel for twenty years. Deborah, a prophet and judge for Israel, instructed the leader of Israel's army, Barak, to attack Sisera because God had promised to give Israel victory. Barak would only agree to go to battle if Deborah went with him. Deborah agreed to go with him, but because Barak was hesitant to trust the Lord, Deborah declared that a woman would receive the honor for the victory instead of the male soldiers or generals.

During the attack, God threw Sisera's army into a panic. Sisera jumped off of his chariot and fled on foot. He escaped to a region near the tent of Jael, the wife of Heber the Kenite, which was a tribe of people who were friendly with the Canaanites. Sisera asked Jael to protect him and tend to him. She invited him into her tent, gave him milk, hid him under a blanket, and promised to keep watch. When Sisera fell asleep, Jael ended Sisera's reign of terror and freed the people of Israel.

When Sisera fell asleep from exhaustion, Jael quietly crept up to him with a hammer and tent peg in her hand. Then she drove the tent peg through his temple and into the ground, and so he died.

Judges 4:21 NLT

By including such graphic details in stories like this, what does God want us to understand about our history with him?

Answer: a tent peg

SEPTEMBER 25

WHAT WE WANT

When the people of Israel told Samuel that they wanted to be like the nations around them, what is it that they specifically demanded?

Samuel was a mighty judge and prophet for Israel, but as he grew old, the people wanted a different arrangement. They looked at the nations around them which all had kings, and they wanted the same thing for themselves. They had grown weary of trusting God as their King; the system of government between the tribes was loosely structured, and they lacked an organized army. They were worried about the next judges, Samuel's two sons, who didn't have the integrity nor the godly power of their father.

The demand broke Samuel's heart, yet the Lord instructed him to grant the people their request. First, however, God wanted Samuel to help them understand what they were truly asking for. A king, God said, would conscript their sons into war and take their daughters into service. A king would take a tenth of their belongings and take away their best properties. He would take their employees into his own possession. It wouldn't be long before the Israelites were searching for a way out from the oppression of a human king.

The people refused to listen to Samuel's warning. "Even so, we still want a king," they said. "We want to be like the nations around us. Our king will judge us and lead us into battle."

1 Samuel 8:19-20 NLT

Why are humans fickle in their desires to be ruled?

Answer: a king

TOWN OF RUTH'S FAME

Ruth married a man named Boaz who was from what town?

A. Nazareth
B. Jerusalem
C. Bethlehem
D. Jericho

Ruth arrived in Bethlehem as a widowed foreigner. Her deceased husband was the Jewish son of the widow Naomi who had extended kin in Bethlehem. When they lost their means of survival, the two women traveled from Moab back to Naomi's family to seek help.

A man named Boaz welcomed them to work his fields, faithfully following the Torah which commanded the Israelites to care for foreigners in the land and to let them pick from the fields. Boaz assumed responsibility for Ruth and soon fell in love with her. They wed and had a son. A few generations later, a man named David would be born in Bethlehem to Ruth's grandson, Jesse. One thousand years later, a man named Jesus would be born in Bethlehem, securing Ruth's fame in Bethlehem forever.

The elders and all the people standing in the gate replied, "We are witnesses! May the Lord make this woman who is coming into your home like Rachel and Leah, from whom all the nation of Israel descended! May you prosper in Ephrathah and be famous in Bethlehem."

Ruth 4:11 NLT

Are you surprised that Jesus was born through the lineage of Ruth, a non-Jewish woman?

Answer: C) Bethlehem

SHARPENING

As iron sharpens _______, so a friend sharpens _______ _______.

An iron tool by itself cannot be sharpened. In fact, with use over time, the tool will become dull, worn, and less effective. But when one iron tool is razed against another one, they become honed for the tasks that they were intended for. The attention given to the grinding process polishes out blemishes and leaves an attractive shine.

A person alone will become worn and less effective in the purpose for which the Lord called them. But when they have someone encouraging them and holding them accountable to pursue what is good and right for their lives, that friend becomes more attuned to God's will. The friction of a good friendship refines dull edges and prepares people for good purposes.

As iron sharpens iron,
so a friend sharpens a friend.
PROVERBS 27:17 NLT

Can you give an example of a true friendship where the other person sharpens you and you sharpen them?

Answer: iron; a friend

WHO BUILT THE TEMPLE

The original temple was built by which king?
A. David
B. Solomon
C. Hezekiah
D. Ahaz

King David desired to build a permanent home in Jerusalem for God to dwell with his people. David reasoned that the king had a palace, but God only had a tent. David concluded that this was unfair. But God did not want David to be the one to build the temple; he had blood on his hands from all his years in battle. It would be David's son, Solomon, who had the honor instead.

Almost five hundred years after God led the Israelites out of Egypt and tabernacled with his people in the desert, King Solomon began construction on a marvelous home for God on earth. Eventually Israel struggled to be faithful to God, and the temple was destroyed. When God brought his people back from the exile in Babylon, a second temple was constructed in the same location, restored and enhanced by Herod the Great. The second temple was destroyed in 70 A.D. by the Romans.

In the four hundred and eightieth year after the Israelites came out of Egypt, in the fourth year of Solomon's reign over Israel, in the month of Ziv, the second month, he began to build the temple of the LORD.

1 KINGS 6:1 NIV

What does it mean in the New Testament when we are called God's temple? (See 1 Corinthians 3:16.)

Answer: B) Solomon

A DONKEY'S JAWBONE

How many men did Samson kill with the jawbone of a donkey?

A. Ten
B. One hundred
C. One thousand
D. Ten thousand

Three thousand men from Judah went to Samson to beg him to chill out a bit. Samson was stirring up trouble with the Philistines. He burned their fields of grain, their vineyards, and their olive groves. The Philistines wanted to take revenge on Samson, or else go to war against the people of Judah.

Of course, it was God's will that Samson deliver his people from the oppressive hand of the Philistines, but the men demanded that Samson let them tie him up and deliver him to the Philistines. He agreed. They bound him with two new ropes and led him to the Philistine army camp. The Spirit of the Lord came upon him, and he snapped the ropes, grabbed a fresh jawbone of a donkey and slaughtered one thousand Philistine men.

Finding a fresh jawbone of a donkey, he grabbed it and struck down a thousand men. Then Samson said,
"With a donkey's jawbone
I have made donkeys of them.
With a donkey's jawbone
I have killed a thousand men."

JUDGES 15:15-16 NIV

Why do you think God allowed Samson to humiliate the Philistines like this?

Answer: C) one thousand

SEPTEMBER 30

HE HAS SHOWN US

FINISH THIS VERSE

He has shown you, O mortal, what is good.
And what does the Lord require of you?
To act _______ and to love _______
and to walk _______ with your God.

God has shown us what is good. After creation, he looked at all he had made and saw that it was very good (Genesis 1). When a man came to him and called him "Good teacher," Jesus replied, "No one is good—except God alone" (Mark 10:17-18). When Jesus described himself, he said, "I am the good shepherd. The good shepherd lays down his life for the sheep" (John 10:11).

And here, the prophet Micah reminds us that God has already shown us the good path. It is good to reflect his very good nature and very good actions. It is good to act justly toward others. It is good to love being merciful. And it is especially good to walk in a humble relationship with the Creator of the universe, the holy God.

He has shown you, O mortal, what is good.
And what does the Lord require of you?
To act justly and to love mercy
and to walk humbly with your God.

Micah 6:8 NIV

Of the three good things mentioned in Micah 6:8, what good thing will you focus on today?

Answer: justly; mercy; humbly

OCTOBER

LYDIA'S JOB

Lydia was a merchant of what kind product?

On one of their missionary journeys, Paul, Silas, and Luke sailed from Troas across the northern part of the Aegean Sea to the region of Macedonia. They made their way to a prominent city called Philippi. On the Sabbath day, they went outside the city to a riverbank where they suspected some Jewish people might be praying. They sat down to speak with some women who had gathered there.

One of the women was named Lydia, a businesswoman who dealt with expensive purple cloth. She was also a devout worshipper of God. She listened intently to Paul and Silas as they shared about Jesus the Messiah. Lydia believed their message. And so did her husband and their whole household, which likely involved family members as well as employed servants. Lydia's whole household were baptized, and she invited them to stay in their home as her guests.

One of them was Lydia from Thyatira, a merchant of expensive purple cloth, who worshiped God. As she listened to us, the Lord opened her heart, and she accepted what Paul was saying.

Acts 16:14 NLT

Read Philippians 1:1-14. What do you notice about the growth of the Philippian Church and Paul's feelings about them?

Answer: expensive purple cloth

BLIND BARTIMAEUS

In what town was Bartimaeus healed?

On his way to Jerusalem, Jesus passed through the town of Jericho. As Jesus was leaving the town with a large crowd of people following him, a blind man named Bartimaeus started shouting, "Jesus, Son of David, have mercy on me!" Some people yelled at Bartimaeus to be quiet. Their attempt to shut him up, however, made him shout louder. When Jesus heard Bartimaeus, he invited him to draw near. Many in the crowd began to encourage Bartimaeus, saying "Cheer up, he's calling you!" Bartimaeus threw aside his coat and came immediately to Jesus.

Jesus asked Bartimaeus a straight-forward, unassuming question. He asked what Bartimaeus wanted. "My Rabbi, I want to see!". Jesus told him to go; his faith had healed him. Instantly Bartimaeus regained his sight, and he followed Jesus down the road.

They reached Jericho, and as Jesus and his disciples left town,
a large crowd followed him. A blind beggar named Bartimaeus
(son of Timaeus) was sitting beside the road.

Mark 10:46 NLT

If Jesus asked you today what you wanted, how would you answer?

Answer: Jericho

OCTOBER 3

STRIKING THE ROCK

Why wasn't Moses allowed into the Promised Land?

As the Israelites wandered in the desert, they grumbled about their poor conditions. They rebelled against Moses and his brother Aaron, complaining that they had it better when they were slaves in Egypt. Miriam, the sister of Moses and Aaron, had died and they were distraught. They fell face down and prayed to God.

God told them to take Aaron's staff and assemble all of the people. At his command, they were to strike a rock so all of Israel could see. God then caused water to gush from the rock, which was intended to satisfy the people and all of the livestock. But when Moses stood before the people, he grew angry and accused them of demanding a sign. "Must we bring water from this rock?" he yelled. And he struck the rock and water gushed out. God was upset with Moses for not demonstrating his holiness, but instead contributing to their sour attitudes. As a consequence, he told Moses and Aaron that they would not be allowed to lead the people into the Promised Land.

The Lord said to Moses and Aaron, "Because you did not trust me enough to demonstrate my holiness to the people of Israel, you will not lead them into the land I am giving them!"

Numbers 20:12 NLT

Why did God respond seriously to Moses' action? How can this event impact your own angry responses?

Answer: he struck the rock with his staff in anger

OCTOBER 4

SIXTH DAY

What did God make on the sixth day of Creation?

The first chapter of the Bible tells us that God created the world in six days. On the sixth day God created his crowning masterpiece. Made in his image, humankind represented God on earth. Mankind was immediately tasked with the responsibility and the authority to govern the planet in a way that would reflect God's love for his creation. Mankind was also commissioned with a unique characteristic of God's nature—the attribute of relationship. He instructed them to be fruitful and multiply.

God created men and women to be close to one another because God is relational. In fact, he walked in the garden he had made to commune with Adam and Eve. All of the preparation of the previous five days of Creation led to this monumental purpose. And he looked on all that he had made and saw that it was very good.

God said, "Let Us make mankind in Our image, according to Our likeness; and let them rule over the fish of the sea and over the birds of the sky and over the livestock and over all the earth, and over every crawling thing that crawls on the earth." So God created man in His own image, in the image of God He created him; male and female He created them.

Genesis 1:26-27 NASB

How would you say humanity has done with the purpose God gave them?

Answer: mankind

OCTOBER 5

MOSES' DEATH

How old was Moses when he died?

After forty years of wandering in the wilderness, God led Moses up Mount Nebo, which sat across from Jericho and the Jordan River to the east of the Promised Land. From there, he showed Moses what was going to happen next. He said the land would be given to Moses' descendants, but Moses would not be able to cross over into it.

Moses died and was buried there in the land of Moab. We are told that he was a hundred and twenty years old, that his eyesight was still clear, and that he was still strong. The people of Israel mourned for Moses for thirty days. There has never been another prophet in Israel like Moses, who knew God face to face or who showed mighty power and performed awesome deeds in the sight of Israel.

> Moses the servant of the Lord died there in Moab, as the Lord had said. He buried him in Moab, in the valley opposite Beth Peor, but to this day no one knows where his grave is. Moses was a hundred and twenty years old when he died, yet his eyes were not weak nor his strength gone.
>
> Deuteronomy 34:5-7 niv

If Moses was one hundred and twenty years old when he died, how old was he when he confronted Pharaoh and led the Israelites out of Egypt? Find the answer in Exodus 7:7.

Answer: one hundred and twenty years old

OCTOBER 6

AFTER SOLOMON

Who was the king that followed Solomon?

When Solomon died and his son, Rehoboam, succeeded him as king, the northern tribes of Israel revolted. They summoned one of Solomon's deposed officials, a man named Jeroboam, who tried earlier to lead a rebellion against Solomon. When that rebellion failed, Solomon had tried to kill him, and Jeroboam fled to Egypt seeking an alliance with Egypt. With Solomon out of the picture, Jeroboam made his way back to Israel with his eye on the ten northern tribes.

While this was happening, Rehoboam assembled the leaders of all the tribes of Israel. They told him that Solomon was a cruel leader with crushing labor demands and heavy taxes. They tried to persuade him that they would be loyal to him if he would lighten the demands on the people. Offended by their request, Rehoboam spoke harshly to the people and increased burdens even more. The people then made Jeroboam the king of Israel in the north (Judah was in the south), and the nation was split into a violent civil war.

> Solomon reigned in Jerusalem over all Israel forty years. Then he rested with his ancestors and was buried in the city of David his father. And Rehoboam his son succeeded him as king.
>
> 1 Kings 11:42-43 NIV

Read 1 Kings 11:29-39. Why did God allow the nation to be divided?

Answer: Rehoboam

OCTOBER 7

FOURTH COMMANDMENT

What is the fourth of the Ten Commandments?

Perhaps it is surprising to discover that the Sabbath commandment is fourth of the Ten Commandments. It follows three major directives about having no other gods, not making idols, and never taking the Lord's name in vain. It would appear that God considers it vitally important to keep one day of the week sacred. He explains, "Six days you shall labor and do all your work, but the seventh day is a sabbath to the Lord your God. On it you shall not do any work" (Exodus 20:9-10). God continued to describe how no one in a person's house, estate, or business, nor any foreigner in the land nor working animal was to work. He said he made the heavens and earth in six days but rested on the seventh. He blessed that day and made it holy (vv. 10-11).

Few people today respect the Sabbath day of rest, keeping it holy. We are forgetting that God wants us to find rest and restoration with him in a weekly rhythm. The commandment doesn't seem as important to people today as it seemed to be for God in his Word.

"Remember the Sabbath day
by keeping it holy."
Exodus 20:8 NIV

What steps can you take this week toward a better rhythm of Sabbath rest?

Answer: remember the Sabbath and keep it holy

OCTOBER 8

JEZEBEL'S DEATH

What did Jezebel do right before she was thrown out of her window to her death?

Jezebel was a Phoenician woman who became the Queen of the northern kingdom of Israel when she married King Ahab. She introduced Israel to her foreign gods and harshly imposed their worship throughout the land. She constructed altars to Baal and Asherah, and seemed to have been a type of priestess, leading people to sacrifice before these idols. She pulled the strings of her malleable husband and ushered in a brutal, violent reign. She severely opposed the prophets that the Lord raised up.

When the great prophet, Elijah, defeated the priests of Baal in a dramatic contest on Mount Carmel, she ruthlessly demanded his execution. Eventually, Israel tired of Jezebel's cruelty and turned against her. When she knew it was the end, she took time to do her makeup and hair and confronted her opponent, Jehu, the former commander of Ahab's armies. Jehu called up to her window asking, "Who is on my side?" The two servants who were attending Jezebel grabbed her and threw her out the window, where she met a grizzly death.

Then Jehu went to Jezreel. When Jezebel heard about it, she put on eye makeup, arranged her hair and looked out of a window.

2 Kings 9:30 NIV

What purpose do these details have in the stories in the Bible?

Answer: put on eye makeup and arranged her hair

GOD'S COVENANTAL SIGN

What was God's sign that he would never again destroy the earth with water?

Because humankind had become so evil, God sent floodwaters to destroy them. He appointed Noah and his family to build an ark to rescue a remnant of humanity and the living creatures on the earth.

After the waters receded from the flood, God caused clouds to form in the sky. He said that never again would floodwaters kill all living creatures or a flood destroy the earth. As a sign that his words were a covenant with humanity and all living creatures for all generations, he orchestrated a rainbow to appear when the atmospheric conditions were right. As sunlight hits water molecules, the light is reflected, and a spectrum of colors appears in the sky. This unique and beautiful sign is a prompt for everyone to remember the covenantal promise God made and a reminder to humanity to be faithful to God.

"I have set my rainbow in the clouds, and it will be the sign of the covenant between me and the earth. Whenever I bring clouds over the earth and the rainbow appears in the clouds, I will remember my covenant between me and you and all living creatures of every kind. Never again will the waters become a flood to destroy all life."

Genesis 9:13-15 NIV

Why is the biblical origin of the rainbow an important foundation in our relationship with God?

Answer: the rainbow

JEPHTHAH'S VOW

Why did Jepthah sacrifice his own daughter?

The king of Ammon was amassing an army to attack several of the tribes of Israel. The Spirit of the Lord compelled Jephthah to rally the people of Israel to fight against the Ammonites. God gave Israel a crushing victory, and devastated about twenty Ammonite towns. This should have been a time of rejoicing for the people of Israel. But Jephthah had made a disturbing error.

Before Israel attacked the Ammonite armies, he made a public vow that if they were successful in battle, he would sacrifice to the Lord the first thing that came out of his house when he returned. When he marched victoriously to Mizpah, his daughter came out of the house first, innocently playing a tambourine and rejoicing. Jephthah did keep his vow. The people of Israel have mourned ever since over this offensive, dishonoring oath.

Jephthah made a vow to the LORD: "If you give the Ammonites into my hands, whatever comes out of the door of my house to meet me when I return in triumph from the Ammonites will be the LORD's, and I will sacrifice it as a burnt offering."

JUDGES 11:30-31 NIV

Describe what you know about the often confused and complicated practice of faith among the leaders of Israel in the Bible. Why does God continue to work his plan with people who are compromised in their faith?

Answer: because he made a foolish vow

OCTOBER 11

WASHING PETER'S FEET

TRUE OR FALSE
At first, Peter had no problem with Jesus washing his feet.

Before the Last Supper, Jesus began to wash the feet of his disciples. It was an action that only a servant would do. It was an indication that those whose feet were being washed were more significant than the one doing the washing. For Jesus, it was a sign that he would serve them by washing away their sins and taking their filth and stains into his own hands.

Peter was indignant. He couldn't bring himself to allow Jesus to stoop so low. He told Jesus he should never wash his feet. But Jesus was insistent. He pointed out that in order to continue in relationship together, Peter had to let him wash his feet. At those words, Peter then wanted to go all in.

"No," said Peter, "you shall never wash my feet."
Jesus answered, "Unless I wash you, you have no part with me."
"Then, Lord," Simon Peter replied,
"not just my feet but my hands and my head as well!"

John 13:8-9 NIV

What did Jesus say to Peter next? Read the answer in verse ten.

Answer: false

OCTOBER 12

PETER'S VISION

TRUE OR FALSE

Peter had a vision of sheet lowered from the heavens and full of fruit to eat.

Peter was staying in a town called Joppa, in the home of a leather tanner named Simon. At midday he went up on the roof to pray. He had a vision of heaven opening up and something like a sheet being lowered with all kinds of four-footed animals as well as reptiles and birds. He heard a voice in his vision say, "Get up, Peter. Kill and eat." In his vision, he protested, "I have never eaten anything impure or unclean" (Acts 10:14). The voice responded two more times, telling him not call anything impure which God made clean.

At that moment, three men arrived from the Roman city of Caesarea. They had been sent by a centurion named Cornelius, and they asked Peter to accompany them so he could speak to Cornelius about God. God told Peter to go with the men. Upon entering the centurion's house—an unclean act in itself—Cornelius and Peter spoke about Jesus. All of Cornelius' household believed in Jesus and were baptized. Peter then realized that God accepts from every nation the one who fears him and does what is right (vv. 1-48).

He saw heaven opened and something like a large sheet being let down to earth by its four corners. It contained all kinds of four-footed animals, as well as reptiles and birds. Then a voice told him, "Get up, Peter. Kill and eat."

ACTS 10:11-13 NIV

How does this event in the book of Acts help launch the spread of Christianity across the earth?

Answer: false

DAVID AND SHIMEI

TRUE OR FALSE
David was pelted with rocks by a member of King Saul's family.

Late in David's reign, there was still some hostility between those loyal to David and those loyal to the former King Saul. Once, as David approached the town of Bahurim, a man from the same clan as Saul confronted him. Shimei cursed David and threw stones at him and at David's officials who were with him. He didn't care that David's elite guards were there. "You murderer," he yelled at David. "The Lord has repaid you for all the blood you have shed!"

Abishai, one of David's leading soldiers, asked permission to go over and cut off his head. But David instructed his men to leave Shimei alone, for perhaps God had told Shimei to curse him. Exhausted, both physically and emotionally, David and his men went on their way.

As King David approached Bahurim, a man from the same clan as Saul's family came out from there. His name was Shimei son of Gera, and he cursed as he came out. He pelted David and all the king's officials with stones, though all the troops and the special guard were on David's right and left.

2 Samuel 16:5-6 NIV

Why do you think David refused to silence Shimei?

Answer: true

A GIRL'S REQUEST

What did Herod's niece request on his birthday?

Herod the Tetrarch, also known as Herod Antipas, was the ruler of the regions around Galilee. He was superstitious and disrespected the Jewish religious practices. His brother's wife, Herodias, was angry with John the Baptist, so she urged Herod to arrest him and put him in prison. Herod wanted to kill John, but he was afraid of John's tremendous influence over the people of Galilee who considered John a prophet of God.

On Herod's birthday, the daughter of Herodias danced for the guests. Herod was pleased with her, and he promised to give her anything she requested of him. Herodias convinced her daughter to request the head of her enemy. She asked for the head of John the Baptist to be put on a platter. This distressed the king, but because of the audience, he ordered her request be fulfilled.

On Herod's birthday the daughter of Herodias danced for the guests and pleased Herod so much that he promised with an oath to give her whatever she asked. Prompted by her mother, she said, "Give me here on a platter the head of John the Baptist."

MATTHEW 14:6-8 NIV

What are your reactions to this dishonorable end to John's life?

Answer: the head of John the Baptist on a platter

LOVE IS

FINISH THIS VERSE

Love is _______, love is _______. It does not _______, it does not _______, it is not _______.

First Corinthians 13, sometimes known as the love chapter, is one of the most famous chapters in the Bible. These poetic descriptions of love have made their way into millions of Valentine's Day cards and have been spoken at countless weddings. But these words weren't directed toward couple romance as much as they were directed toward community unity. The Christians in Corinth were experiencing tensions due to selfish attitudes and malicious behaviors.

But love, as the apostle Paul taught, is the great unifier. It does not keep a record of wrongs. It does not hold grudges nor create divisions. Love does not fail others. In fact, love is best represented in Jesus Christ. Every description of love in 1 Corinthians 13 is embodied in him. Jesus is patient, kind, not self-seeking, and he rejoices in truth. He always protects, always trusts, always hopes, and always perseveres.

Love is patient, love is kind. It does not envy,
it does not boast, it is not proud.

1 Corinthians 13:4 niv

In what specific ways has Jesus exhibited love for you?

Answer: patient; kind; envy; boast; proud

HOSEA'S WIFE

What was the name of Hosea's wife?

God asked the prophet Hosea to marry a promiscuous woman named Gomer. The couple had three children, each with a special prophetic name symbolic to the people of Israel. But it is his marriage that is the most vividly symbolic message which God wanted Hosea to manifest through his life. Gomer continually cheated on Hosea. At one point, Gomer went to live with another man. Hosea had to pay the man fifteen shekels of silver as well as some barley in order to buy Gomer back. Hosea told her, "You are to live with me; you may not be a prostitute or be intimate with any man, and I will behave the same way toward you" (3:3).

Hosea's marriage with Gomer was a living parable of the relationship that God had with the children of Israel. His people were not faithful and were intimate with other gods. They lived with idols and became captive to their prostituted lifestyle. But God still wanted Israel to know that he was willing to pay the price to free them because he loved them and was committed to the covenant he had made with them.

When the Lord began to speak through Hosea, the Lord said to him, "Go, marry a promiscuous woman and have children with her, for like an adulterous wife this land is guilty of unfaithfulness to the Lord." So he married Gomer daughter of Diblaim, and she conceived and bore him a son.

Hosea 1:2-3 NIV

Do you ever think about how much pain has God endured in his relationship with his people?

Answer: Gomer

OCTOBER 17

AFTER HOSEA

What book follows the book of Hosea?

The book of Joel is a book of judgment and love mingled together. God loved his people, but they were struggling to love him. At some point, the consequence of unfaithfulness fell upon the children of Israel.

God will not relent in his loving pursuit of his people. His promise to bless them and bless the world through them stands. "Rend your heart and not your garments. Return to the Lord your God, for he is gracious and compassionate, slow to anger and abounding in love, and he relents from sending calamity" (Joel 2:13). Those who heed his invitation and receive his forgiveness will certainly rejoice. They will again know the abundance of life with him. Symbolically, Joel proclaims that the trees are bearing fruit and the people should be glad because God, in his faithfulness, had given them rain. Everyone who calls on the name of the Lord will be saved.

The word of the LORD that came to Joel son of Pethuel.

JOEL 1:1 NIV

Why are people resistant to return to God?

Answer: Joel

BI-VOCATIONAL PROPHET

Which prophet was bi-vocational as a shepherd as well?

Amos was called by God to speak to the northern tribes in Israel. At the time, he was working as a shepherd in a small town a few miles south of Bethlehem. Amos also occasionally took care of a grove of sycamore fig trees, just like the kind that Zacchaeus climbed up in order to see Jesus hundreds of years later. But God told him to go prophesy to his people.

True faith in God throughout the northern tribes was compromised. Not only were they worshipping other gods and building pagan shrines, but they had turned their backs on those in need. While the greedy grew more powerful, the poor grew more oppressed. Amos continued to encourage the people to seek God so they would live. The people of the north struggled to listen to the shepherd-prophet from Judah, but God assured Amos that someday he would restore Israel in the land.

> Amos answered Amaziah, "I was neither a prophet nor the son of a prophet, but I was a shepherd, and I also took care of sycamore-fig trees. But the LORD took me from tending the flock and said to me, 'Go, prophesy to my people Israel.'"
>
> AMOS 7:14-15 NIV

What kind of focus in life does it take to work a steady job and also serve the Lord in ministry?

Answer: Amos

BOOKS OF THE BIBLE

How many books are in the Bible?

The Old Testament is made up of thirty-nine books from Genesis to Malachi, and with nine hundred and twenty-nine chapters, which accounts for seventy-eight percent of the chapters in the Bible. The New Testament is made up of twenty-seven books from Matthew to Revelation, and these contain two hundred and sixty chapters. The Bible was written over a period of about fifteen hundred years by multiple authors in different locations using primarily Hebrew and Greek languages.

The word *testament* refers to the evidence of someone's will, or a covenant. The Old and New Testaments together reveal God's redemptive plan for the world through the death and resurrection of Jesus Christ. The Bible is God's inerrant Word, given to humanity so they might be restored to a relationship with him.

All Scripture is breathed out by God and profitable for teaching, for reproof, for correction, and for training in righteousness, that the man of God may be complete, equipped for every good work.

2 Timothy 3:16-17 ESV

In what ways is 2 Timothy 3:16-17 a good summary to describe the whole Bible?

Answer: sixty-six books

BEFORE JONAH

What is the book before Jonah?

Obadiah prophesied around the time of the destruction of Jerusalem in 586 B.C. As the Babylonian Empire was conquering Judah and destroying the temple, the nearby nation of Edom was mocking God's people. God sent Obadiah to silence them. Edom was a relatively small and insignificant nation to the south of Judah and the Dead Sea. Obadiah told the Edomites, "On the day you stood aloof while strangers carried off his wealth and foreigners entered his gates and cast lots for Jerusalem, you were like one of them" (1:11).

The pride of their hearts deceived them. They didn't think anyone could destroy them. But God told them just as they had done, it would be done to them. He explained that Edom itself would also be conquered, but unlike Israel which would have a surviving remnant, no one would be left alive in Edom.

The vision of Obadiah.
This is what the Sovereign Lord says about Edom—
We have heard a message from the Lord:
An envoy was sent to the nations to say,
"Rise, let us go against her for battle."

Obadiah 1:1 NIV

What kind of courage must it have taken to deliver this message to the people of Edom?

Answer: Obadiah

THE LAST FIVE

Put the last five books of the Old Testament in their proper order:

A. Habakkuk, Zephaniah, Haggai, Zechariah, Malachi
B. Zephaniah, Habbakkuk, Zechariah, Haggai, Malachi
C. Malachi, Haggai, Zechariah, Zephaniah, Habakkuk
D. Habakkuk, Haggai, Malachi, Zechariah, Zephaniah

The twelve minor prophets of the Bible are the collection of prophetic books from Hosea to Malachi. The term comes from St. Augustine who determined that they stood apart from the four longer prophetic books—Isaiah, Jeremiah, Ezekiel, and Daniel. This does not mean, however, that the minor prophets are less important. It only means that the size and scope of their books is smaller. The minor prophets include Hosea, Joel, Amos, Obadiah, Jonah, Micah, Nahum, Habakkuk, Zephaniah, Haggai, Zechariah, and Malachi.

Each minor prophet book contains a first-person account from a specific prophet and occurs in a particular place and time, such as during the time of Israel's divided kingdom, or during the exile or return from exile. Each minor prophet confronts the deteriorating spiritual conditions of God's people. They speak about God's people in Israel and Judah, but some also addressed neighboring nations. Each book also contains future prophetic promises regarding the restoration of God's kingdom and salvation in the land of Israel.

Then the Lord replied:
"Write down the revelation
and make it plain on tablets
so that a herald may run with it."

Habakkuk 2:2 NIV

How many of the minor prophet books can you explain?

Answer: A) Habakkuk, Zephaniah, Haggai, Zechariah, Malachi

JEREMIAH AND THE PEOPLE

TRUE OR FALSE
The prophet Jeremiah was always well received by the people.

A prophet is like a lightning rod. He speaks the words of God whether people want to hear or not. If they don't want to hear what the prophet has to say, people usually do not respond kindly. The anger of kings and crowds can be turned toward the prophet. Jeremiah prayed that the people would be overthrown. They made his prophetic task difficult and very dangerous.

People did not like Jeremiah's message. He spoke about their sins and warned them of impending calamity at the hands of the neighboring nations. He told the people of Judah that God would scatter them for their sins as the east wind scatters dust. The people of Judah then began to undercut Jeremiah's ability to communicate effectively.

"Come, let's make plans against Jeremiah; for the teaching of the law
by the priest will not cease, nor will counsel from the wise,
nor the word from the prophets. So come, let's attack him
with our tongues and pay no attention to anything he says."

Jeremiah 18:18 NIV

How difficult is it for you to stand up for God's message in a culture that undercuts you and your faith?

Answer: false

DRESSED-UP WOLF

Who first said the famous phrase, "a wolf in sheep's clothing?"

If you aren't careful, Jesus warned, you could be tricked by religious leaders who present themselves as a friend but are actually looking for prey. They'll mimic your heart's desires, tricking you into thinking they are on your side. They'll draw you in with promises of fellowship and lull you into a sense of comfort. Only when it is too late do they reveal their fangs.

Jesus warned that there are people who present themselves as his representatives, but in truth they seek to devour the devout. These false prophets claim to speak for God, but their intentions are selfish and destructive. Ironically, many people accused Jesus of being a false prophet. It seems that humans lack discernment when it comes to detecting who is speaking for God.

"Watch out for false prophets.
They come to you in sheep's clothing,
but inwardly they are ferocious wolves."
MATTHEW 7:15 NIV

How do you become an expert at spotting the wolf in sheep's clothing?

Answer: Jesus

REDUCING GIDEON'S ARMY

In Gideon's army, how many men drank from their hands rather putting their mouths in the stream?

Gideon had thirty-two thousand troops ready to go to war against the Midianites, but God told him that was too many! God's concern was that the Israelites would boast of their own power when they were victorious on the battlefield. God then asked Gideon to reduce the size of his army.

First, God told Gideon to inform his soldiers that whoever was timid or afraid could simply go home. Astonishingly, twenty-two thousand troops went home. Next, he asked Gideon to take his men down to a spring to observe how they drank. Whoever got on their knees and drank by putting their mouths in the stream should be sent home, but whoever cupped water in their hands would be led by God to victory over Midian. That night, Gideon and his three hundred remaining men scattered around the enemy camp and lit torches and blew horns. The startled Midianites, thinking they were under attack by a massive army, went into confusion and began killing each other in the chaos.

Only 300 of the men drank from their hands. All the others got down on their knees and drank with their mouths in the stream.

JUDGES 7:6 NLT

Why do we want to take credit for success rather than giving glory to God?

Answer: three hundred

KING SAUL'S HEIGHT

Was King Saul taller or shorter than most other Israelite men?

Saul, the son of Kish, was an impressive figure. The Bible described him as very handsome; it also mentions twice that he stood head and shoulders above anyone else in the land. He was an imposing soldier and gifted strategist. God frequently placed his Spirit on Saul to lead with might and prophetic power.

And yet, Saul was a conflicted leader. When the time came to choose a king, he hid himself amongst the baggage of the large crowd that had gathered for the ceremony. He was found, however, because he was so tall. His reign as king was similar. He led with a natural ability and impressive skills, and he certainly had the most impressive armor in the land. Regretfully, King Saul often cowered, made poor decisions, and compromised situations. Later he grew increasingly paranoid and turned his back on God more frequently.

They found him and brought him out,
and he stood head and shoulders above anyone else.

1 Samuel 10:23 NLT

Why is it more important to keep the inner character of a person right with God even if they look impressive in their outward appearance?

Answer: taller

OCTOBER 26

JEREMIAH'S CALLING

TRUE OR FALSE
Jeremiah was selected after he was born to be a prophet to the nations.

God had a long-term plan for Jeremiah. The entirety of his life was to be dedicated to God. While he was still a boy, he was commissioned by God to become a prophet and speak the message of God to the nations.

At first Jeremiah protested, saying he didn't know how to speak—he was too young. But God assured him that he would be with him and protect him, that he would put his words in Jeremiah's mouth, and he would enable him to stand up against nations and kingdoms. Jeremiah's service spanned the reigns of three kings in Judah. As an old man, he was forced to exile in Egypt where he likely died while still prophesying and urging God's people to turn back to him.

The word of the Lord came to me, saying,
"Before I formed you in the womb I knew you,
before you were born I set you apart;
I appointed you as a prophet to the nations."

Jeremiah 1:4-5 NIV

How can you explain what God has called you to do with your life?

Answer: false

OCTOBER 27

SELLING LAND

Hanamel sold his land to his cousin, a prophet named _______.

When God told Jeremiah to buy some land, it must have seemed like a questionable investment. Jeremiah was imprisoned by King Zedekiah because he told the king that the Babylonians were soon going to conquer Jerusalem, and Zedekiah himself would be carried off into exile. While in prison, God told Jeremiah about his cousin's land in Anathoth, and he instructed Jeremiah to buy it. He paid the full price and sealed the deed before several witnesses. Jeremiah then asked his scribe to put the deed into a pottery jar to preserve it for a long time.

This prophetic real-estate parable shows that God always intended to bring his people back to the land of Israel. Even if the nation was conquered and people taken into exile, he would one day restore his throne in Jerusalem.

"Just as the Lord had said, my cousin Hanamel came to me in the courtyard of the guard and said, 'Buy my field at Anathoth in the territory of Benjamin. Since it is your right to redeem it and possess it, buy it for yourself.'"

Jeremiah 32:8-9 NIV

What questionable things has God asked you to do in your lifetime?

Answer: Jeremiah

JEREMIAH'S SCRIBE

What was the name of Jeremiah's scribe?

Jeremiah the prophet had a lot to say. The book of Jeremiah is one of the longest books in the Bible in terms of sheer volume. The book has the third most chapters in the Bible and the second most words. Jeremiah spent a significant amount of his time imprisoned for preaching God's message to the kings and the people of Judah. He needed a loyal scribe to get the words down and follow through with some of the edicts.

Baruch, son of Neriah, was that faithful servant. The book of Jeremiah reveals several personal conversations and struggles as Jeremiah and Baruch had to confront the people with bitter reminders and unpopular warnings. At times Baruch even had to put his life on the line in order to deliver Jeremiah's words of warning. His work was exhausting and costly, but he was as committed as his master was to being faithful to God. Read Jeremiah 45 for more about Baruch.

Jeremiah called Baruch son of Neriah, and while Jeremiah
dictated all the words the LORD had spoken to him,
Baruch wrote them on the scroll.

JEREMIAH 36:4 NIV

For what reasons do you think Jeremiah was thankful to have a faithful partner like Baruch?

Answer: Baruch

JEREMIAH'S NICKNAME

Jeremiah was known as the ________ prophet.

A. joyful
B. weeping
C. wild
D. respected

Jeremiah was tasked with a difficult job. He was appointed by God to deliver miserable news to the kings and the people of Judah. Because of their insolent attitudes, God was going to deliver them over to be conquered by the neighboring nations, the temple would be destroyed, and they would be killed or taken into exile. For years, Jeremiah had to keep sharing this news. And it broke him. Often in the book of Jeremiah, he expresses sorrow. His soul was heavy and downcast. "I hurt with the hurt of my people. I mourn and am overcome with grief" (8:21).

Later, Jesus and his message would be compared to Jeremiah (Matthew 16:14). Jesus was a man of sorrows and acquainted with deepest grief (Isaiah 53:3). Hes also wept over Jerusalem (Luke 19:41-44).

If you still refuse to listen,
I will weep alone because of your pride.
My eyes will overflow with tears,
because the LORD's flock will be led away into exile.

JEREMIAH 13:17 NLT

What does it mean to you that Jesus, like Jeremiah, experienced times of intense sadness?

Answer: B) weeping

DEN OF THIEVES

TRUE OR FALSE

When Jesus turned over the tables in the temple, he quoted the prophet Jeremiah.

In Jeremiah's day, the people in Jerusalem had a hard time fathoming that there could be anyone or anything that could destroy the temple. It had withstood many challenges over hundreds of years. It was the sign of God's throne in Judah. It was the site of God's kingdom promises for his people. And yet, the people had become lazy and compromised in their commitment to the Lord. "Don't be fooled into thinking that you will never suffer because the Temple is here," Jeremiah warned. "Do you really think you can steal, murder, commit adultery, lie, and burn incense to Baal and all those other new gods of yours, and then come here and stand before me in my Temple" (7:8-10). Soon after this, the Babylonians conquered Jerusalem and destroyed the temple.

Six hundred years later, in a temple built by King Herod the Great, Jesus entered the outer court and turned over merchants' tables. He drove out those who were changing money and buying and selling goods. Then he quoted Jeremiah 7:11. (Read Matthew 21:12-13.)

"Don't you yourselves admit that this Temple, which bears my name, has become a den of thieves? Surely I see all the evil going on there. I, the Lord, have spoken!"

Jeremiah 7:11 NLT

How does the background of Jeremiah help you better understand the context of Jesus turning over the tables in the temple?

Answer: true

NEW TABLET

The old laws of God were written on stone tablets, but the new covenant for Israel will be written on _______ _______.

The book of Jeremiah is filled with sorrow on page after page of dire warnings and horrible judgments. And yet, the book also contains verses of the most inspirational glimmers of hope. These passages of Scripture shine brightly against the backdrop of Jeremiah's darkness and depression: "Do not weep any longer. Your children will come back to you. There is hope for your future! God will cause something new to happen" (Jeremiah 31:15-22).

God said he would make a new covenant that would allow everyone, from least to greatest, to know him personally. No longer would they need to practice the old ways of sacrifice and religious decrees and laws written on stone. Instead, he said he would put his instructions on their hearts, so it would be a much more intimate relationship.

"This is the new covenant I will make with the people of Israel after those days," says the LORD. "I will put my instructions deep within them, and I will write them on their hearts. I will be their God, and they will be my people."

JEREMIAH 31:33 NLT

How did Jesus usher in this new covenant?

Answer: people's hearts

NOVEMBER

NOVEMBER 1

BE THANKFUL

The Bible says that we should be thankful in ______ circumstances.

A. good
B. some
C. most
D. all

Paul told the believers in Thessalonica to live to the extreme. We should be joyful always, pray always, and give thanks in all circumstances. Not some. Not most. But all.

As followers of Jesus, this means we live a 24/7 lifestyle. Everything we do, everything we think, everything we say is to be saturated in a pattern that is being transformed by Jesus Christ. Everywhere we walk, everywhere we drive, everywhere we go is a place we can live for Jesus. The idea of joy in the midst of frustration, or the notion of unceasing prayer, or the concept of giving thanks during times of loss can seem very difficult and foreign. But there is something in the thankful Christian life that begins to produce this sort of attitude.

> Rejoice always, pray without ceasing, in everything give thanks; for this is the will of God for you in Christ Jesus.
>
> 1 Thessalonians 5:16-18 NASB

Which of these three do you think you most need to work on: joy, prayer, or thankfulness?

Answer: D) all

CURSED TREE

What kind of tree did Jesus curse?

It was the final week of Jesus' ministry. As he entered Jerusalem, the crowds praised God and heaped blessing on him. They waved leafy branches to honor him along the road. But by the end of the week, he was rejected and crucified by these very same crowds of people.

The morning after his triumphal entry into Jerusalem, Jesus noticed a leafy fig tree. When he found that it had no fruit, he cursed it. He then went into the temple in Jerusalem, where he found money changers and merchants making deals and profiting from the complicated religious systems that people had put in place. It all looked very spiritually vibrant and productive, but it was fruitless. Jesus disrupted the market, turning over the tables. His temple was supposed to be a house of prayer for all nations, but they had turned it into a den of thieves. The next morning as they passed by the fig tree again, the disciples noticed that the fig tree had withered.

The next morning as they were leaving Bethany, Jesus was hungry. He noticed a fig tree in full leaf a little way off, so he went over to see if he could find any figs. But there were only leaves because it was too early in the season for fruit. Then Jesus said to the tree, "May no one ever eat your fruit again!" And the disciples heard him say it.

MARK 11:12-14 NLT

What is the significance of the visual parable Jesus told by cursing this fig tree?

Answer: a fig tree

CITIZENSHIP

Paul told the Philippians of Macedonia that we are citizens of ________.

A. the Roman Empire
B. Israel
C. heaven
D. the earth

Throughout his letters to the early Christians, Paul taught the theme that followers of Jesus belonged to heaven more than to the world. "We are citizens of heaven," he told the Philippians even though they were in the province of Macedonia, which was part of the Roman Empire. Paul was from Tarsus and was technically a Roman citizen. But he believed that our true home and identity is found in Christ.

It doesn't matter where we are living or where we were born, if we are followers of Jesus, we are citizens of heaven. And while here on earth we are on assignment. We are Christ's ambassadors (2 Corinthians 5:20) and messengers (1 Thessalonians 2:4). This world is not our permanent home; we are looking forward to a new home (Hebrews 13:14).

We are citizens of heaven, where the Lord Jesus Christ lives. And we are eagerly waiting for him to return as our Savior.

Philippians 3:20 NLT

With this theme in mind, read Matthew 6:19-21. How does this affect the way you live?

Answer: C) heaven

SEVENTH DAY

After God made the world, what did he do on the seventh day?

After God created the heavens and the earth, the Bible says he rested. It's not that God was tired from his labor or that he had grown weary and needed to be refreshed. It is simply that God established a rhythm for people to have a relationship with him and with the world which he made for them.

In the Bible, God told the Israelites repeatedly that they were to do all their work over six days, and rest on the seventh day. God instilled his creative and collaborative image into humankind, and he had commissioned them to care for the world the way he had during the creation. But every week, God wanted his people to be restful and restored. He wanted them to trust in him and enjoy a relationship with him.

> By the seventh day God completed His work which He had done, and He rested on the seventh day from all His work which He had done. Then God blessed the seventh day and sanctified it, because on it He rested from all His work which God had created and made.
>
> Genesis 2:2-3 NASB

How is your rhythm of work and Sabbath? What better patterns do you need to put in place each week?

Answer: he rested

THREE EXAMPLES

Who are the three people Paul mentioned in Philippians 2?

In Philippians 2, Paul urged the Christians in Philippi to be encouraging, humble, and considerate. He instructed them to live innocent lives as an offering to God. In fact, he said, they needed to have the same attitude that Christ Jesus had. And then Paul commends three individuals.

First, he commends Jesus himself. Though he is God, he chose to become human, taking on the nature of a servant and going to the cross. Second, he commends Timothy. Though times were difficult, Timothy cared deeply for the Philippian believers and also for Paul. He proved himself loyal, like a son with his father. And he preached the Gospel through all circumstances. Third, he comments Epaphroditus. Though he was near death, he was a faithful coworker and helper in Paul's times of need. He also was worried about the Philippian believers and longed to get better so he could return to them. He risked his life for the work of Christ and would continue to do so.

Don't be selfish; don't try to impress others. Be humble, thinking of others as better than yourselves. Don't look out only for your own interests, but take an interest in others, too.

Philippians 2:3-4 NLT

How do Jesus, Timothy, and Epaphroditus all exemplify God to the Philippians?

Answer: Christ Jesus, Timothy, and Epaphroditus

NOVEMBER 6

WHAT I CAN DO

FINISH THIS VERSE

I can do ____ _______ through Christ, who gives me _______.

Sometimes Paul was in prison. Sometimes he was free to travel. Sometimes he was shipwrecked. Sometimes he was alone. Sometimes he was beaten. Sometimes he was blessed. Sometimes he was starving. Sometimes he was fed. Sometimes he was lonely. Sometimes he was surrounded by friends. Sometimes he was ignored. Sometimes he was the center of attention.

In all circumstances, Paul had a secret. He knew that he could endure anything, good or bad, empty or full, because he had Christ. The same God who took care of Paul will supply our needs from his glorious riches, given to us in Christ Jesus.

I know how to live on almost nothing or with everything.
I have learned the secret of living in every situation,
whether it is with a full stomach or empty, with plenty or little.
For I can do everything through Christ, who gives me strength.

PHILIPPIANS 4:12-13 NLT

What kind of circumstances do you find yourself in today? According to Paul, what can Christ do for you?

Answer: all things; strength

SEVENTH COMMANDMENT

What is the seventh of the Ten Commandments?

When we promise to love another person in marriage, we agree to submit ourselves to a covenant relationship. We declare before witnesses that we will not love someone else. In effect we are saying, "You are my one love." To break this vow is to break the infrastructure of relationship.

The greatest commandment of all is to love God wholly. The Bible refers to God's people as the bride, and Jesus as the groom. When we agree to love God, we agree to love him alone. We don't have other gods, misuse his name, or miss a day of being with him. We don't dishonor the people he's put in our lives, or hurt his other children, or break the integrity of our relationship. The Ten Commandments are a covenant. They are far from being restrictive or burdensome because they are a freeing promise of loving relationship. They are, in fact, a marriage vow with Jesus himself as the groom.

"You shall not commit adultery."

Exodus 20:14 NIV

How can you grow deeper in your relationship with God?

Answer: you shall not commit adultery

NOVEMBER 8

SET YOUR FACE

Where did Jesus set his face to go?

As the time of the Passover celebration in Jerusalem grew closer, Jesus turned his focus on the troubled task ahead. He had ministered around Israel for three years, preaching the kingdom of God, healing the sick, demonstrating his power, and boldly claiming to be the Son of God and the Son of Man, the Messiah, and God in the flesh. He had certainly gained quite a following. Thousands upon thousands of people had seen him and interacted with him, Jew and Gentile, sinners and tax collectors, centurions and zealots, male and female, young and old. But he had also gained enemies. And he knew it was time to begin making his way to the cross.

Jesus set his face to go to Jerusalem. He was resolutely determined to go. He did not waiver. He did not question. He knew it was what he had come to earth to do.

When the days drew near for him to be taken up,
he set his face to go to Jerusalem.

Luke 9:51 ESV

Jesus knew during his years of ministry that he had come to give his life as a ransom for many (Mark 10:45). What does this statement stir in you as you think about him?

Answer: Jerusalem

JESUS BREATHED ON THEM

When Jesus breathed on his disciples, was it before or after the resurrection?

On the same day as his resurrection, Jesus appeared to his disciples. They were meeting behind locked doors, reeling from the violent events of the three days before when Jesus was beaten and crucified. They were afraid of more persecution and were certainly distraught. But then Jesus appeared in their midst! "Peace be with you," he said in an almost matter-of-fact manner. He showed them the wounds in his hands and sides. To say it must have been quite a moment is an eternal understatement.

Then Jesus commissioned them. "Just as the Father has sent me, so I am sending you," he told them. John, an eyewitness of this moment, stated that Jesus breathed on them. What a memorable thing to do. Jesus breathed his last breath on the cross, his dead lungs collapsed and punctured by a Roman spear, his dead body sent to a grave. And now he breathed on them. A resurrection breath!

"Peace be with you. As the Father has sent me,
so I am sending you." Then he breathed on them and said,
"Receive the Holy Spirit."

John 20:21-22 NLT

The Hebrew word for spirit is ruach, which also means "breath" or "wind." What deep significance did Jesus' breathing on the disciples have in this moment?

Answer: after the resurrection

NOVEMBER 10

THE VINE

Jesus taught that he is the vine and we are the _______.

A. fruit
B. branches
C. leaves
D. vineyard

Jesus compared himself to the true vine, God the Father to the vinedresser, and his followers to the branches. Every branch that does not bear fruit he takes away, but those that bear fruit are pruned so they can bear more fruit. Either way, we are getting cut. The question is whether we'll be cut off and thrown in a fire or trimmed so the fruitfulness of our lives can become even more abundant.

We can do nothing if we do not abide, or remain, in Jesus. We have to be part of the vine in order to produce fruit. Abiding in Jesus means we stay close in his love. We connect with him in daily, authentic relationship. That is what he wants from us. To be with us.

"I am the vine; you are the branches.
Whoever abides in me and I in him,
he it is that bears much fruit,
for apart from me you can do nothing."

John 15:5 ESV

Read John 15:1-17. What do you notice about the honesty and intimacy of Jesus' heart for you?

Answer: B) branches

MOST MENTIONED

What three names of people are mentioned more than any others in the Bible?

The name of Moses is mentioned significantly more than all but two others in the Bible. It is used around eight hundred times, depending on the translation consulted. The fourth most mentioned, interestingly, is Jacob with over three hundred and fifty references. The story of the Bible cannot be told without Moses, who led the Israelites out of Egypt and then gave them the law of God. His face-to-face relationship with God is a picture of what everyone can have through Jesus. The second-most mentioned name in the Bible is David. It is used almost a thousand times. His significance as a biblical fulcrum figure cannot be underestimated. He was the king from whom the King of kings would be born. He was the man after God's own heart and the one who united Israel into a single nation.

The most mentioned name of a person in the Bible is Jesus. His name is used around thirteen hundred times. This is appropriate after all since the Bible is ultimately about Jesus—the fulfillment of the Law and the Prophets. Interestingly, while he is foreshadowed and referenced frequently throughout the Old Testament, the name *Jesus* is only used directly in the New Testament.

Whoever confesses that Jesus is the Son of God,
God abides in him, and he in God.

1 John 4:15 ESV

In a couple of sentences, can you explain how Moses and David prepared the way for Jesus?

Answer: Jesus, David, and Moses

NOVEMBER 12

STONE PAVEMENT

What was the Hebrew name for the stone pavement platform that held Pilate's judgment seat?

Pilate was concerned that Jesus wasn't talking. He knew Jesus was innocent, but the religious leaders were demanding his crucifixion, and the crowds that were gathered for the Passover festival were turning into a bloodthirsty mob. They accused Jesus of calling himself God.

Pilate tried to release him, but the leaders put the charges against Jesus in Roman terms. "He has declared himself the King of the Jews. Only Caesar is king!" they challenged Pilate. Pilate brought Jesus out again and he sat down on the judgment seat on the platform called Gabbatha. "Look, here is your king." "We have no king but Caesar!" So, Pilate from his judgment seat turned Jesus over to be crucified.

When Pilate heard these words, he brought Jesus out and sat down on the judgment seat at a place called The Stone Pavement, and in Aramaic Gabbatha.

JOHN 19:13 ESV

From what you know of the biblical story, was Gabbatha the true judgment seat in God's eyes?

Answer: Gabbatha

PAUL'S WRITING PARTNER

Who wrote 1 Corinthians along with Paul?

The name of Sosthenes appears in two separate places in the Bible. Once is here in 1 Corinthians. No background or insight is given as to who he is or why he is helping Paul send a letter to the believers in Corinth. The other time the name of Sosthenes is mentioned, intriguingly, is at an earlier date in the city of Corinth. Acts 18 records Paul's missionary journey to the city. The leader of the local synagogue, a man named Crispus, believed in Jesus and his whole household was baptized.

Paul stayed in Corinth for the next eighteen months sharing the Gospel. But some Jewish leaders seized Paul and brought him before the local governor in an attempt to have him arrested. When the governor told them to release Paul and take care of the disturbances themselves, the mob seized the new leader of the synagogue, Sosthenes, and beat him in the courtroom. Some scholars suspect that Sosthenes had permitted Paul to continue preaching about Jesus.

This letter is from Paul, chosen by the will of God to be an apostle of Christ Jesus, and from our brother Sosthenes.

1 Corinthians 1:1 NLT

If these two references are about the same Sosthenes, what would this reveal about the transforming power of the gospel?

Answer: Sosthenes

RICH IN GOOD WORKS

Paul says that those who are rich should not trust in _______ but trust in _______.

Having a lot of money is not a problem according to Paul. Trusting in money, however, is. Paul urged Timothy to help those who were wealthy to use their money to do good, to be rich in good works, to be generous, and ready to share.

When we behave this way, we are storing up our treasure in heaven instead of on earth. Money is temporary and unreliable. It can give people a false sense of security and a sick sense of arrogance. But if the wealthy are generous, they will become more satisfied with their lives, and they will be rewarded later by God.

As for the rich in this present age, charge them not to be haughty, nor to set their hopes on the uncertainty of riches, but on God, who richly provides us with everything to enjoy.

1 Timothy 6:17 ESV

What has God blessed you with? How could you use your richness generously today?

Answer: money; God

LOVED FIRST

FINISH THIS VERSE

God demonstrates His own love toward us, in that while we were still sinners, Christ ________ ________ ________.

Even while we were in the midst of rejecting him, Jesus Christ gave up his life so we could be restored to a relationship with God. While we mocked him, ridiculed him, and spat on him, he still chose to hang on the cross.

Jesus could have gotten himself off the cross. He could have freed himself. He could have defended himself. But he wasn't interested in saving himself. He wanted to save us. That's how much he loves us—unto death.

God demonstrates His own love toward us,
in that while we were still sinners, Christ died for us.

ROMANS 5:8 NKJV

Considering the truth of Romans 5:8, what words of prayer do you want to lift up to Jesus?

Answer: died for us

NOVEMBER 16

PICKING UP STONES

Why did the Jews pick up stones to kill Jesus when he said, "I and the Father are one?"

One winter, during Hanukkah, Jesus was walking around a part of the temple called Solomon's Colonnade. Crowds gathered around him and demanded that he be straight forward with them and tell them whether or not he was the Messiah. Jesus responded that he had already told them and already showed them. They didn't believe him because they weren't his sheep. He said he had given his followers eternal life, and no one could take them away from him. He then said that he and the Father were one.

At this, the crowd picked up stones to kill Jesus. He reminded them that he had done many good works and asked which of those works they were stoning him for. "We're stoning you for blasphemy! You, a mere man, claim to be God!" (John 10:33)

"I and the Father are one."
The Jews picked up stones again to stone him.
John 10:30-31 ESV

Why did people have such extreme reactions to Jesus' claims?

Answer: he was blaspheming by saying he was God

NOVEMBER 17

POINT OF SCRIPTURE

Jesus said that the Scriptures point to ________.

A. Israel
B. mankind's purpose
C. creation
D. him

Sometimes even the most well-intentioned believers can miss the point. Many people jump into the Bible searching for hope and encouragement, wisdom and truth. They'll pour over passages and try their best to memorize inspirational verses. But all spiritual practice can be meaningless in the long run if it fails to recognize Jesus. No amount of Bible knowledge can save someone from their sins unless that person sees Jesus in the Scriptures and calls out to him.

Jesus wants us to receive the life he offers by seeing him in the Bible. From Genesis to Revelation, all of the Scriptures point to him. The Bible itself is not the lifesaver. Jesus is.

"You search the Scriptures because you think they give you eternal life. But the Scriptures point to me!"

John 5:39 NLT

Why is it easier for some people to study the Bible than it is for them to know Jesus?

Answer: D) him

NOVEMBER 18

WHAT MATTERS

TRUE OR FALSE
Paul wrote that it doesn't matter if you are a Jew or a Gentile.

Every single person is invited to receive Jesus as their Savior. It doesn't matter if that person is rich or poor, powerful or weak, healthy or sick. Everyone is invited to believe in Jesus and to be made right with God. The sinners and the tax collectors, the lepers and the lame, they all are invited to dine with Jesus. The promiscuous and the prideful, the religious and the rude, they all are able to give their lives over to Jesus Christ, their Redeemer.

The invitation of Jesus disrupts the class systems and the prejudices of the world. People find their true worth not in the infrastructures and perceptions of mankind, but in Jesus Christ. Paul urged us to come to Christ and put on our new nature and be renewed as we learn to know our Creator and become like him. In terms of your identity, Christ is all that matters.

In this new life, it doesn't matter if you are a Jew or a Gentile, circumcised or uncircumcised, barbaric, uncivilized, slave, or free. Christ is all that matters, and he lives in all of us.

COLOSSIANS 3:11 NLT

You are defined not by who you are but by whose you are. How does this change your view of yourself?

Answer: true

NOVEMBER 19

LONGEST SENTENCE

What verses contain the longest sentence in the Bible?

Scholars have generally agreed that Ephesians 1:3-4 is one long sentence in the original Greek writing. The apostle Paul's lengthy stream of Greek words at the beginning of his letter to the Christians in Ephesus, in most of our modern English translations, has been broken into multiple, bite-sized, sentences. Still, even the modern translations have the verse markers in awkward mid-sentence locations that steer the reader to the larger context of the verses around it.

Today, we would perhaps consider Paul's lengthy sentence to be more like a paragraph containing a bullet-point list of punchy statements, or even a series of dashes and colons filled with witty commentary. No matter the exact grammatical structure, certainly this section of Ephesians, along with the long sentence-like list that follows it in Ephesians 1:15-21, is a brilliant theological summary of who Jesus is and what he has done.

Blessed be the God and Father of our Lord Jesus Christ, who has blessed us with every spiritual blessing in the heavenly places in Christ, just as He chose us in Him before the foundation of the world, that we would be holy and blameless before Him.

EPHESIANS 1:3-4 NASB

Take a few minutes to read all Ephesians chapter one. What points stand out to you the most?

Answer: Ephesians 1:3-4

CHRIST LIVES IN ME

Paul told the Galatians, "My old self has been _______ with Christ."

A. crucified

B. won

C. wrestling

D. at odds

When we give our lives to Jesus we are made right with God. Before that, even if we tried to be good enough and follow God's commands, we would still have fallen short of God's standards. We couldn't help but occasionally mess up and sin, disobeying something in God's commandments. Because of Jesus' death on the cross, our missteps and sins against the law of God are forgiven.

Paul taught the Galatian church that no one would ever be made right with God by obeying the law. We are only made right with God by faith in Jesus Christ. As those who have accepted Jesus as the Savior, we can allow him live within us today. Let's give Christ full rule of our hearts and minds.

> My old self has been crucified with Christ. It is no longer I who live, but Christ lives in me. So I live in this earthly body by trusting in the Son of God, who loved me and gave himself for me.
>
> GALATIANS 2:20 NLT

What difference will it make to you today that Jesus lives in you?

Answer: A) crucified

FOUR LIVING CREATURES

In Revelation 4, what did the four living creatures keep saying day after day and night after night?

John was overwhelmed by his vision. He heard a voice that sounded like a trumpet blast. He saw a throne in heaven and someone sitting on it. The throne was shining brilliantly with a spectrum of light emanating from it, and there were four living creatures around the throne. The first looked like a lion, the second an ox, the third had a human face, and the fourth looked like an eagle in flight. Each of the creatures had six wings covered with eyes inside and out.

Whenever these creatures sang, John says that there were twenty-four elders who would fall down to worship the one who was sitting on the throne. God is worthy to receive all the glory and honor and power because he is the Creator of all things.

Each of the four living creatures had six wings and was covered with eyes all around, even under its wings. Day and night they never stop saying: "'Holy, holy, holy is the LORD God Almighty,'
who was, and is, and is to come."

REVELATION 4:8 NIV

What do you think is happening in this vision and how does it impact you today?

Answer: Holy, holy, holy is the Lord God Almighty

THE GATEKEEPERS

How many gatekeepers did David and Samuel appoint to guard the tabernacle of the Lord?

When the people of Judah began to return to Jerusalem after the exile to Babylon, they needed to rebuild the walls of the city and restore it to safe, defensible conditions. An important step in this process was to organize a group of armed gatekeepers who would watch those who entered the temple mount.

When the gatekeepers were first organized, Samuel set up two hundred and twelve gatekeepers for the city, and David followed that pattern. The records of 1 Chronicles inform us that in early times Phinehas, son of Eleazar, was the official in charge of the gatekeepers, and the Lord was with him. The descendants of the original gatekeepers who were able to return to Jerusalem, such as Zechariah son of Meshelemiah, Shallum, Akkub, Talmon, Ahiman, and others, were commissioned with the responsibility.

Altogether, those chosen to be gatekeepers at the thresholds numbered 212. They were registered by genealogy in their villages. The gatekeepers had been assigned to their positions of trust by David and Samuel the seer.

1 Chronicles 9:22 NIV

Read 1 Chronicles 9 and consider how strategically important the gatekeepers were. What roles in modern churches might be similar today?

Answer: two hundred and twelve

NOVEMBER 23

RETURN TO WHAT

As a dog returns to its _______, so fools repeat their folly.

A. master
B. vomit
C. dog bowl
D. home

Occasionally the Bible can be shocking with its raw depiction of real-life stories and honest articulation of life's truths. The book of Proverbs, in particular, can be brutally graphic with its words of wisdom.

In the verse today we are given a visual presentation of the disgusting nature of foolish behavior. A dog that has regurgitated its food will return to it afterward with compulsive curiosity. It's as if the dog cannot keep itself from sniffing and examining the mess, testing whether it should be ingested again. This is how fools behave. Fools do something idiotic or reckless and fail to learn from their mistakes. A fool repeats the same sort of idiotic, reckless behavior again and again without recognizing the damage he is causing to himself or to those around him.

As a dog returns to its vomit,
so fools repeat their folly.

PROVERBS 26:11 NIV

Examine your own life. What foolish, repetitive habits might you have? Ask the Lord to point them out to you and equip you to avoid the same mistakes.

Answer: B) vomit

NOVEMBER 24

GIDEON'S REQUEST

When Gideon asked God for a sign, what did he use for the test?

Twice Gideon tested God. The Lord had empowered him with his Spirit as Israel's judge against their eastern enemies. But Gideon was apprehensive and wanted to make sure that God really was going to use him to rescue Israel as promised. So, Gideon devised a test.

He told God he would put out a wool fleece at night. In the morning, if the fleece was wet and the ground was dry, then Gideon would know God was with him. When Gideon got up the morning, the ground was dry, and he wrung out a whole bowlful of water from the fleece. Still anxious, he begged for God's patience. He wanted to make sure. Gideon told God he would put the fleece out again, but this time he wanted to see the fleece dry and the ground wet in the morning. The Lord passed Gideon's test, proving he would be with him.

Gideon said to God, "Please don't be angry with me, but let me make one more request. Let me use the fleece for one more test. This time let the fleece remain dry while the ground around it is wet with dew."

JUDGES 6:39 NLT

Why do you think God was patient with Gideon's request for a sign?

Answer: a wool fleece

SAUL'S REIGN

How old was Saul when he became king? And how many years did he reign?

Saul became king at thirty years old and reigned for forty-two years. His reign was marked by tremendous successes, but also remarkable failures. He united and divided Israel with his inconsistent dedication to God. He rallied armies to impressive victories, but also led them into terrible defeats. His back-and-forth battles against the Philistines were a constant thorn in his side. At times he was filled with the Spirit of the Lord and showed awesome power and charisma. At other times, he pursued pagan rituals, struggled with paranoia, and showed more interest in protecting himself than the people of Israel.

Saul's reign grew more complicated after God rejected him as king and asked the prophet Samuel to anoint David as the new king. David's victory over Goliath, his musical skills, and his popularity ate away at Saul's soul. Saul conspired against David and dedicated much of his remaining reign to hunting him down. At seventy-two years old, dejected, weakened, and wounded by an arrow in battle, Saul fell on his own sword rather than be captured by the enemy.

Saul was thirty years old when he became king,
and he reigned for forty-two years.

1 Samuel 13:1 NLT

How can someone stay faithful to God for the duration of their life?

Answer: thirty years old; forty-two years

NOVEMBER 26

BIBLICAL LANGUAGES

In what three languages was the Bible was originally written?

The two primary languages of the Bible are Hebrew and Greek; a few passages are in Aramaic. Hebrew was the primary language of the Old Testament. It was the language of the Jewish people, but Aramaic was present. "Then Eliakim…said to the Assyrian chief of staff, 'Please speak to us in Aramaic, for we understand it well. Don't speak in Hebrew, for the people on the wall will hear'" (2 Kings 18:26). Hebrew fell into some disuse during the exilic period, when the men of Judah had married women from Ashdod, Ammon, and Moab. "Furthermore, half their children spoke the language of Ashdod or of some other people and could not speak the language of Judah at all" (Nehemiah 13:24). As a result, for quite some time of history, Aramaic became the more popular spoken language in Israel.

Before the Romans conquered Israel, Greek culture had spread and taken root. The koine Greek, the common language, became the universal language spoken throughout the Middle East and the Mediterranean regions. Therefore, the New Testament was written in Greek.

The LORD said to Moses, "Write down all these instructions, for they represent the terms of the covenant I am making with you and with Israel."

EXODUS 34:27 NLT

What role do the biblical languages play in God's Word?

Answer: Hebrew, Aramaic, and Greek

SAYINGS OF ECCLESIASTES

TRUE OR FALSE
King Solomon's wisdom made him always see the bright side of life.

Ecclesiastes repeats several phrases that give voice to some of the most disparaging thoughts of humankind. Solomon concluded that everything is meaningless; it's like chasing the wind. The king bemoaned that as his knowledge increased, so did his sorrow. "There is nothing new under the sun," he cried over two dozen times.

Overwhelmingly, he used the word *meaningless* nearly forty times. The book weighs against cheerfulness and challenges any attempt at an optimistic view of life. And yet, it is not an aimless book that wallows in despair. It is instead a raw and honest look into the eternal mystery of God, and the fragile existence of mankind. There is an unmistakable trust in the Lord that serves as a through-line for the book. God is an unshakable truth, which causes the uncertainty of human experiences to quiver. The final conclusion is to fear God and keep his commandments.

The words of the Teacher, son of David, king in Jerusalem:
"Meaningless! Meaningless!"
says the Teacher.
"Utterly meaningless!
Everything is meaningless."

ECCLESIASTES 1:1-2 NIV

Which saying or verse in Ecclesiastes resonates the most with you?

Answer: false

SHORTEST SONG

What is the shortest recorded song in the Bible?

The year that Solomon finished constructing the temple, he gathered the men of Israel during the Feast of Tabernacles. He had the Levites carry the ark of the covenant into the inner sanctuary of the temple. Everyone purified themselves, showing the sacredness of this dedication day. The Levites who were musicians, including Asaph who wrote many of the Psalms, were dressed in fine linen robes and stood on the east side of the temple playing their instruments including cymbals, lyres, harps, and trumpets.

Along with the instruments, a large choir of musicians raised their voices and praised the Lord. Amazingly, at that moment a thick cloud filled the temple. The priests could not continue their service because of the cloud—the glorious presence of God was too strong.

The trumpeters and singers performed together in unison to praise and give thanks to the Lord. Accompanied by trumpets, cymbals, and other instruments, they raised their voices and praised the Lord with these words:
"He is good! His faithful love endures forever!"
At that moment a thick cloud filled the Temple of the Lord.

2 Chronicles 5:13 NLT

Why is it important for God's people to sing praise songs?

Answer: 2 Chronicles 5:13

REVELATION SONGS

TRUE OR FALSE
There are several songs recorded in the book of Revelation.

Many people often assume that the book of Revelation is a weird apocalyptic vision filled with ominous predictions about the end of the world. While that is one aspect of the book, there are several other key themes and sections that may be surprising to contemporary readers.

Revelation 4-7 contains several poetic stanzas of songs. Most of the songs are about Jesus, the Lamb, and they praise him and recognize his place on the throne of God. They bestow blessing and honor upon him and are sung in a posture of awe, often with angels and people falling to their faces in worship.

Then I heard every creature in heaven and on earth and under the earth and in the sea. They sang:
"Blessing and honor and glory and power
belong to the one sitting on the throne
and to the Lamb forever and ever."

REVELATION 5:13 NLT

What song can you think of that uses the words from the songs of Revelation?

Answer: true

MOST EXCELLENT

Which books of the Bible are addressed to Theophilus?

Luke wrote two books to Theophilus. The first book was about the ministry of Jesus from his birth through his resurrection. In this second book, Luke informs him about the dynamic spread of the gospel through the power of the Holy Spirt, and the final half of it through Luke's eyewitness account.

Very little is known about Theophilus. He does not appear anywhere else in Scripture except in the greeting addresses of Luke and Acts. He is called "most excellent Theophilus" in Acts, or "most honorable Theophilus" in Luke 1:3. This may indicate that he was a man of importance like a nobleman or a high-ranking Roman official. Around that time, there are references to a wealthy man in Antioch named Theophilus who some have speculated was a major benefactor of the dynamic Christian movement which was launched from there. It would fit that Luke was commissioned by such a man to write down a historical account of the life, death, and resurrection of Jesus as well as the spread of his message across the Roman Empire.

In my first book I told you, Theophilus, about everything Jesus began to do and teach until the day he was taken up to heaven after giving his chosen apostles further instructions through the Holy Spirit.

Acts 1:1-2 NLT

Even if we can't be sure who Theophilus was, how does knowing that Luke and Acts were written to a real person in a real time period change the way you read these books?

Answer: Luke and Acts

DECEMBER

DECEMBER 1

FORSAKEN LOVE

Which of the churches mentioned in the book of Revelation is accused of having forsaken their first love?

The gospel established deep roots in city of Ephesus. Paul used it as a base of operations for branching the missionary work throughout the world. A fruitful and productive church community emerged which impacted Christians for generations. Paul's letter to the Ephesians is one of the most personal, encouraging, and theologically enlightening sections of the whole Bible. The followers of Jesus in that city led the way for other believers elsewhere to endure hardships in cultures that made a lifestyle of faith in Jesus difficult.

By the time John wrote his Revelation, Jesus had a worrying critique. The church had forsaken the love it had at first. Jesus wanted the Ephesians to rekindle the love they once had for him and get back to doing what they had been good at—living out the gospel and being a light in a dark world.

"I hold this against you:
You have forsaken the love you had at first."
REVELATION 2:4 NIV

Why do we let the vibrancy of our faith grow dim?

Answer: the church in Ephesus

NUMBER OF FISH

How many fish did the disciples catch when the Resurrected Jesus told them to throw their nets on the right side of the boat?

After Jesus' resurrection, Peter and several of the disciples went fishing in the Sea of Galilee. They were out all night but caught nothing. In the morning as they returned, a man on the beach asked them if they had caught any fish. Not realizing that the man was Jesus, they told him they had not caught anything. The man told them to throw their net on the right-hand side of the boat and they would get some. When they did, they couldn't haul in the net because it was too full of fish.

That's when Peter realized it was Jesus. He jumped straight in the water and swam the hundred yards to the shore. The others pulled on the nets and made their way in the boats. Once back on the beach, the disciples found Jesus already preparing a breakfast of fish and bread, cooked over a charcoal fire. When they counted their catch on the beach, the catch numbered 153 large fish.

Simon Peter went aboard and dragged the net to the shore. There were 153 large fish, and yet the net hadn't torn.

JOHN 21:11 NLT

Why do you think Jesus waited to appear until after they had fished all night without catching anything?

Answer: one hundred and fifty-three

DECEMBER 3

BOUND FOR THE ABYSS

In the book of Revelation, the angel binds Satan and throws him into the Abyss for what length of time?

In Revelation, a mighty cosmic war is waged between the Lamb of God and the forces of Satan. After Jesus' victory in the final battle, an angel comes down from heaven holding the key to the abyss in one hand and a great chain in the other. He seized the dragon, the ancient serpent, who is the devil, or Satan, and bound him for a thousand years. Like a prison guard, the angel throws him into the abyss and locks and seals him inside. While imprisoned, Satan will not be able to deceive the nations any more.

John saw that after a thousand years, Satan would be released and allowed to gather his massive forces from all over the earth. But Jesus will then rain down fire upon them. The devil will be thrown into the lake of burning sulfur to be tormented forever.

He threw him into the Abyss, and locked and sealed it over him, to keep him from deceiving the nations anymore until the thousand years were ended. After that, he must be set free for a short time.

REVELATION 20:3 NIV

Why is this vision an important bookend to the Bible?

Answer: one thousand years

DECEMBER 4

BEGINNING OF KNOWLEDGE

What does the Bible say is the beginning of knowledge?

The purpose of the book of Proverbs is not to demonstrate how great Solomon's wisdom was. It is true that he was very wise. The Bible even claims that he was the wisest person in the world and that people would come from around the world to listen to his measureless insight (1 Kings 4:29-34). But Solomon also came to realize how foolish he was. As is often the point of several of the saying in Proverbs, Solomon failed to follow through on his much of his own wisdom.

The purpose of the book of Proverbs is to live a life that respects God and walk in step with his guidance. It is the foolish person who fails to heed the insight of this collection. But it is the wise person who pursues God's patterns in humility with a posture of learning. A disciple of Jesus is a learner of him. Disciples assume a posture of submission to God's will for their life. God's way gives understanding to why we are here and what we are to do.

The fear of the Lord is the beginning of knowledge;
but fools despise wisdom and instruction.

Proverbs 1:7 NIV

What is your favorite saying from the book of Proverbs?

Answer: the fear of the Lord

DECEMBER 5

THE MESSIANIC ANGEL

Which angel who appeared to Daniel, later appeared to Zechariah and the virgin, Mary?

Daniel was terrified when Gabriel first appeared to him. But Gabriel assured him with a gentle touch and helped him to his feet. "I am here," Gabriel told Daniel, "to tell you what will happen later" (8:17-19). The second time Gabriel appeared to Daniel, he revealed that the Messiah, the Anointed One, would come to Jerusalem and be killed, appearing to have accomplished nothing, and the temple would then be destroyed by a ruler and his armies.

Later, Gabriel appeared to Zechariah to let him know that his son, John, would prepare the way for the Messiah. Zechariah was overwhelmed by this encounter and couldn't speak until the child was born (Luke 1:5-25). Gabriel then appeared to Mary in Nazareth to tell her that she would be the mother of Jesus, the Son of the Most High, whose kingdom would never end.

As I was praying, Gabriel, whom I had seen in the earlier vision, came swiftly to me at the time of the evening sacrifice. He explained to me, "Daniel, I have come here to give you insight and understanding."

DANIEL 9:21-22 NLT

How do you see the Old and New Testaments working together in the story of Gabriel?

Answer: Gabriel

DECEMBER 6

THE ARCHANGEL

Besides Gabriel, who is the only other unfallen angel to be mentioned by name in the Bible?

The Bible teaches that angels have great purpose. Angels appear frequently throughout the Bible, but only two are mentioned by name. Gabriel introduced Daniel to God's plans for the future Messiah and played an important role in the nativity of Christ. His presence stirred fear in Daniel, Zechariah, and Mary.

In addition to the fearsome Gabriel, is the angel Michael. His name is mentioned in Daniel 10, 12, Jude 1, and Revelation 12. He is called the *archangel*, or "chief angel." He is a warrior, fighting spiritual battles against the devil and evil forces. He is also called "the great prince who protects Israel." He will lead the battle that overcomes the dragon in the book of Revelation. As one of the commanders of God's armies, he works with other angels to do God's will.

"At that time Michael, the archangel who stands guard over your nation, will arise. Then there will be a time of anguish greater than any since nations first came into existence. But at that time every one of your people whose name is written in the book will be rescued."

Daniel 12:1 NLT

Do you think about the spiritual battles that are happening around you every day?

Answer: Michael

EIGHTH COMMANDMENT

What is the eighth of the Ten Commandments?

Jesus compared Satan to a thief who comes only to steal and kill and destroy where Jesus had given life to the full (John 10:10). According to 1 Corinthians 6:10, because of the wickedness of their hearts, thieves will not inherit the kingdom of God. Their attempt to grasp things on earth will prove to be their eternal ruin. God will not reward those who betray him and others by raiding the storehouses prematurely.

The thieves who come to Christ have an opportunity to use their hands for work. In fact, they can use their talented hands for works of service, sharing with people in need. This can be seen in the life of Zacchaeus, who realized he had stolen from the poor and cheated people out of their possessions. He was profoundly changed by Jesus, and voluntarily began to give away his estate and pay people back generously (Luke 19).

"You shall not steal."

Exodus 20:15 NIV

There is a stark contrast between the way of Jesus and the way of the thief. What do you need to do today to walk in the way of Jesus?

Answer: you shall not steal

DECEMBER 8

CROWN HIM KING

When a crown was first placed on Jesus' head, what was it made of?

The first crown given to Jesus during his earthly ministry was in ridicule. As the soldiers ripped apart his back with a lead-tipped whip, they crudely wove together branches of thorns into a crown and pressed it down on his head. They put him in a purple robe, symbolizing royalty, hailed him the king of the Jews and slapped him repeatedly across the face.

Jesus wears other crowns in the Bible too. For instance, in John's Revelation, Jesus wears a gold crown and holds a sharp sickle as he prepares for the harvest of the nations. Later he also wears many crowns on his head as he goes into battle with eyes of fire, a robe dripping with blood, and a sword coming out of his mouth. He is the King of all kings and the Lord of all lords.

Pilate had Jesus flogged with a lead-tipped whip. The soldiers wove a crown of thorns and put it on his head, and they put a purple robe on him. "Hail! King of the Jews!" they mocked, as they slapped him across the face.

John 19:1-3 NLT

Consider the crowns Jesus wears. What does this reveal about who he is and the mission he is on?

Answer: thorns

DECEMBER 9

SPOKEN OF

In his third letter, does John speak highly of Diotrephes and poorly of Demetrius, or the other way around?

Besides John himself, three names are mentioned in the short letter of 3 John. First is Gaius, John's dear friend, to whom John sent this letter. This was a popular name and is not necessarily the same Gaius as the others who appear throughout the New Testament. Many of these men named Gaius were instrumental in supporting and organizing the growth of Christianity across the Roman Empire.

Second, John mentioned Diotrephes, who appears to have been a self-proclaimed leader in the church. He is a bad example, John said. He made accusations against John and the church. He refused to help people and divided the church. Third, in contrast to Diotrephes, John mentioned Demetrius. "Everyone speaks highly" of him, "as does the truth itself."

I wrote to the church about this, but Diotrephes, who loves to be the leader, refuses to have anything to do with us.

3 John 9 NLT

If your name were included in a letter that talked about your church, what would be said of you?

Answer: other way around

PAUL'S HANDWRITING

In which three letters does Paul finish by pointing out his own handwriting?

Paul often used a scribe to write his letters. In Romans 16, for instance, a man named Tertius identified himself as the one writing the letter for Paul. But Paul usually wanted to be the one to finish the letters, giving a greeting to his friends along with a final blessing.

In 1 Corinthians 16:21 Paul simply wrote, "Here is my greeting in my own handwriting—Paul." In Galatians 6:11 Paul wrapped up the letter by writing, "Notice what large letters I use as I write these closing words in my own handwriting." Whenever he made this note, he wanted to make sure that the readers knew the letter came from him. It was a way for him to personally authenticate the message to the recipients of the letter.

Here is my greeting in my own handwriting—Paul.
I do this in all my letters to prove they are from me.

2 Thessalonians 3:17 NLT

Why do you think it was important to Paul to end his letters in his own handwriting?

Answer: 1 Corinthians, Galatians, and 2 Thessalonians

DECEMBER 11

JESUS' BAPTISM

What did the voice from heaven say when Jesus was baptized?

John the Baptist prepared the way for Jesus. He preached about the kingdom of God and encouraged people to repent of their sins. Baptism is a symbolic practice people use to declare that they wanted to be washed of their sins, to die to themselves, and to be made clean and alive again through God's forgiveness and mercy. As he did this ministry, John told people that the true Lamb of God who takes away the sins of the world, was about to arrive.

When Jesus came to the Jordan river to be baptized by John, John tied to deter him. Jesus, after all, had nothing to repent of. Jesus told John that it must happen as a fulfillment of what was to come. This act is rewarded in a moment of remarkable insight into the Trinity, Father, Son, and Holy Spirit together in the mission to save humanity.

> As soon as Jesus was baptized, he went up out of the water. At that moment heaven was opened, and he saw the Spirit of God descending like a dove and alighting on him. And a voice from heaven said, "This is my Son, whom I love; with him I am well pleased."
>
> MATTHEW 3:16-17 NIV

Why does the Bible encourage all believers to be baptized?

Answer: This is my Son, whom I love; with him I am well pleased.

DECEMBER 12

PERSONAL NATURE

Which of the following people are included in the letter to Titus?

A. Zenas
B. Apollos
C. Artemas
D. Tychicus

Many people don't realize that much of the Bible was written in a personal, social manner. Many of the Psalms are intimate prayers of connection with God. The Song of Songs is blushingly relational. The book of Job is a conversation—or rather, an argument?—between friends. The books of Luke and Acts were written to a friend named Theophilus, so that he would know about Jesus and the spread of Christianity.

Likewise, the Epistles in the New Testament are personal letters. James, Peter, and John each wrote some of them. Paul wrote at least thirteen of them, and in each he addressed a particular group of people. In his letter to Titus, he added personal notes about other people. He ended his letter to Titus by telling him that everyone he was with also sent their greetings and asked that Titus give his love to everyone in Crete.

> As soon as I send Artemas or Tychicus to you, do your best to come to me at Nicopolis, because I have decided to winter there. Do everything you can to help Zenas the lawyer and Apollos on their way and see that they have everything they need.
>
> TITUS 3:12-13 NIV

Why is it important to read the Bible as a personal message and not a textbook?

Answer: all of them

DECEMBER 13

BOOK OF EZRA

The book of Ezra occurs during the reign of which king?

As Jeremiah prophesied, God orchestrated events so the people of Israel could return to Jerusalem and begin rebuilding the temple. The Lord moved the heart of Cyrus king of Persia to make a proclamation that the Jewish people were allowed to return to Judah to resurrect their nation and their livelihood in Jerusalem. King Cyrus, Ezra the priest tells us, also allowed Israel to carry back many of the items that Nebuchadnezzar had stolen from the temple.

The book of Ezra is precise in many of the details of the return from exile. It records census data, lists of items that were returned to Jerusalem, and the names of project managers, priests, servants, and so on, needed for the reconstruction efforts. Ezra's skill and deliberate care helped organize the nation and defend Israel from the local nations that tried to disrupt the rebuilding. In his role as priest, Ezra also led the people into a reconstructed relationship of faith in God.

In the first year of Cyrus king of Persia, in order to fulfill the word of the LORD spoken by Jeremiah, the LORD moved the heart of Cyrus king of Persia to make a proclamation throughout his realm and also to put it in writing.

EZRA 1:1 NIV

In what ways do you need to be more deliberate about the construction of your faith in God?

Answer: King Cyrus of Persia

LAMENTATIONS

What is the book of Lamentations lamenting about?

The overwhelming heartache in the book of Lamentations is difficult to absorb. People don't typically put any verses from this book on their inspirational posters or social media posts. In its pages, Jeremiah the prophet empathized deeply with the pain that the people of Jerusalem were experiencing. He looked out over the city and wept. There is nothing he could say to make things better. The people had turned their backs on God and were therefore destroyed as conquering nations came rolling in.

In its context, this book is one of the most profound glimpses into the heart of a man of sorrows. Jeremiah longs to send a comforter who can heal the wounds of his people.

What can I say for you?
With what can I compare you, Daughter Jerusalem?
To what can I liken you, that I may comfort you,
Virgin Daughter Zion?
Your wound is as deep as the sea.
Who can heal you?

LAMENTATIONS 2:13 NIV

How is Jesus the fulfillment of this overwhelmingly honest and gut-wrenching book?

Answer: the destruction of Jerusalem

DECEMBER 15

NO ANXIETY

FINISH THIS VERSE

Do not be anxious about anything, but in every situation, by ____________ and ____________, with ____________, present your requests to God.

Perhaps the most difficult thing to do is to trust God enough so that we avoid anxiety. It is really easy to be overwhelmed with worry. There are many reasons to be stressed and many burdens that we bear.

Jesus encouraged his followers to not worry; Matthew wrote about this at length in his gospel. In Philippians 4, Paul encourages us to not let anything overwhelm us, but instead to give every situation over to God. We are to do this by prayer and petitioning with an attitude of thanksgiving. We can hand our worries over to God because he is capable of handling them. And when we trust our cares to God, he will guard our hearts and minds with his full peace.

Do not be anxious about anything, but in every situation, by prayer and petition, with thanksgiving, present your requests to God. And the peace of God, which transcends all understanding, will guard your hearts and your minds in Christ Jesus.

PHILIPPIANS 4:6-7 NIV

What worries do you need to cast on God today?

Answer: prayer; petition; thanksgiving; peace of God

DECEMBER 16

ZEPHANIAH'S HERITAGE

Zephaniah, the prophet, had a royal lineage that was traced back to which king?

King Hezekiah led some instrumental reforms in Judah which brought the nation back to a righteous standing with the Lord for a time. Eventually the people fell away from their faith again and turned to sin and other gods. Early in the reign of Josiah, God tapped on the shoulder of one of Hezekiah's great-great grandsons to have him prophecy to the people.

Zephaniah's message must have influenced the heart of his distant cousin, Josiah, who during his reign led Judah in a dramatic reformation. Zephaniah prophesied with hopefulness, telling the people that God would take away their punishment, keep them from harm, and always be with them. He talked about God taking great delight in his people and singing over them (3:15-17).

The word of the Lord that came to Zephaniah son of Cushi, the son of Gedaliah, the son of Amariah, the son of Hezekiah, during the reign of Josiah son of Amon king of Judah.

Zephaniah 1:1 NIV

Which verses in Zephaniah strike you the most?

Answer: Hezekiah

ZERUBBABEL AND JOSHUA

What are Zerubbabel, son of Shealtiel, and Joshua, son of Jehozadek, known for?

God told Haggai to give this message directly to the governor of Judah, Zerubbabel, and the high priest, Joshua, who were both still living in Jerusalem after it was destroyed and people had been carried into exile. He passed on the challenge from God asking why they were living in luxurious homes while his house lay in ruins.

Zerubbabel and Joshua quickly got the message and began to obey. They faced difficult conditions but set out to work. Even though the new temple was not as glorious as the first, God wanted them to be encouraged. Because of Zerubbabel and Joshua's obedience and leadership, the book of Haggai is an exceptionally bright spot amidst the stark messages of the other books of the prophets.

The LORD stirred up the spirit of Zerubbabel son of Shealtiel, governor of Judah, and the spirit of Joshua son of Jozadak, the high priest, and the spirit of the whole remnant of the people. They came and began to work on the house of the LORD Almighty, their God, on the twenty-fourth day of the sixth month.

HAGGAI 1:14-15 NIV

What do you learn about God in the book of Haggai?

Answer: starting the work to rebuild the temple

THE ROYAL RIDE

What did the prophet Zechariah predict Israel's king would ride on?

Hundreds of years before Jesus rode into Jerusalem on the foal of a donkey, the prophet Zechariah was speaking about him. His message was for the people of Israel to let them know that God would restore them to him. Israel had effectively been destroyed. The people had rebelled against God, turned to worshiping idols, split the country into two kingdoms, and been overrun by one neighboring nation after another. A majority of the people of Israel and Judah had been killed or scattered across the Middle East. God's promise that Israel would be the light of the world and the source of blessing for all nations seemed bleak.

Zechariah hinted that the cornerstone was coming. God would save them, as the flock of his people. When they looked at the one they pierced, they would mourn for him. But they wouldn't be left hopeless. There would be a fountain opened for the house of David and the inhabitants of Jerusalem to cleanse them from sin and uncleanliness.

Rejoice greatly, O daughter of Zion!
Shout aloud, O daughter of Jerusalem!
Behold, your king is coming to you;
righteous and having salvation is he,
humble and mounted on a donkey,
on a colt, the foal of a donkey.

ZECHARIAH 9:9 ESV

Look through the encouraging Messianic glimpses provided in the book of Zechariah. Where do you see Jesus?

Answer: the foal of a donkey

DECEMBER 19

NO MENTION

Which book of the Bible does not mention God?

The book of Esther is unique in all of the Bible in that God is not mentioned. The story took place during the Persian Empire, when Jewish people from the Israel and Judah had been taken captive, scattered, and persecuted across the regions. The story is one of political intrigue, conspiracy, deception, violence, drama, oppression, and vengeance. It is a story of how two Jewish people, Mordecai and his niece, Esther, shrewdly saved God's people from genocide at the hands of an evil political advisor named Haman.

While God's name is not mentioned in the book, the holy design and the protection of his people, and therefore the covenant of his plan for salvation, is clearly evident. The book of Esther is ultimately the story of how God, once again, raised up unexpected people in unexpected places to bring about justice and redemption for his people. And because of his provision, the Jews were eventually restored to the land of Israel where the promised coming of the Messiah would take place.

The king loved Esther more than any of the other young women. He was so delighted with her that he set the royal crown on her head and declared her queen instead of Vashti.

ESTHER 2:17 NLT

How will your actions today fit into God's design to restore people to him?

Answer: Esther

IMMANUEL

What does the name *Immanuel* mean?

While Joseph was engaged to Mary, she was found to be with child. Joseph did not want to shame Mary, so he considered ending the engagement quietly. But an angel appeared to him and told him not to be afraid of taking Mary as his wife, for that which was conceived in her was from the Holy Spirit. The angel told Joseph that Mary would bear a son, and he should be called Jesus because he would save his people from their sins.

The book of Matthew tells us that this fulfilled what Isaiah had prophesied over seven hundred years earlier. Isaiah told Israel that their Messiah would be born to a virgin and that he would be given the name *Immanuel*, meaning "God with us."

All this took place to fulfill what the Lord
had spoken by the prophet:
"Behold, the virgin shall conceive and bear a son,
and they shall call his name Immanuel"
(which means, God with us).

MATTHEW 1:22-23 ESV

As you consider the name *Immanuel*, why do you think God chose to dwell among us as a baby?

Answer: God with us

DECEMBER 21

NAME OF THE CHILD

When Isaiah prophesied of the child to be born, what titles did he say the child would have?

Of all the remarkable prophecies about the Messiah, one of the most astonishing is in Isaiah 9. The Messiah would be a child. He would be a great light born for the people who walk in darkness. He would reign forever with justice and righteousness. And, he would have incredible titles.

Wonderful Counselor is a reference to the Holy Spirit who is an Advocate and Comforter for God's people. *Mighty God* was an alarming title to give to a human being—a title which would be blasphemous unless true. *Everlasting Father* was another breathtaking title that would have only been reserved for the One True God of Israel. The *Prince of Peace* would bring shalom to the whole world.

To us a child is born, to us a son is given;
and the government shall be upon his shoulder,
and his name shall be called
Wonderful Counselor, Mighty God,
Everlasting Father, Prince of Peace.

Isaiah 9:6 ESV

Which Messianic name of Jesus is most astonishing to you today?

Answer: Wonderful Counselor, Mighty God, Everlasting Father, Prince of Peace

DECEMBER 22

MEANING OF BETHLEHEM

The town where Jesus was born is called Bethlehem,
which means ________.

A. house of bread
B. Beth's place
C. little town
D. shepherd's hamlet

Bethlehem may have seemed like an unimportant dot on the map to many people, but it had a significance that outmatched its small size. It was near Bethlehem that Jacob's beloved wife, Rachel, died after giving birth to Benjamin (Genesis 35:19). It was in Bethlehem that the redemptive story of Ruth took place (Ruth 1:19), and there her great-grandson, David, was born, raised, and anointed king of Israel (1 Samuel 16:4-13).

It was in Bethlehem that the Messiah was born. When Mary and Joseph returned there for the national census, since Joseph was a descendant of David, Mary gave birth to Jesus. Later, Jesus would proclaim, "I am the bread of life. Whoever comes to me will never be hungry again" (John 6:35). Because of this, Bethlehem truly lives up to its name as the house of bread.

You, O Bethlehem Ephrathah,
are only a small village among all the people of Judah.
Yet a ruler of Israel, whose origins are in the distant past,
will come from you on my behalf.

Micah 5:2 NLT

How do these details cause you to see the sovereign plan of God?

Answer: A) house of bread

TURTLEDOVES OR PIGEONS

According to the law, how many turtledoves or pigeons were Mary and Joseph supposed to offer as a sacrifice when Jesus was eight days old?

In the "Twelve Days of Christmas," have you ever wondered why the singer's true love sent two turtle doves on the second day of Christmas? Maybe you have wondered more about the partridge in a pear tree or the eight maids a-milking.

Well, there is a biblical precedent for two turtle doves as a Christmas gift. When it came time for Mary and Joseph to present Jesus at eight days old for circumcision in the temple, it was customary that they should offer a sacrifice of either two turtle doves or two young pigeons. This sacrifice indicated that they were very poor. Leviticus 12 states that the proper offering after the birth of a firstborn male child would be a lamb, but if a mother could not afford a lamb, then she could take either two turtledoves or two pigeons instead as a purification ritual.

> They offered the sacrifice required in the law of the Lord—
> "either a pair of turtledoves or two young pigeons."
>
> Luke 2:24 NLT

Are you surprised that Jesus was born in poverty? Why or why not?

Answer: two

DECEMBER 24

NAMED OFFICIALLY

When did Mary and Joseph officially give Jesus his name?

While Mary was a virgin and engaged to be married Joseph, she was told by the angel, Gabriel, that she found favor with God and would conceive and give birth to a son; she would name him Jesus. The angel told her that Jesus would be very great and called the Son of the Most High. God would give Jesus the throne of his ancestor, David, and he would reign over Israel forever; his Kingdom would never end. The angel told Mary that Jesus would be holy and called the Son of God.

The name of Jesus is deliberate. *Jesus* is the English way of saying *Yeshua*, a Hebrew name meaning "God saves." According to Jewish ceremonial laws, Mary and Joseph had their baby circumcised on the eighth day after he was born, and then gave him the name that Gabriel had said.

Eight days later, when the baby was circumcised,
he was named Jesus, the name given him by the angel
even before he was conceived.

LUKE 2:21 NLT

Why is the meaning of Jesus' name significant to you personally?

Answer: eight days after he was born

(EXTRA)ORDINARY BIRTH

When the angels appeared to the shepherds in Bethlehem, what sign did they say would help them recognize the Messiah?

A. a "No Vacancy" sign in the window of the inn
B. a baby wrapped in strips of cloth, lying in a manger
C. a home filled with well-wishing family members
D. gathering of barn animals and wise men

When Jesus was born, he was wrapped snugly in cloth and likely held in the arms of his exhausted but excited parents. He was treasured by his mother, Mary. His birth was, in many respects, another ordinary delivery of another ordinary child in another ordinary town.

Yet, his birth was also far from ordinary. As the angel appeared, the radiance of God's glory surrounded the shepherds, and they were terrified! The angel tried to calm their fears with a message of good news and great joy for all people on the earth, but then the armies of heaven burst onto the scene and praised God for bringing peace on earth. The ordinary birth of Jesus marks an extraordinary turning point for every human in all of history.

> The Savior—yes, the Messiah, the Lord—has been born today in Bethlehem, the city of David! And you will recognize him by this sign: You will find a baby wrapped snugly in strips of cloth, lying in a manger."
>
> Luke 2:11-12 NLT

Why would the shepherds find it extraordinary that Jesus was born in such normal circumstances?

Answer: B) a baby wrapped in strips of cloth, lying in a manger

DECEMBER 26

GIFTS OF THE MAGI

What three gifts did the magi present to Jesus?

Upon seeing a mysterious star appear, some wealthy and wise leaders from the east interpreted the heavenly event as indicating that the long-prophesied king of the Jews was finally due to be born. We don't know how many magi were in this entourage, but a tradition started in the Middle Ages that there were three wise men because they gave Jesus three kingly gifts: gold, a sign of wealth and royalty; frankincense, an extravagant oil; and myrrh, an aromatic spice.

Each of these gifts is mentioned in the Old Testament as being royal: gold is mentioned in Psalm 72:15; gold and frankincense is in Isaiah 60:6; and myrrh is in Psalm 45:8. Song of Solomon 3:6 talks about myrrh and frankincense, and spices and gold are in 1 Kings 10:2. The magi clearly meant to praise and honor Jesus as the king of the Jews. Because they chose to serve the child rather than the reigning ruler, Herod, who was disturbed by the news of the star and the possible Messiah, the Magi returned back home by a secret route without notifying Herod.

On coming to the house, they saw the child with his mother Mary, and they bowed down and worshiped him. Then they opened their treasures and presented him with gifts of gold, frankincense and myrrh.

MATTHEW 2:11 NIV

What gifts can you offer Jesus today?

Answer: gold, frankincense, and myrrh

DECEMBER 27

THE ACCUSERS

When Jesus defended the woman caught in adultery, who left the scene first, the older accusers or younger ones?

When trying to trap Jesus, some Pharisees and religious teachers brought a woman to him. They said she had been caught in the act of adultery, and she should be killed by stoning. The Gospel of John tells us that Jesus then bent down and wrote with his finger on the ground. What he wrote, we don't know. But when he spoke, he dumbfounded the accusers, who were clamoring for a response. He said, "Let him who is without sin among you be the first to throw a stone at her" (John 8:7). And once more he bent down and began to write on the ground (v. 8).

The older accusers realized Jesus had outplayed them once again, so they started to go away, one by one. The younger ones were a little slower, and perhaps more reluctant, to give up. They eventually walked away leaving only the woman and Jesus. He turned to her and said, "Has no one condemned you?" She replied, "No one, Lord." Jesus told her he didn't condemn her either; she should go and sin no more.

When they heard it, they went away one by one, beginning with the older ones, and Jesus was left alone with the woman standing before him.

John 8:9 ESV

What do you find most remarkable about Jesus in this passage?

Answer: the older accusers

THE DISCIPLES

What were the names of the twelve disciples?

Each of the twelve men that Jesus selected to be a disciple had a story. Each one left family or friends, a career or responsibilities, in order to follow him. Peter and Andrew, along with James and John, left their fishing businesses. Matthew left a lucrative tax-collecting career. Simon set aside his passion to revolt as a Zealot.

These men were to accompany Jesus, and he would eventually send them out to preach. He gave them authority to cast out demons and to represent him during and after—except for Judas Iscariot—his ministry.

He appointed the twelve: Simon (to whom he gave the name Peter); James the son of Zebedee and John the brother of James (to whom he gave the name Boanerges, that is, Sons of Thunder); Andrew, and Philip, and Bartholomew, and Matthew, and Thomas, and James the son of Alphaeus, and Thaddaeus, and Simon the Zealot, and Judas Iscariot, who betrayed him.

Mark 3:16-19 ESV

As the new year approaches, what will you give up in order to follow Christ?

Answer: read Mark 3:16-19

RANDOM PEOPLE

Who did Paul leave sick at Miletus?

The Epistles are the twenty-one letters from Romans to Jude in the New Testament. They contain unique greetings from the writer to the recipients. These personal letters were meant for particular audiences in a time and place, but they were also distributed and shared with leaders of various churches, so they spread further throughout the world.

Today's verse in 2 Timothy is an example of the personal nature of the letters in the Bible. Paul, writing from Rome, addressed this letter to his dear son Timothy (2 Timothy 1:2) and talked about Timothy's mother and grandmother. At the end of the letter, he asked Timothy to give his greetings to his friends and partners in ministry: Priscilla and Aquila. He also said hello to those who live with Onesiphorus. He mentioned that their friend, Erastus, stayed in Corinth and that Trophimus had to stay in Miletus because he was sick. He spoke of several others with him that sent greetings: Eubulus, Pudens, Linus, Claudia, and all the rest of the church.

Give my greetings to Priscilla and Aquila and those living in the household of Onesiphorus. Erastus stayed at Corinth, and I left Trophimus sick at Miletus.

2 Timothy 4:19-20 NLT

How can you encourage someone in their faith today?

Answer: Trophimus

WHAT TO LISTEN TO

In 2 Timothy, Paul predicted that people would turn from listening to sound teaching and instead listen to ________.

A. whatever their itching ears want to hear
B. good music
C. the most popular influencers
D. bad advice

"Preach the word of God," Paul urged Timothy. "Be prepared, whether the time is favorable or not. Patiently correct, rebuke, and encourage your people with good teaching" (v. 2). This is the job of a pastoral leader, to equip the people with God's Word so they may live for Jesus.

There will come a time, Paul said, when people—even people in churches—will only want their ears scratched. People will follow their own desires and look for teachers who will tell them what makes them feel better or who will affirm their opinions. It will be difficult at times to reveal the truth of God's Word because it will go against what they want to hear. Be ready. "Keep a clear mind in every situation," Paul urges. "Don't be afraid of suffering for the Lord. Work at telling others the good news."

A time is coming when people will no longer listen to sound and wholesome teaching. They will follow their own desires and will look for teachers who will tell them whatever their itching ears want to hear.

2 Timothy 4:3 NLT

How do you know when a sermon has been a "good sermon"?

Answer: A) whatever their itching ears want to hear

DECEMBER 31

HOUSE OF ANOINTING

In whose house did the woman anoint Jesus' head with expensive perfume?

Simon the leper lived in Bethany: the same village the sisters, Mary and Martha, lived in with their brother, Lazarus. There is not much to be known about Simon other than the fact that he was known as the leper, and that Jesus reclined at a table in his home.

In Simon's home, a woman poured very expensive perfume on Jesus' head. This was a sign of an extravagant anointing, indicating the extreme respect she held for Jesus. The disciples, however, didn't see her anointing as sacred. They were indignant and saw her action as wasteful. They thought the perfume could have been sold and the money given to the poor. But Jesus told them that the woman had done a beautiful thing for him. She recognized how special it was to be in the presence of Jesus, and she lavished him with her most expensive possession. He said what she had done would be preached throughout the world.

While Jesus was in Bethany in the home of Simon the Leper, a woman came to him with an alabaster jar of very expensive perfume, which she poured on his head as he was reclining at the table.

Matthew 26:6-7 NIV

As you end this year and begin the next, how will you choose to recognize the presence of Jesus in your life on an ongoing basis?

Answer: Simon the leper's home

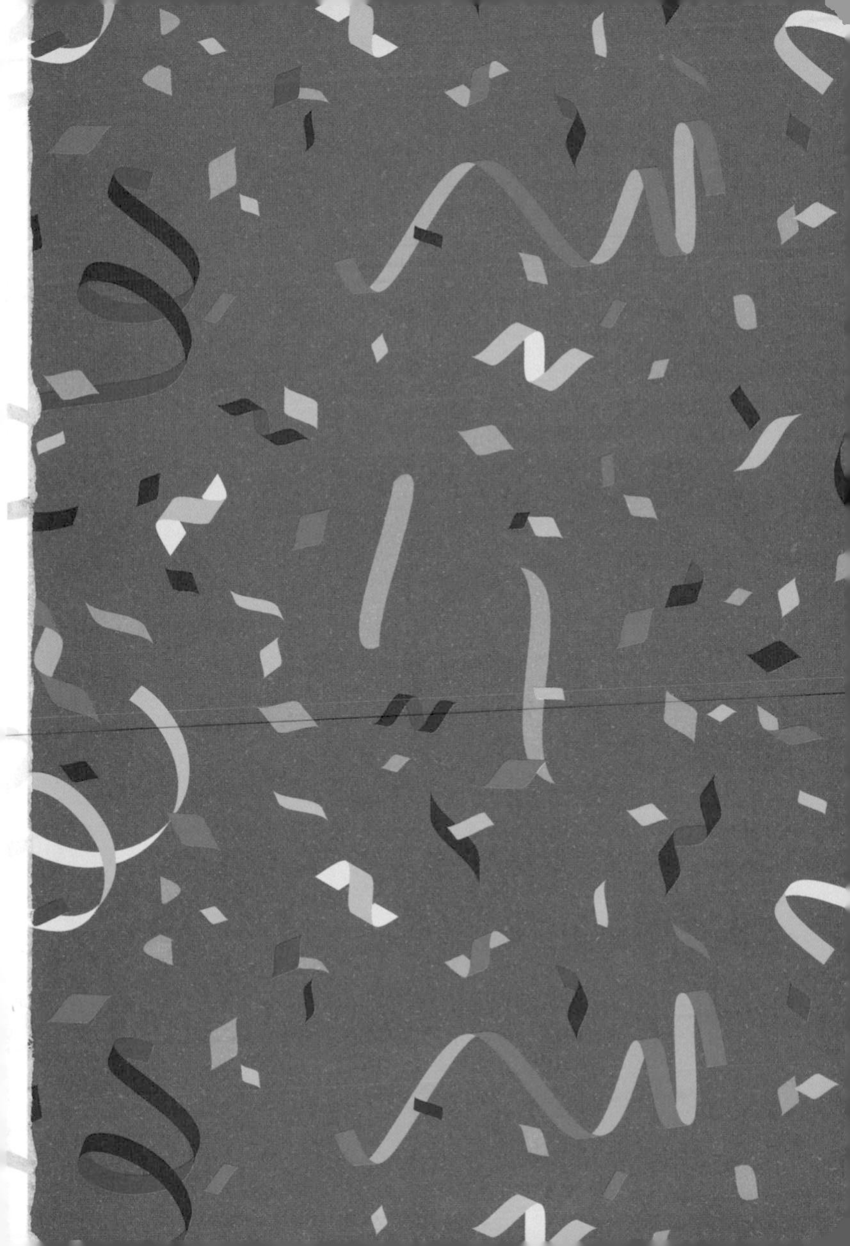

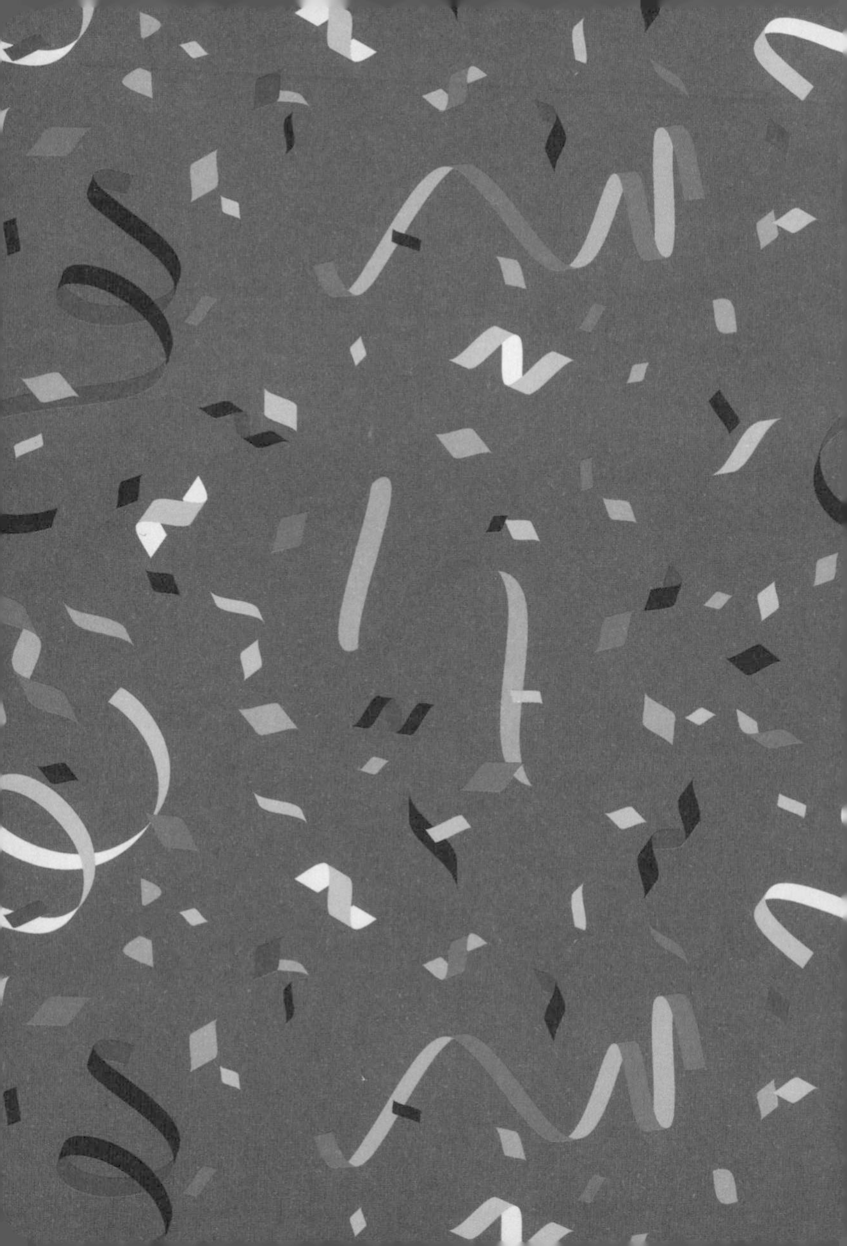